Crusades

Crusades

*Terry Jones and
Alan Ereira*

Facts On File®

Crusades
Published by arrangement with BBC Books,
a division of BBC Enterprises Ltd
Copyright © 1995 by Fegg Features Ltd and Alan Ereira
For information contact:
Facts On File, Inc.
460 Park Avenue South
New York NY 10016

Library of Congress Cataloging-in-Publication Data
Jones. Terry. 1942–
    Crusades / Terry Jones & Alan Ereira.
        p.   cm.
    Includes bibliographical references (p.) and index.
    ISBN 0-8160-3275-0 (acid-free paper)
    1. Crusades.   I. Ereira, Alan.   II. Title.
D157.J66   1995
909.07—dc20   94-31748

Facts On File books are available at special discounts when purchased in
bulk quantities for businesses, associations, institutions or
sales promotions. Please call our Special Sales Department
in New York at 212/683-2244 or 800/322-8755.

Designed by Tim Higgins
Picture research by Deirdre O'Day
Maps by Andrew Farmer

Manufactured by Butler & Tanner Ltd
Printed in Great Britain
Color separations by Radstock Reproductions
Jacket printed by Lawrence Allen Ltd

10 9 8 7 6 5 4 3 2 1

This book is printed on acid-free paper.

Frontispiece
Pope Urban II at Clermont Cathedral in 1095
preaching the sermon that launched the First Crusade.
This illustration comes from a French illustrated
manuscript, *Les Passages faits Outremer par les Français
contre les Turcs et autres Sarrasins et Maures outremarins*,
produced about 1490. Like all medieval illustrations,
it is not concerned with literal accuracy. In reality,
Clermont Cathedral was unfinished in 1095 and was
too small to hold the crowd that attended. Urban
preached in the open air.

Contents

List of Maps

Preaching St Louis' Crusade in France,
from the fifteenth-century *Les Passages faits Outremer* . . . .

Acknowledgements

This book is the product of a collaborative venture, not just by the two people who actually put the words on paper, but by the production team of the BBC *Crusades* series. In particular, we want to thank David Wallace, who produced and directed half the series, Sarah Lambert, who provided much of the academic research, and Rod Williams and Lucy Jago, who also helped with research.

We are also heavily in debt to the many writers and researchers on the Crusades who gave us insights and access to their own work, including Sir Stephen Runciman and Professor Suheil Zakkar (who acted as our overall consultants), Karen Armstrong, Dr Dan Bahat, Dr Meron Benvenisti, Matthew Bennett, Dr Kamel Abdul Fatah, John France, Professor Isiltan, Dr Zehava Jacoby, Professor Benjamin Kedar, Professor Jonathan Riley-Smith and Christopher Tyerman. Dr Susan B. Edgington allowed us to read and use her unpublished work, including her translation of the chronicle of Albert of Aix.

Despite this impressive galaxy of willing and profoundly knowledgeable advisors, the judgements and errors in this book are all our own.

T J and A E

Introduction

The eleventh-century Syrian poet Abu 'l-'Ala al-Maarri wrote:

> *The world is divided into two sects:*
> *Those with religion but no brains*
> *And those with brains but no religion.*

Some forty years after his death, the town where he had lived and from which he takes his name, Maarrat an-Numan, was invaded by cannibals. These cannibals were Christians who had marched three thousand miles on their way to save the Holy Land in the name of Jesus.

One couldn't get much further away from the teachings of the Sermon on the Mount, yet these people were probably sincere in their belief and convinced they were doing the right thing. New forces of bigotry and righteous savagery were unleashed by Pope Urban II when he preached what later came to be called 'the Crusades'. These forces are still with us.

The Crusades have never been without a contemporary significance. Right now, that significance is associated with the emergence of Islamic fundamentalism, and the new confrontations between Christian and Moslem societies in our post-Communist world. It is important to know how the old confrontation affected Christian and Islamic society and how it contributed to the present mess.

In this book, and in the television series which gave rise to it, we have tried to break away from a purely Euro-centric outlook and to tell the story of the Crusades from the Moslem point of view as well as from the Christian.

We make no pretensions to extending the bounds of scholarship. This is a book for the reader with little or no knowledge of the subject. For those who want to read more there is plenty. We hope that this book may be a help in reading the others.

1

The World of a Crusader

Friday is the most important day in the Moslem week. It is a day of prayer and in Jerusalem Moslems stream to the Temple Mount to worship.

The Temple Mount is dominated by the Dome of the Rock, built over 1300 years ago. An immense rotunda, decorated with magnificent golden mosaics and surmounted by a golden dome, stands over a bare rock. This is the Foundation Stone, the rock where, for Jews, Christians and Moslems, heaven and earth meet. It is the rock on which Abraham is said to have been ready to sacrifice his son: Ishmael, according to the Koran, Ishmael's brother Isaac according to the Bible. It is the rock from which Mohammed is said to have made a miraculous night flight to heaven.

On Friday, 15 July 1099, shortly after midday prayers, a twenty-one-year-old Norman knight called Tancred burst onto the Mount with a band of heavily armed men. The Crusaders had reached their goal. After three years of marches and battles, and having lost perhaps four out of every five who left Europe, they had arrived to protect the Holy Places of Jerusalem.

Tancred and his men smashed their way into the Dome of the Rock and stripped it of *'more than forty silver candelabra, each of them weighing 3600 drams, and a great silver lamp*

The Foundation Stone in the Dome of the Rock, Jerusalem. This bare rock is a focal point for three religions: Judaism, Christianity and Islam. Until 586 BC it was surmounted by the fabric of Solomon's Temple, from 516 BC to AD 70 by the Second Temple, and from AD 132 by a Roman Temple of Jupiter until the construction of the present-day Islamic monument in AD 691.

weighing forty-four Syrian pounds, as well as a hundred and fifty smaller silver candelabra and more than twenty gold ones, and a great deal more booty'. The Moslems fled into the other great structure on the Mount, the al-Aqsa Mosque. There they surrendered, promising a great ransom for their lives and accepting Tancred's banner as the symbol of his protection. Before the sun set, Tancred's flag, hoisted by Moslems, was flying over the most sacred site in Jerusalem.

The following morning the Crusaders re-entered the al-Aqsa Mosque and slaughtered every Moslem sheltering there. No-one knows how many died; the Moslem chronicler reports seventy thousand. One of the Crusaders reports picking his way through a mess of blood and bodies more than knee-deep.

The impact of that conquest and that slaughter still reverberates. It began the strange history of the Latin Kingdom of Jerusalem – a kingdom which lasted for almost two hundred years and which transformed the worlds of Christianity and Islam.

Tancred the Norman

Tancred came originally from Normandy, in northern France. He was born about 1076; his ancestors were Vikings, Northmen, and none of them would have been Christian two hundred years before he was born. They were a practical people, and their religion was practical. Its purpose was to get you easily and efficiently into heaven, avoiding the danger of hell-fire. That was why they were baptized. Christianity offered a very direct route to the afterlife, with firm guarantees, and since the Church also allowed these newly-settled landowners to nominate their own priests and bishops, the Normans took to it with enthusiasm.

One of the unforeseen consequences of interesting the Northmen in Christianity was that they became keen on pilgrimage. Travel may or may nor broaden the mind, but it certainly expands one's knowledge of which parts of the world are worth plundering or taking over. The pilgrimage to Jerusalem became quite popular among the Normans, especially on a route which passed through the wealthy and militarily weak region of southern Italy.

Tancred was named after his maternal grandfather, a minor Norman baron called Tancred de Hauteville, who had more sons than his land would support. In 1040, three of Tancred de Hauteville's six sons took part in the seizure of the town of Melfi in Apulia. Nineteen years later a fourth brother was proclaimed ruler of Apulia by the Pope, and a fifth was about to embark on the conquest of Sicily.

Carving out a new Normandy in southern Italy meant war against two empires, one Latin, the other Greek.

The two Roman Empires

Start with the Greeks.

They called themselves Romans.

The Roman Empire had divided into Eastern and Western halves in the third century. The Western Empire had long ago been overrun by pagans in Europe, but the Eastern Empire continued. Its capital was New Rome, Byzantium, the great city on the Bosphorus.

Byzantium was also known as Constantinople, after its founder Constantine, the first Christian Emperor. The language of the Eastern Empire had become Greek but its identity was still imperial Roman. In fact, even today, the Greek word for Greekness is *Romiosini*.

The Western Empire had been Latin, not Greek, and Charlemagne had re-launched it in AD 800 as the 'Holy Roman Empire'. Its churches used a Latin liturgy and the Holy Roman Emperors saw themselves as the protectors of the Pope in Rome, equals in theory to the Emperor in Byzantium.

Although the city of Byzantium remained huge, wealthy and militarily impreg-nable, the frontiers of Byzantium were crumbling. In the seventh and eighth centuries Arabs had occupied central Anatolia, and taken Crete, Sicily and the whole of Syria, Egypt and North Africa from the Empire, but between 976 and 1025 the Empire reasserted itself. The Arabs were driven back to Jerusalem, Crete was recovered and so too was central Anatolia.

It may have looked as though the Byzantine Roman Empire was being restored, but the de Hauteville boys, Tancred's great-uncles, did not think so. They could tell an over-extended, clapped-out power when they saw one, and that was exactly what they saw in southern Italy. Italy was divided between the two Empires. It was Latin down almost to Bari, and then Byzantine Greek in the south.

To begin with, the Holy Roman Emperor and the Pope were happy to support the de Hautevilles, since they would extend the Roman Catholic influence into a region that had been under the religious control of Byzantium.

As the campaign went on, however, it became clear that the Normans were not acting out of duty to the Church, but purely in their own interests. They began to look more like a serious bandit-power in Italy. The Pope travelled around their territory and complained to the Byzantine Emperor that the Normans *'with an impiety which exceeds that of pagans, rise up against the Church of God, causing Christians to perish by new and hideous tortures, sparing neither women, children nor the aged, making no distinction between what is sacred and profane, despoiling churches, burning them and razing them to the ground'*.

The Pope and the Holy Roman Emperor realized they had a tiger by the tail. In 1053 the Pope personally marched south with an army, intending to combine with a Byzantine army and put the Normans back in their place. The Pope actually declared that this was a Holy War, or at any rate one being fought in the name of the 'patrimony of St Peter'.

The de Hautevilles did not see any of this as much of a problem: they smashed the Pope's forces before he was able to join up with his Byzantine allies, took him prisoner and persuaded him to agree that, on mature consideration, it was a very fine thing to have Normans in control of southern Italy. Tancred's family may have been Christian but they would never let that interfere with more important matters.

The Challenge to the Eastern Empire

'Meanwhile a different variety of barbarian had smashed into the Byzantine Empire from the east. The Seljuk Turks had taken over central Armenia and advanced almost to the Bosphorus itself.

The vast steppe-lands of Eurasia had produced, and would continue to produce, hordes of horseback warriors who could do as they pleased with settled civilizations. The Goths, Huns, Alans and Vandals – the ancestors of the Franks, Germans, Lombards and Spaniards – had all come from this immense territory. The bulwark against these hordes had been the Caliph of Baghdad. His power had bottled up the gap between the Caspian Sea and the Persian Gulf, and stopped the steppe horsemen from raiding westwards towards the Mediterranean. But in the eleventh century

---

A page from Matthew Paris's itinerary from London to Jerusalem which laid out the journey for medieval pilgrims in the form of a strip-map, *c.* 1250. Each town marked is a day's journey from the last (indicated by the word *Jurnee* alongside the road). This section starts from the walled City of London (bottom left) to Rochester, Canterbury and Dover (top left), and then south from Wissant (bottom right) on the French coast, between Boulogne and Calais, to Montreuil, St-Riquier, Poix de Picardie and as far as Beauvais on the road to Paris.

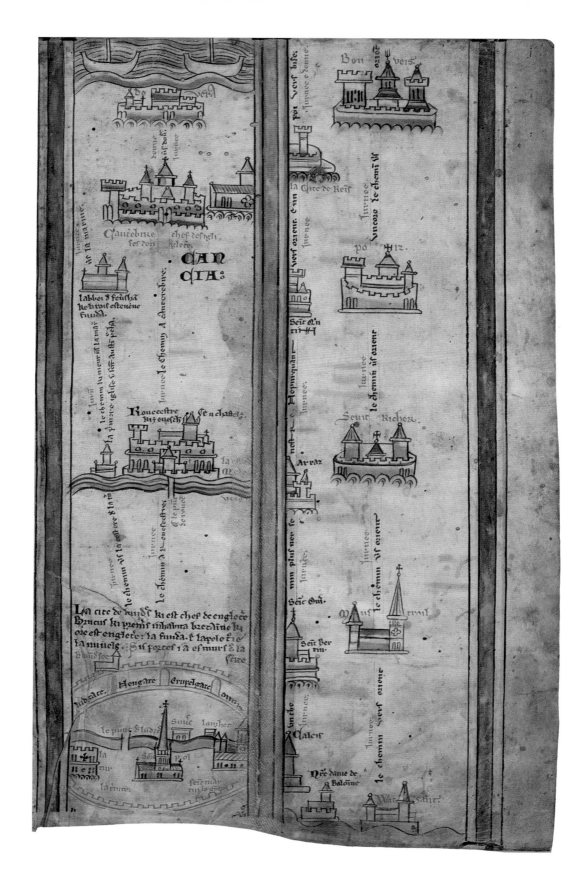

Baghdad was disintegrating; the cork was rotting in the bottle. The Turks of central Asia, who had already established an empire that stretched from the Punjab to eastern Iran, had converted to Islam, moved into Iraq as mercenaries of the Caliph, and begun eyeing possibilities further west.

One clan, who called themselves Seljuks, made themselves masters of Baghdad in 1055. Over the next fifteen years they began invading Anatolia and in 1071 confronted the most impressive force the Byzantine Empire could muster. They destroyed the Emperor's army at Manzikert and took him prisoner. There was nothing to stop their advance towards Constantinople.

One of Tancred's great-uncles, Robert Guiscard, saw this as a golden opportunity. He took his son across the Adriatic to begin his own assault on the Byzantine Empire. As a caring father Guiscard wanted to provide for his son's future. So he decided to give him Greece. All he had to do was conquer it.

The son's name was to ring through the history of the Crusades for generations to come: Bohemond.

Fortunately for Byzantium, the conquest of Greece was simply too large a task for Robert and Bohemond, and by the time of Guiscard's death in 1085 it was as far off as ever. Bohemond turned his attention back to southern Italy.

There were other power struggles going on there which could keep a fighting knight like Bohemond well occupied. The most interesting was the bitter conflict that had developed between the Pope and his would-be protector, the Holy Roman Emperor.

The Revolutionary Pope

It all started because of one man – Pope Gregory VII – Europe's first revolutionary leader. Before he became Pope he had been associated with the abbey of Cluny in central France. Cluny had begun a new kind of monastic movement, committed not simply to quiet withdrawal from the world but to the regeneration of Christian society in a centralized authoritarian structure under the Pope as Christ's Viceroy.

In an age of chaotic violence and banditry, in which the law was simply an instrument used by the strong, there was a yearning for some kind of order and settled life. Many people, including a large number of knights, began to support the Church reformers for the same reason that many people in South America supported Communism in the 1960s and 1970s. It offered the only credible programme for ending the corruption and violence that surrounded them.

Since a knight was trained to understand authority as a hierarchy, with lords who had overlords and greater lords over the overlords, he could easily grasp the authority of Christ. And, since the Church was Christ's mouthpiece, Pope Gregory insisted that secular lords, including the Emperor, were subject to the authority and judgement of the Church.

On 8 December 1075 Pope Gregory launched his bid for supreme authority on earth by threatening the Holy Roman Emperor with *'the fate of Saul'* (i.e. the destruction of himself and his heirs) unless he stopped appointing bishops and abbots. That, Gregory insisted, was the Church's prerogative. Emperor Henry denounced Gregory as a *'false monk'*. Gregory then excommunicated the Emperor, condemning him to eternal damnation, and declared that he was deposed as King of Germany and that no-one was obliged to obey him.

This was spectacular stuff; nothing like it had ever happened before.

The Emperor, a thousand miles from Rome, declared that, on the contrary, it was Gregory who was deposed. Every lord of Church and state in the West was going to have to take sides. It was the Emperor who lost.

The symbolic moment of victory came in 1077, when Emperor Henry IV humbly waited on the Pope in the snow-bound castle of Canossa and begged for absolution. From that point on, it was clear that the Pope was capable of limiting the Emperor's power. The de Hautevilles, who were always in favour of weakening emperors, suddenly became serious supporters of organized religion.

In a few years Henry was back on the warpath and Gregory needed military help from wherever he could get it. Although Gregory had excommunicated him twice over, Tancred's great-uncle Robert Guiscard went to war on the Pope's behalf. In return Gregory recognized Robert as Duke of Apulia. Two years later, when Henry actually captured Rome, it was Robert who rode to the rescue. He released Gregory from imprisonment and gave him back his throne. At the same time, his troops looted and ravaged Rome, and when the desperate population rose against them, the Normans set fire to the city and destroyed the entire area between the Colosseum and the Lateran.

Pope Gregory had been restored to Rome, but his benefactors had demolished the city to do it. Understandably, Gregory was profoundly unpopular with the Romans; he could not stay once his protectors left and he died in Salerno, the guest – if not the puppet – of the de Hautevilles.

Gregory was shortly followed by Pope Urban II, who, like Gregory, was a Frank, a product of Cluny and was deeply committed to the reform programme and the vision of the Pope as supreme monarch. It was Urban who would launch the Crusade. He would never have been able to do so without the de Hautevilles.

The Holy Roman Emperor controlled Rome and for some years Pope Urban wandered round southern Italy, dependent on Tancred's relatives. In 1093 Bohemond and his half-brother brought him into Rome by military force. In fact Urban could still not get into the Lateran Palace, and it was not until 1094 that he was able to take his place on the papal throne – thanks be to God and a little judicious bribery.

Tancred's Dilemma

It was around this time that Tancred was sent from Normandy to be educated in Italy. He joined the household of his uncle Bohemond at Taranto. It was Bohemond who would take him crusading.

Tancred's biographer, Radulph of Caen, paints an interesting picture of the state of the young man's mind in 1096:

> Frequently he burned with anxiety because the warfare he engaged in as a knight seemed to be contrary to the Lord's commands. The Lord, in fact, ordered him to offer the cheek that had been struck together with his other cheek to the striker, but secular knighthood did not spare the blood of relatives. The Lord urged him to give his tunic and his cloak as well to the man who would take them away; the needs of war impelled him to take from a man, already despoiled of both, whatever remained to him. And so, if ever that wise man could give himself up to repose, these contradictions deprived him of courage.

Given the history of the de Hautevilles, this may seem surprising. Conscience, after all, was not one of their strong points. But these feelings of Christian anxiety were clearly affecting a significant number of knights and played a large part in launching the Crusade movement.

It is worth rereading what Radulph says, putting aside the idea that it describes a guilty conscience. It doesn't. It describes the dilemma of a man with two overlords who are giving him different orders. One is his knightly master, his feudal overlord on earth, who is telling him to kick ass. That, he is told, is his job. The other is his Lord in heaven, Christ enthroned on the summit of the feudal hierarchy, who appears to have laid out a quite different set of orders in the Sermon on the Mount.

In 1095, the year after taking his throne, Urban explained how the conflicting claims of knighthood and Church could be reconciled. He had obviously given the matter a great deal of thought and produced a wholly original solution. The Crusade.

Preaching the Crusade

On Tuesday, 27 November 1095, Pope Urban made the speech which changed Tancred's life. Urban had summoned a great Council to Clermont in central France and word had gone out that he was going to make a major announcement at the end of the meeting. There was tremendous excitement and when the day came, the new cathedral was not large enough to hold the crowds. The papal throne had to be set up in a field.

Urban revealed that he had received an embassy from the Emperor of Byzantium asking for help in driving back the Turks. It may be that the ambassadors overdid the urgency of the situation. It may be, since they were addressing the Pope, that they emphasized the need to protect Christians in the East from savage Moslems. Whatever

An example of Christian propaganda against the Turks. The decapitation of a Christian at the order of the Turkish 'king' in front of a golden idol indicates Europe's enduring ignorance of Islam.

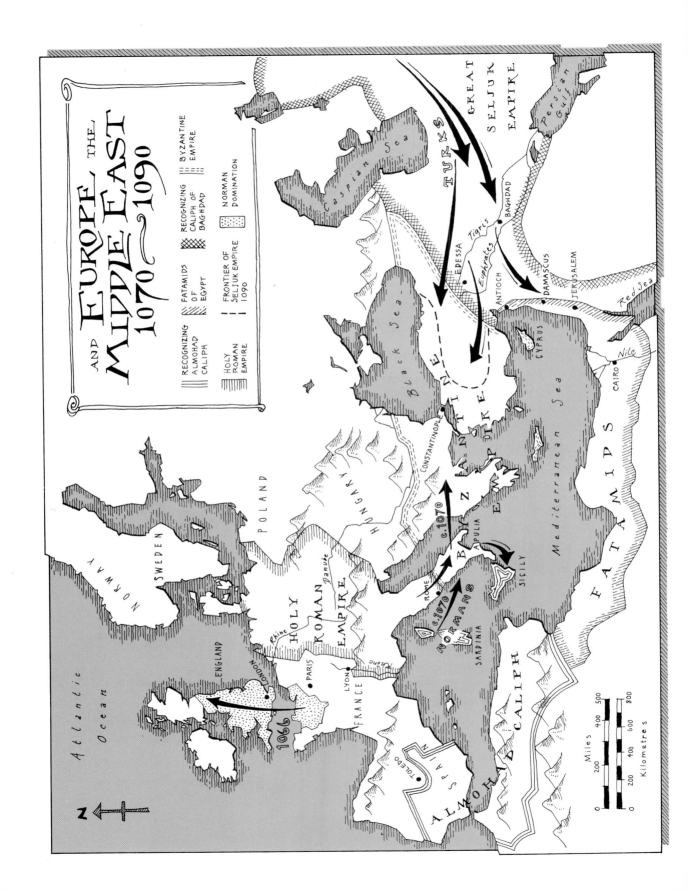

←——————————————————————————→

it was they said, they certainly fired Urban's imagination and he, in turn, was to fire the imagination of the whole of Europe.

The help the Emperor of Byzantium had in mind was probably a couple of thousand mercenaries. What Urban saw in the request, however, was the chance to make himself the saviour of the Eastern Church and thus move closer to his goal of supremacy over the whole Church. So instead of writing a few letters to the Western barons, requesting them to send forces east, the Pope stood up on the rostrum in that field outside Clermont, before that vast multitude buzzing with anticipation, and made an announcement that would change the world. He summoned all Christian warriors to arms in the name of the Church to go and rescue their brothers in the East.

He described, in highly misleading terms, the Seljuk conquests in Christian Byzantine lands:

> They have circumcised the Christians, either spreading the blood from the circumcisions on the altars or pouring it into the baptismal fonts. And they cut open the navels of those whom they choose to torment with a loathsome death, tear out their most vital organs and tie them to a stake, drag them around and flog them, before killing them as they lie prone on the ground with all their entrails out. They tie some to posts and shoot at them with arrows, they order others to bare their necks and they attack them with drawn swords, trying to see whether they can cut off their heads with a single stroke.

(that comes, admittedly, from the most lurid of the accounts of Urban's speech to have survived – we do not have a reliable copy of what he said).

By summoning an army under the banner of the Cross, the Pope was extending the Church's mantle over all Christendom. This was the idea at the very heart of the revolutionary papacy; in place of separate local churches at the centre of discrete communities, there was to be one overarching Church, ruled by one overarching Pope. The Crusade was to be its expression and its instrument.

Urban's army would also rescue Jerusalem, the spiritual (and therefore the physical) centre of the Universe. He hoped that the redeemed Jerusalem would be directly ruled by the Church.

Every man who enrolled for the struggle must mark himself out by wearing a cross and, most important, vow to continue on his way until he reached Jerusalem.

Urban's method of raising this army was completely original; as well as pay, he could offer paradise – anyone who took part had all their sins forgiven. *'Whoever for devotion alone, not to gain honour or money, goes to Jerusalem to liberate the Church of God can substitute this journey for all penance.'*

By saying that carrying out a military/political enterprise would make you a better person, wiping out past sins, Urban had invented a way by which every person could internalize papal policy. Fighting in the Pope's cause was not only an obligation, it made you righteous. With that one idea, mass political action was launched. With that one idea, ideology was born. With that one idea, the Crusade was set in motion. Urban did not understand what he had done.

The Pope's Crusaders

Adhemar, the Bishop of Le Puy, immediately rose and asked to join the expedition; it had been privately agreed that he was to be Urban's deputy in constructing the seat of the papal monarch in Jerusalem. A few days later messengers from Raymond of Toulouse confirmed that he would be joining with many followers. He was in his fifties and as the most senior aristocrat involved he expected to be appointed as leader of the expedition. Urban, however, would not appoint any layman to that role.

For the next eight months the Pope toured France, wearing a crown and accompanied by a huge retinue of Church dignitaries, repeating his message. In place of the remote figure of the King, known to most people only from his head on a coin, people saw — in the flesh — the representative of God on earth, calling them to war. The response to his appeal was quite beyond anything that anyone could have imagined.

The nobility flocked to take the Cross. The younger brother of the King of France, Hugh of Vermandois, announced that he would go; like Raymond of Toulouse, he had been fighting the Moslems in Spain and saw this as an extension of that war. Crusaders also volunteered from inside the Holy Roman Emperor's own domains; the main body was based around the households of three brothers, Godfrey de Bouillon, the Duke of Lower Lorraine, Eustace, Count of Boulogne, and Baldwin of Boulogne.

The medieval world-map was based on a schematic circle, in which a
T-shaped body of water separated Europe (bottom left) from Africa
(bottom right) and Asia (the top half of the circle). Jerusalem was in the
centre of the circle, England on the bottom edge at seven o'clock.
Assorted monsters were located on the right-hand edge.
From a thirteenth-century English psalter.

←————————————————————→

Godfrey, the oldest of the three, was in his mid-thirties. He was sympathetic to Urban's ideas and embraced the Crusade with enthusiasm, selling off various of his estates to equip a large army. Eustace was not so keen, but was bullied into it.

Baldwin was as keen as Godfrey, but for quite different reasons. As a landless younger son he had been put into the Church, but had a run-in with the reform movement and quit. Now he had no job and no land, so the Crusade was his opportunity to carve out a new future.

In Normandy, both William the Conqueror's eldest son, Robert, Duke of Normandy, and his daughter, Adela, reacted favourably to Urban's call. Robert put his duchy in hock to his brother, William Rufus, King of England, to finance his army, while Adela simply told her reluctant husband, Stephen of Blois, that he had to join up and that was the end of it.

Tancred Reborn

The Normans of southern Italy were less interested. In the summer of 1096 Bohemond and Roger Borsa were busy crushing a rebellion in the merchant town of Amalfi. Bohemond had taken Tancred along and they were all camped in the hills behind the town, bogged down in a long, boring siege, when parties of armed men, with red crosses on their armour, began passing through on their way to Byzantium. Tancred's brother William was among them. And this was how Tancred learnt of Pope Urban's solution to his dilemma.

Tancred's problem had been simple. Killing was the duty of a knight but killing was wrong in the eyes of the Church. When the Normans killed the English in the Battle of Hastings, they had committed a sin and had to do penance for it. But killing, the Pope now declared, need not be a sin after all. It depended on who you killed. In fact, if you killed the enemies of Christ, killing did not require a penance – it *was* a penance. Holy slaughter could be as effective a devotional activity as prayer, or fasting, or pilgrimage.

> *Until now you have fought unjust wars: you have often savagely brandished your spears at each other in mutual carnage only out of greed and pride, for which you deserve eternal destruction and the certain ruin of damnation! Now we are proposing that you should fight wars which contain the glorious reward of martyrdom, in which you can gain the title of present and eternal glory.*

Or, as one report put it, *'Soldiers of Hell – become soldiers of the Living God!'* Tancred, according to Radulph of Caen, suddenly realized that all his problems had been solved: '*At last as if previously asleep, his vigour was aroused, his powers grew, his eyes opened, his courage was born.*'

The Pope had also pointed out the importance of rescuing Jerusalem from the infidel. He seems to have suggested that 'rescue' meant 'seize and keep'.

> *This land you inhabit is everywhere shut in by the sea, is surrounded by ranges of mountains and is overcrowded by your numbers . . . This is why you devour and fight one another, make war and even kill one another . . . let all dissensions be settled. Take the road to the Holy Sepulchre, rescue that land from a dreadful race and rule over it yourselves.*

Suddenly the idea of the Crusade seemed to capture the imaginations of the Normans of southern Italy too. In October 1096, a year after the Pope had issued his call, Bohemond abandoned the siege of Amalfi and led a large and powerful body of fighters across the Adriatic. Among them was Tancred.

Peter the Hermit, shown here in clerical garb and
with a monk's tonsure, points the way for his
motley collection of followers. He is shown
without his customary donkey and the knight's
horse appears to be his most enthusiastic follower.
At the bottom of the picture, women react with
apprehension. From an early fourteenth-century
French manuscript.

2

The Great Adventure

O f course, Urban had not intended that ordinary people should just down their hoes and spades and go on this expedition as individual volunteers. That was not how society worked in the eleventh century. People were locked into strict patterns of obligations. It was necessary for great landowners to accept the Cross and then to order their retainers and followers, who owed them duties of military service, to come with them.

But Urban's words and ideas, repeated by preachers and priests throughout the length and breadth of Christendom, touched a chord amongst the common folk. The least looked-for response of all came from north-east France and north Germany, where evangelical monks began preaching in town after town that people should abandon everything and walk to Jerusalem. The most celebrated of these preachers was Peter the Hermit (who was actually known by his contemporaries as 'Little Peter').

Peter was a small, dirty man with a long face similar to that of the donkey he always rode; he went barefoot and lived on a diet of wine and fish. These eccentricities, plus a charismatic speaking voice, enabled him to move crowds even if they could not understand the language he spoke. Guibert of Nogent, who knew him, said that *'whatever he said or did, it seemed like something half divine'.*

Peter's obsession was pilgrimage. He had almost certainly tried to make a pilgrimage to Jerusalem, but found his journey blocked by the breakdown of authority in Seljuk-invaded territory. Now he was travelling round north-east France urging people to move *en masse* and re-open the route.

Pilgrimage was of great importance in the eleventh century. There were good maps, and a chain of pilgrim hostels, one day's journey apart along virtually the whole route.

←――――――――――――――――――――――――――→

The Church encouraged the journey as a penance (it got troublemakers out of the way for many months), and because travelling in a group of holy pilgrims was a useful moral exercise.

Other preachers took up Peter's message. Wandering through lands ravaged by floods and pestilence in 1094, and drought and famine in 1095, they began to attract a following who believed that the end of days was at hand and that they were being urged by the Pope to liberate the heavenly Jerusalem.

The air was thick with future marvels. Europe had been swept by millenarianism. It was being said that a huge body of Christian pilgrims assembling in Jerusalem could hasten the return of the Messiah; in 1064–5 a party of some seven thousand pilgrims had travelled to Jerusalem from Germany. The Messiah did not appear in Jerusalem. The Seljuks did.

Although there is no reason to believe that Christians in Jerusalem were having a particularly hard time in the 1090s, pilgrimage had become very difficult as a result of the disintegration of authority along the route, as Peter had discovered. Strange bands of visionaries, often led by minor German knights from the edge of Christian Europe, began converging. Hairs said to be from the tail of Peter's donkey were venerated. One group of pilgrims were said to be following a goose inspired by God.

These bizarre fantasists were the first forces to advance eastward. They did not wait for the official departure date, even if they knew of it. The daughter of the Byzantine Emperor, Anna Comnena, did not even connect the Crusade with her father's request to Pope Urban. She believed that it had been conjured into existence by the preaching of Little Peter.

> *Full of enthusiasm and ardour they thronged every highway, and with these warriors came a host of civilians, outnumbering the sand of the sea shore or the stars of heaven, carrying palms and bearing crosses on the shoulders. There were women and children, too, who had left their own countries. Like tributaries joining a river from all directions they streamed towards us in full force.*

The First Holocaust

The first victims of the Crusades, however, were not Turks or Arabs, they were not even Moslems, they were the Jews of Germany.

The systematic persecution and killing of Jews has been such a feature of European history that it can be a surprise to realize that it is an inheritance from the Crusades. Jewish communities had long been seen as economic assets and were allowed to own

The Massacres of the Jews

What is the significance of the massacres of Jews, which were to become a hallmark of all Crusades? One answer must be that at the heart of crusading lay a deep ambivalence about Christianity and Christ (who was, after all, a Jew). On one level, perhaps it was a projection of the Crusaders' own unease about themselves onto their parent faith. They were not really killers, it was the Jews who were killers, because they had killed Christ. They were not really greedy for wealth; it was the Jews who must be greedy. To purge these unclean things about themselves, they must project them onto others who could be exterminated. And, of course, the Jews were aliens – so Christ could not really be thought of as a Jew.

Similar anxieties were projected onto the Moslems. Praying to a wooden image of Christ could not be idolatry; it was the Moslems who must be idolaters. Worshipping the Son, the Father and the Holy Ghost could not be denying the single nature of God; it must be the Moslems who worshipped many gods.

How else can one explain the fact that the author of the *Gesta Francorum* – who came from southern Italy, where Moslems were not unknown, and fought for three years against the Turks – assumes that the Moslems were polytheists? He has the Seljuk leader Kerbogha swear *'by Mohammed and by all the names of our gods'* – ignoring the most basic tenet of Islam that there is only one God. He also refers to them as *'Christ's enemies'* – again completely ignoring the high regard in which Christ is held by Moslems.

And how can one explain the fact that another famous eyewitness, Fulcher of Chartres – who not only went on the Crusade but lived for twenty-seven years in Jerusalem, which gave him every opportunity to gather at least a superficial picture of Islam – insists that the Moslems worship Mohammed, and not only worship him but worship idols in his likeness? *'All the Saracens held the Temple of the Lord* [the Dome of the Rock] *in great veneration. Here rather than elsewhere they preferred to say the prayers of their faith although such prayers were wasted because offered to an idol set up in the name of Mohammed.'*

The Crusaders had not only taken into themselves the notion that they would become better people through violence; they also projected onto the victims of their violence their own inner demons. This is probably the most obvious and long-lasting heritage of the Crusade. We still do it.

Peter's pilgrim army being attacked by Bulgarians on the road through the Balkans. Their white garb is, of course, an outward sign of their inner purity. From *Les Passages faits Outremer . . . , c.* 1490.

land, houses and businesses. In 1048, for example, the Bishop of Spier issued a charter which reads: *'Desiring to make a city out of the village of Spier, I have admitted the Jews . . . I have thought to multiply one thousand times the honour of our city by gathering the Jews within its walls.'*

In 1096 the Jewish inhabitants of Spier, along with those of Worms, Mainz, Cologne, Trier, Metz and many smaller Rhineland towns, were slaughtered by Crusaders as a curtain-raiser to their journey of holy murder. The killings were done by bands of apocalyptic enthusiasts, loose followers of Peter the Hermit; these were people who lacked the cash to go on Crusade and their hatred of the Jews was clearly associated with love of, and desire for, gold. There were also some who could not understand why, if it was right to kill the enemies of Christ abroad, they should not also kill Christ's enemies at home.

When bishops defended the Jews, they were attacked too. At Spier the Bishop's intervention saved many lives but at Worms the killers were more determined. Led by Count Emich of Leisingen, a petty lord with a reputation for brigandage, they invaded the Bishop's palace and killed some five hundred Jews sheltering there. At Mainz they drove out the Archbishop and destroyed his palace in order to remove the Jews' protector.

The Chief Rabbi of Mainz escaped with some fifty followers to Rudesheim, where the Archbishop had taken refuge in his country villa, and begged asylum there. Unfortunately the Archbishop could not resist using this golden opportunity to try to convert them, whereupon the Chief Rabbi was so enraged that he seized a knife and attacked his protector — with the result that he and all his followers were also killed.

Count Emich and his followers, their pogrom accomplished, moved into Hungary. They were not the only ones. Another group, having moved on from killing Jews in the Rhineland to killing Jews in Prague, tried to do the same in the Hungarian town of Nitra but was scattered by the Hungarian army. Another, led by an old sidekick of Peter the Hermit, Gottschalk, made itself so unpopular during its brief march across Europe (massacring Bavarian Jews for example) that it was disarmed by the Hungarians and then was itself massacred. When Emich arrived with the largest force so far — and equipped with siege artillery — the King of Hungary decided he had had enough. He refused the Crusaders entry and when they forced their way over the border he finally destroyed them.

These bands of German thugs offered easy ammunition to Pope Urban's enemies, who were particularly numerous inside the Holy Roman Emperor's own German kingdom. Ekkehard, the Abbot of Aura in Germany, writing in about 1115, reported that many people thought the whole idea of the Crusade was vain and frivolous. The short life of the German Crusaders was seen by some as proof of God's disapproval. But the dominant mood was of feverish support for the Crusade.

Peter's March

In the meantime the biggest unofficial army of all, led by Peter the Hermit, was taking the traditional pilgrim route through Hungary into Byzantine territory. The first Byzantine city they came to was Belgrade. The Empire was taken completely by surprise by an advance group of Frenchmen under Walter Sans-Avoir (Walter the Penniless). Since the harvest was not in, and the local governor had no instructions, they were blocked and food was refused them. So Walter's men started pillaging around Belgrade. There was a violent clash, in which several of his followers were killed, before the Emperor got his act together and had them escorted to Constantinople. They had set out in April 1096 and arrived in July.

Peter was a few days behind with a much larger party. It was so much larger that the governor of the Hungarian border town of Semlin was frightened by it and tried to limit its freedom of movement. Bad temper and a complete absence of discipline soon led to a riot in which Peter's pilgrims stormed the citadel, killed four thousand Hungarians and then forced their way over the River Save and on to Belgrade.

Belgrade was hurriedly evacuated; the pilgrims sacked and burned it. On they marched, to be met by an imperial escort which they soon began to fight. The escort was left with no choice but to be ruthless. By the time Peter's force reached Sophia it had been subdued but a quarter of his enthusiastic volunteers had been killed or taken into slavery.

They arrived at Constantinople on 1 August, to be greeted by a politic message from Emperor Alexius saying that the expedition had suffered enough and the pilgrims were forgiven for their outrages. But the Emperor was not taking any chances. Peter's followers were causing enough trouble camped outside the city walls, burgling suburban villas and stripping the lead off church roofs. Small parties were allowed in for sightseeing, but most were kept firmly shut out.

There was plenty for the sightseers to gawp at.

Latin Europe had nothing to compare with Constantinople. London and Paris might have had ten thousand inhabitants, Cologne twenty thousand, Rome thirty thousand. The triple walls of Constantinople enclosed at least a quarter of a million people. The city was dominated by the huge new palace complex, the Blachernae, whose gardens housed a menagerie of exotic beasts, by the Emperor Justinian's great church of Haghia Sophia, whose immense dome appeared to float weightless over the space below; and by the gigantic sports arena, the Hippodrome. They could also see the collection of holy relics, which included the Crown of Thorns, the Seamless Garment, a cloth imprinted with Christ's face, Saint Luke's portrait of the Virgin, the hair of John the Baptist and many other wonders. It was a pilgrim's paradise.

But were Peter's followers pilgrims or invaders? Alexius could not take any chances, nor could he risk Peter's violent rabble being augmented by even larger armies which, he was told, would soon be on their way.

Just five days after Peter's force arrived everyone who had come to Constantinople was ferried over the Bosphorus into Asia. Alexius warned Peter that he should wait close to the shore for more professional forces to arrive, but Peter was not in charge of his army.

No-one was.

Into Asia

The land the Crusaders now entered, Anatolia, was controlled by the Turks to within a few miles of the Bosphorus. Most of the population were Christians, but they had not felt any need to appeal for help when they found the Turks in charge. On the contrary, since many of them followed heretical Christian sects – Jacobites, Nestorians, Armenians – they found life much easier under Islamic law. They were allowed freedom of worship and found their taxes somewhat lower; their writers, far from protesting about the rule of their conqueror, Malik Shah, sang his praises for bringing a restoration of order after the chaos of invasion.

Sultan Malik Shah had died in 1092. His sultanate was one of the great empires of history, stretching across Anatolia, down into Syria and Palestine, and eastward

---

Overleaf
The walls of Constantinople. This restored section
shows the triple line of defences built by Theodosius II in the
first half of the fifth century AD, which successfully protected
the city for eight hundred years. It was actually more impressive
than it looks, as the moat has been filled in.

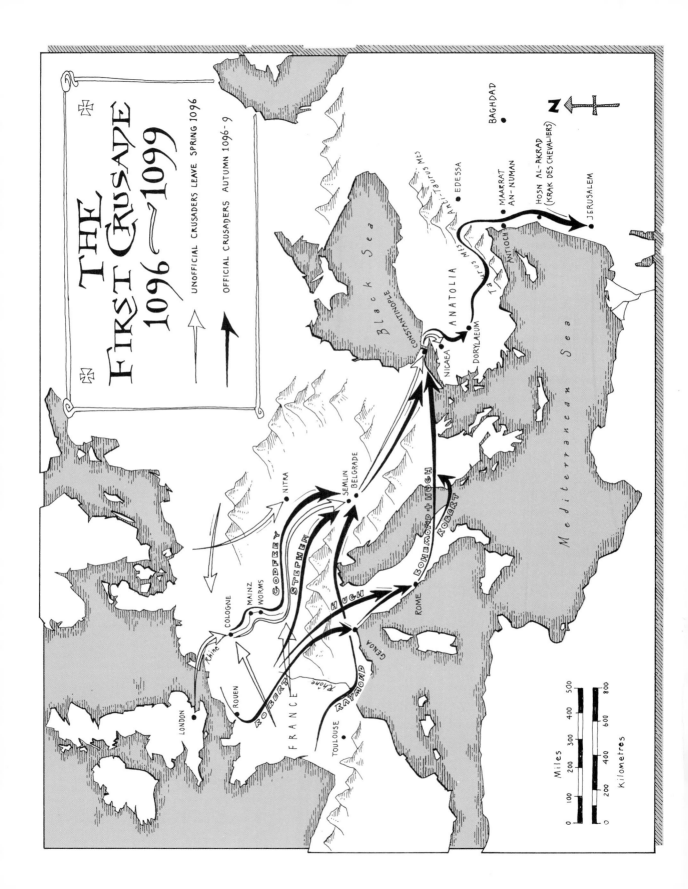

THE FIRST CRUSADE 1096~1099

⊳ UNOFFICIAL CRUSADERS LEAVE SPRING 1096

→ OFFICIAL CRUSADERS AUTUMN 1096-9

BAGHDAD

Black Sea

CONSTANTINOPLE

ANATOLIA

NICAEA

DORYLAEUM

Anti-Taurus Mts

EDESSA

Taurus Mts

ANTIOCH

MAARRAT AN-NUMAN

HOSN AL-AKRAD (KRAK DES CHEVALIERS)

JERUSALEM

Mediterranean Sea

SEMLIN

BELGRADE

NITRA

GODFREY

STEPHEN

BOHEMOND + HUGH

ROBERT

MAINZ

WORMS

COLOGNE

HUGH

ROME

Rhine

ROBERT

GENOA

FRANCE

Rhone

RAYMOND

ROUEN

LONDON

TOULOUSE

N

Miles
0   100   200   300   400   500

Kilometres
0   200   400   600   800

←—————————————————————→

through Baghdad across Persia, Afghanistan and northern India. His power, exer-
cised in the name of the puppet Caliph of Baghdad, covered the whole region from
the Mediterranean to China. His name really says it all – *Malik* is Arabic for King,
Shah is Persian for King and *Sultan* is Arabic for Ruler.

When he died in 1092, his empire disintegrated into competing emirates. Western
Anatolia became the Sultanate of Rum – 'Rum' being Rome. Its sultan was a
teenager, Kilij Arslan ibn Suleiman, the son of the emir who had conquered Anatolia
for Malik Shah. His capital was Nicaea (the modern Iznik), a historic Byzantine city
less than a hundred miles from Constantinople.

Alexius and Kilij Arslan were, when push came to shove, enemies, but they were
not on particularly bad terms. Indeed, it was on Alexius's advice that Kilij Arslan
had killed his father-in-law, the powerful and ambitious Emir of Smyrna (Izmir).
They both benefited from his death.

The Crusaders, of course, had no grasp of the niceties of politics in the region.
They could not even tell Christians from Turks.

The horde that Peter now led into Anatolia consisted of Germans, Italians and
Frenchmen. It was not really an army, though it included many knights; it was a vast
pilgrim force including many women, children and old people. The different groups
had little in common; the French quickly quarrelled with the others, who broke away
and elected an Italian, Rainald, as their leader. The rival groups shared a camp at
Civetot, on the Sea of Marmora. From there they set about what they saw as their
God-given mission to torture, pillage and massacre the locals. The snag, of course,
was that most of the locals were Christians.

In September the French raided the suburbs of Nicaea, treating the Christians of
the region with legendary nastiness: burning babies on spits, that sort of thing. They
returned to camp very pleased with themselves and their booty. Whereupon the other
lot decided to go one better.

A force of several thousand, including priests and bishops, marched beyond
Nicaea to a castle called Xerigordon, where they settled in. Kilij Arslan sent a force
to surround the castle and the Crusaders then discovered that they had made a serious
miscalculation. Xerigordon's water came from outside the castle. It took eight days
for them to surrender, by which time they were dying of thirst, having learned that
the blood of their animals and their own urine was no substitute for cool water. The
terms of surrender were straightforward; either convert to Islam (and be sent into
captivity) or die.

Conversion to Islam is very simple. All that is involved is to say 'God is great and

Mohammed is his prophet' and, if you are an uncircumsised male, to undergo a simple operation. Rainald, the leader of the gang, decided that the Pope's guarantee of a place in heaven had lost its appeal; he gritted his teeth and offered up his foreskin. Others found it easier, for whatever reason, to embrace martyrdom.

Kilij Arslan then sent agents into Civetot to spread rumours that Nicaea had been captured and that the victorious Crusaders were keeping all the loot for themselves. This triggered such excitement amongst the French that, even when they learned the terrible truth, the cries for booty turned into cries for vengeance and they set off anyway.

Peter had gone back to Constantinople to try to get some help from Alexius; he was not around to try to restrain them. Some twenty thousand men set out at dawn on 21 October and walked straight into a trap. They were ambushed three miles down the road and the People's Crusade was wiped out.

The Turks then stormed the camp. The entire process of destruction took about five hours. *'When they gathered up the remains of the fallen ....'* wrote Anna Comnena, *'they heaped up, I will not say a mighty hill or peak, but a mountain of considerable height and depth and width, so huge was the mass of bones.'* Alexius sent ships to gather up the few survivors and bring them back to safety. Meanwhile much more menacing forces were advancing on Constantinople.

The Official Crusade

The first of the official armies to arrive was led by Hugh of Vermandois. He had written ahead to the Emperor of Byzantium to tell him exactly who he was: *'Know, Emperor, that I am the King of Kings, the greatest of all beneath the heavens. It is my will that you should meet me on my arrival and receive me with the pomp and ceremony due to my noble birth.'*

Hugh's letter may have been written to impress on Alexius that his expedition was properly organized and financed, and not to be confused with the rabble that had accompanied Peter the Hermit, but it roused the scorn of the Emperor's daughter

---

Raymond of Toulouse and Bishop Adhemar
on their way to the Holy Land
being ambushed in Bulgaria.
From *Les Passages faits Outremer ..., c.* 1490.

Anna, who ridiculed it as 'absurd'. Perhaps Anna embellished on its absurdity when she recorded the letter for posterity – but hers is the only version we have.

Whatever his intentions, Hugh's arrival was anything but dignified. He was shipwrecked on the eastern coast of the Adriatic. The local Byzantine Governor rescued the bedraggled Count and entertained him to a magnificent banquet and 'fine promises'. He was then escorted under close surveillance to Byzantium. Once there, he was showered with gifts and fine words, but he was kept under such close supervision that he was virtually a prisoner – a fact which apparently rankled with some of his followers but which Hugh seems to have been happy to ignore.

In fact, Hugh felt honoured to swear an oath, when asked, that he would be the Emperor's liege-man. It would be his duty to return to the Emperor any lands taken from the Turks. This was to be the Emperor's policy to all those who were to follow. But, of course, it was not going to be as simple as all that.

The next army to arrive was from the Channel coast and Lorraine: the brothers Godfrey, Eustace and Baldwin with a substantial following of leading knights. Hugh was sent to invite Godfrey to take the oath of homage to Alexius.

Northern Europeans were not generally broadminded people and they did not like Byzantine civilization. It was court-based, dense with etiquette and ordered by a bureaucracy that had about a thousand years of experience to draw on. Back in the 960s Bishop Liudprand of Cremona had visited Constantinople and reported that in his objective view the inhabitants were *'soft, effeminate, long-sleeved, bejewelled and begowned liars, eunuchs and idlers'*. (He had been arrested trying to smuggle Imperial purple silk out of the country.) Most Franks and Germans shared Liudprand's view.

Godfrey had no intention of becoming the Emperor's liege-man. He wanted to wait for the other Crusading lords to arrive, which was exactly what Alexius was anxious to avoid. The Emperor wanted to get the oath and move this dangerous force over the Bosphorus before they received reinforcements. Above all, he wanted to prevent Bohemond from meeting up with Godfrey's army under the walls of Con-stantinople. Alexius tried cutting off their food supply.

Since Godfrey and his men had expected to be welcomed with open arms (after all, they had come a huge distance at their own expense to help the Empire and were about to fight its battles), this did not go down at all well. The army responded with a little controlled ravaging, and Alexius restored the food supply.

But the stand-off continued and in March 1097 Alexius heard that more armies were on their way. In desperation, he cut off supplies once more. This time God-frey, by way of further demonstration, launched a full-scale assault on the city. It created panic among the populace and Alexius sent out messengers to say that he would transport the Crusaders over the Bosphorus without waiting for Godfrey's oath.

The messengers, however, were attacked before they could open their mouths, whereupon Alexius had had enough. He sent out a real army to teach Godfrey's followers a lesson. On Easter Sunday, a chastened Godfrey, Baldwin and their followers swore to acknowledge Alexius as overlord of any conquests and to return to the Empire lands which they took from the Turks. They were immediately shipped over to Asia.

When new groups of Crusaders loosely attached to Godfrey arrived in unruly bands over the next couple of days, they were brought to heel and taken to the Palace to make the same oath. Godfrey and Baldwin were brought back to watch. When one of these knights insisted on sitting on the Emperor's throne, Baldwin had to explain to him that he must not be deliberately offensive. Their resentment of the court manners of Byzantium was profound.

Bohemond at Constantinople

On 9 April, just three days after Godfrey's army was ferried over the Bosphorus, Bohemond arrived. Alexius had just managed it in time.

Bohemond may have come on his way to attack the Turks but that did not mean he hated Islam. Sicily had been ruled by Arabs until his uncle conquered it, and mosques were allowed to continue there after the conquest. Indeed, he used Moslems to run his administration and southern Italy had begun to flourish with a stunningly brilliant *mélange* of Arab science and architecture, Byzantine craftsmanship and Norman practical sense. A Moslem source recounts how, when he was urged to attack North Africa and Christianize it, the Norman ruler of Sicily *'lifted his foot and made a great fart, saying "By my faith, here is far better counsel than you have given".'*

Unlike the Byzantines, the Arabs did not make it quite so obvious that they regarded Europeans as smelly, ignorant barbarians. The Normans did not hate the Arabs, but they did hate the Greeks of Byzantium. And here they were in Byzantium.

Bohemond's army, which waited under Tancred's command some distance away, was smaller than Godfrey's, but it was well equipped and effective. Bohemond was about twenty-two years older than Tancred and a striking figure. Normans were generally short and stocky — the Germans used to make fun of them for it — but

Bohemond was an exception. Anna was fascinated by him, and described him in detail in the memoirs she wrote in her old age:

> *Bohemond's appearance was, to put it briefly, unlike that of any man seen in those days in the Roman world, whether Greek or Barbarian. The sight of him inspired admiration, the mention of his name terror. I will describe in detail the Barbarian's characteristics. His stature was such that he towered almost a full cubit over the tallest men. He was slender of waist and flanks, with broad shoulders and chest, strong in the arms; in general, he was neither skinny nor heavily built and fleshy, but perfectly proportioned . . . His hair was lightish-brown and not as long as that of other barbarians (that is, it did not hang on his shoulders); in fact, the man had no great predilection for long hair, but cut his short, to the ears . . . His eyes were light blue and gave some hint of the man's spirit and dignity . . . There was a certain charm about him, but it was somewhat dimmed by the alarm his person as a whole inspired; there was a hard savage quality to his whole aspect, due, I suppose, to his great stature and his eyes; even his laugh sounded like a threat to others. Such was his constitution, mental and physical, that in him both courage and love were armed, both ready for combat.*

Bohemond was no boor; he knew exactly how to behave. That made him all the more threatening. Alexius had no doubt about Bohemond's intentions; the question was, how was he going to try to achieve them? Alexius asked indirectly. Bohemond smiled. *'I come of my own free will as Your Majesty's friend.'* He would take the oath without question. Of course. After all, it meant no more to him than it did to Alexius.

Bohemond was taken to luxurious quarters, but refused to touch the food prepared for him. Alexius had expected that; the chefs produced the raw ingredients for Bohemond's own cooks. The next day the charade continued. After the oath-taking, Bohemond was led to a chamber filled with gold, silver, rich cloths and other luxuries. *'If I had such wealth'*, he said, *'I would long ago have become master of many lands.' 'All this'*, said the man, *'is yours today – a present from the Emperor.'*

Finally, Bohemond issued his terms: he wanted to be Alexius's deputy in Asia. Alexius prevaricated, as Bohemond had expected. On 26 April his army was ferried over the Bosphorus to join Godfrey's Lorrainers. Tancred, who was baffled by what was going on, slipped through the city by night to avoid taking the oath.

Emperor Alexius standing before the throne of Christ.
His daughter Anna described Alexius as 'not very tall',
broad-shouldered and deep-chested, with curving eyebrows
and flashing eyes, a high colour and a thick
beard. From a twelfth-century Greek manuscript.

There were two more armies to come – the Franks, under Raymond of Toulouse, and Robert of Normandy's Normans. Raymond arrived on the day Bohemond's forces crossed the Bosphorus. He did not like the idea of taking an oath to Alexius and modified it so that he did not acknowledge the Emperor as an overlord, but Alexius was satisfied. Privately, Alexius told him that he would never give an imperial command to Bohemond and Raymond decided that he and Alexius could get on just fine together.

Finally Robert of Normandy's group arrived, after spending many months with their relatives in southern Italy. Alexius treated them warmly (he had got rid of the main forces by now) and gave each of the leaders the feeling that he was the Emperor's special, trusted ally. Stephen of Blois was particularly susceptible to this and wrote an enchanting letter to his wife revealing that he had fallen hook, line and sinker for Alexius's flattery. Adela would not have been pleased by Stephen's comparison between Alexius and William the Conqueror: *'Your father, my love, made many great gifts, but he was almost nothing compared to this man.'*

3

War in Anatolia

The force that was now assembled on the western edge of Asia was not a single army. It was an international gathering, divided by language, culture and loyalties. The latest estimate of this uncounted host is that it may have included sixty thousand combatants, but to those must be added women and children (some of them families of Crusaders who intended to settle in Jerusalem), old people who were making the pilgrimage as a final act of piety, clerics and vague hangers-on, including the remnants of Peter the Hermit's horde of enthusiasts.

Their leaders were at least as suspicious of each other as they were of the Turks or Byzantines. But for now they agreed that their first objective was to take the town of Nicaea – the capital of Kilij Arslan's Sultanate, which stood proudly on the eastern shore of Lake Iznik.

The Capture of Nicaea

Kilij Arslan had not expected this lot to be any more problem than the last bunch and had gone off to fight his neighbour, the Emir Danishmend. When he heard that the Crusaders had launched an attack on Nicaea, he patched up a hasty alliance with Danishmend, hurried back to raise the siege, and found he had been wrong.

Kilij Arslan threw his forces against the section of besiegers commanded by Raymond of Toulouse. This was the first battle between a full army of European knights and Turkish horsemen, and there was not simply a clash of arms, there was a clash of fighting cultures.

The Normans had brought to horse-riding the mentality of boat crews. They expected to work together as a group and that was how they worked as cavalry. Instead of throwing their lances and wheeling away, they preferred to bear down on the enemy in a massed charge with their lances firmly wedged under their arms or held aloft ready for pig-sticking.

They had developed deep saddles and long stirrups so that the rider could be wedged firmly into place, bracing himself between stirrup and saddle-back. Since there was no easy way of getting off, these soldiers did not even think of fighting on foot.

Their horses were little fighting stallions, selected for power, weight, and a broad flat back that could support a man wearing a mail shirt that came down to his knees. This, with his thick padded long jerkin (an *aketon* – a corruption of the Arabic *al-Qutun*, meaning cotton), added two stone to the rider's weight. All European knights now fought this way, riding in tight formation, galloping straight at the enemy and expecting to demolish him by sheer power; Anna Comnena wrote that *'a Frank on horseback could knock a hole in the walls of Babylon'*.

But the knights' charge was only effective against an enemy who stood still to be charged at – and the Turks could and did get out of the way. They rode long-legged mares, chosen for speed, agility and responsiveness; they did not fight in formation, but wheeled in and away, shooting arrows from their short, highly tensioned bows. They depended above all on numbers – an endless, terrifying assault by wave after wave of deadly sharpshooters, who could fire as readily when they were retiring as when attacking. The whole emphasis was on speed; they wore little armour and used small, light shields.

The real deciding moment of a conflict between the two forces would be when the knights had finished their charge. If they remained together as a pack, and used their swords on horseback as an armoured group, they were virtually invulnerable, but if they broke apart they could be individually surrounded and brought down.

This battle was a learning exercise on both sides. The Crusaders suffered heavy casualties, but there was no way the Turks could break up their force and Kilij Arslan had to withdraw.

The Crusaders could now concentrate on breaking into the city. The trouble was that their siege artillery only hurled small rocks. It was excellent for forcing defenders to keep their heads down, but could make little impression on a thick wall. It was used as a crude form of psychological warfare lobbing fire bombs, severed heads, and even beehives at the besieged. The Crusaders' best hope was to starve the city out, but since they had no boats, they could not stop the Nicaeans getting supplies from across the lake.

In this thirteenth-century version of the Crusaders' attack on
Nicaea, baskets of severed heads are being hurled at the walls.
Early siege artillery was not much use at demolishing masonry:
the most effective ammunition was either psychological (as
here) or bacteriological – infected or rotting animals
were popular for this. Even hives of bees were sometimes thrown
onto the defenders. From William of Tyre's *History of Deeds
done beyond the Sea*.

Six weeks later they were still stuck there. Emperor Alexius decided it was time he showed the Crusaders how to do it. He transported a fleet of boats overland, put them on the lake, made a secret deal with the Turkish commanders in Nicaea and then slipped his men across the lake in the dead of night. When dawn broke on 19 June 1097, the Crusaders, who were all geared up for a final assault on the walls, saw to their dismay the Emperor's flag flapping languidly over Nicaea.

The Crusaders were not overjoyed by this victory, even though it secured the first strategically vital city on the road to Jerusalem. They were livid. Alexius had snatched their booty. According to the accepted conventions of the time, a city that was stormed could also be sacked. A city that surrendered would only yield a ransom for its leading citizens. And the Byzantines had even rescued those, hustling Kilij Arslan's wife and children and all their movable property off to Constantinople.

So far as Alexius was concerned, Nicaea was his city (most of its inhabitants were still Greeks) and the prisoners would be extremely useful to him. In fact he exchanged Kilij Arslan's wife for the Emirate of Smyrna. But to many Crusaders it seemed ridiculous to protect the infidel from their holy wrath and criminal to deprive them of their sacred right of plunder.

Alexius acted as a generous feudal lord. He presented food to every Crusader and offered large gifts of gold to their leaders. But he also insisted that Tancred would only receive his portion once he gave the oath that he had so far evaded. Tancred insisted that his loyalty lay to Bohemond, not Alexius, and he demanded that he be given as much gold as everyone else combined, plus the Emperor's own tent filled with gold. It took serious pressure from Bohemond before he gave in. Tancred took oaths and obligations very seriously; that was what had so troubled him in the past. But he was young and would learn.

The Battle of Dorylaeum

It was the end of June 1097; the coast of Anatolia was at its most pleasant, and the Crusaders were only about seven hundred miles from Jerusalem. *'In five weeks' time,'* wrote Stephen of Blois to his wife, *'we shall be at Jerusalem, unless we are held up at Antioch.'* It was going to take two years.

Kilij Arslan had retreated into the mountains. As the Crusaders began their eastward march, he and his new ally, Danishmend, brought their combined forces into an ambush position. The Crusaders' force was too large to travel as a single mass, and the Franks and Lorrainers formed a rearguard group under Raymond, one day behind the Normans and others who accepted Bohemond's leadership. Four days from Nicaea, on the road to Dorylaeum (Eskiehir), the Turks fell on the leading group.

There was panic among the Christians when the attack began and if it had been allowed to continue, the Crusade would have been over in an hour. But Bohemond immediately took command. He had seen what had happened at Nicaea and had no intention of fighting with half an army. Instead, he invented the tactic that would be reinvented eight hundred years later to fight the horse-archers of the American West. He drew the wagons into a circle and sent an emergency message to the cavalry over the hill. Bohemond forbade anyone to charge the Turks and those who disobeyed soon found themselves in deep trouble. The Crusaders suffered terribly under the assault, but their will to fight was unbreakable. After all, they were fighting in a holy cause.

During the battle a Norman eyewitness noticed that the Turks went into the attack with a distinctive war-cry: *'These Turks began, all at once, to howl and gabble and shout, saying with loud voices in their own language some devilish word which I do not understand.'* Tancred's biographer, Radulph of Caen, explained that this 'devilish word' was *'Allachibar'*, that is, *Allah al-Akhbar* or 'God is great'. The two sides were hurling themselves into battle against each other, one side yelling 'God's will! God's will! God's will!' and the other 'God is great!' Both sides were addressing the same god. Neither could understand what the other was saying.

After about six hours God's forces were definitely winning. The Turks were breaking through the Crusaders' defences. Then, suddenly, God's other forces came to the rescue. Raymond's men appeared, fresh and eager for battle. Now Bohemond brought out his line of knights, which joined with the newcomers to form an ap-parently endless wall, thundering forward against the tiring Turks. The Turks broke.

The Crusaders had suffered significant casualties (including Tancred's brother, William), but this had been a battle of wills and their will had proved the stronger. The Turks would not seriously challenge them again on the long march through Anatolia.

Overleaf A head-to-head conflict between charging lines of knights and 'Saracens', as depicted here, was not a likely event as Turkish horsemen preferred to swoop in and out again. The battle of Nicaea must have been enlivened by the fact that the knights' chargers were stallions, whereas Turkish archers rode mares; as the battle took place in June, many of the mares may well have been on heat. From the fourteenth-century *Chronicles of Godfrey of Bouillon.*

The March across Anatolia

The fastest route was straight through the middle. It had to be fast, as it crossed a waterless salt desert. The huge, slow-moving body of Crusaders could not hope to survive it in midsummer. So, instead, they skirted the edge of the desert, lumbering along an endless, hot, difficult road under the foothills of the Taurus mountains.

The temperature mounted steadily through August; the chronicler Albert of Aix describes the suffering on a single day in August as men, women, children and animals died of thirst, women gave birth at the roadside and abandoned their infants. When they finally reached a river, *'many who had been weakened, as many men as beasts of burden, died from drinking too much'*.

Finally, in September, they reached the Cilician Gates, the only pass over the Taurus mountains towards Antioch, and decided not to take it. They had just been attacked by the first substantial Turkish force since Dorylaeum and although they had sent it packing, they were in poor shape. The pass was steep and narrow, ideal ambush territory. It was also very hot and dry. Many of the pilgrims were severely weakened; horses and donkeys had perished in such numbers that some knights were riding oxen and carts were being pulled by dogs. Instead of attempting another endurance test, they turned towards the woods and pastures that lay to the north-east. This route would take them into friendly Armenian-held lands. They would find a pass up there, over the Anti-Taurus mountains, and approach Antioch from the east.

The Armenians were Christians who felt no loyalty to Byzantium. Driven from their homeland in the southern Caucasus by Byzantine armies as well as Islamic ones, they disliked the Greeks as much as the Crusaders did. They now lived in the mountains and coastal plain of Cilicia, in the area of the Anti-Taurus to the north-east, and across to the Euphrates. The Crusade leaders were very interested in the Armenians.

Baldwin, the young brother of Godfrey of Lorraine, was particularly interested in the Armenians. At Nicaea he had become friendly with an Armenian called Bagrat whose brother was Vasil the Robber (Kogh Vasil), a princeling who ruled to the east of the Anti-Taurus. Bagrat had been in Alexius's service; now he was in Baldwin's. He was urging Baldwin to go to the aid of the Armenians. It was a proposition that held rather attractive possibilities for a fortune-hunter like Baldwin.

Tancred also had a pet Armenian. This man told Tancred that the inhabitants of Tarsus, the town immediately to the south of the Cilician Gates, were prepared to throw off their Turkish garrison and welcome him as their overlord. So Tancred persuaded his uncle Bohemond to let him take a party of a hundred knights and two hundred infantrymen through the Cilician Gates to Tarsus. Unfortunately it was not a large enough force to dispatch the Turks of Tarsus quickly. After three days, however, a more substantial army of five hundred knights and two thousand infantrymen was spotted coming to join him. The Turks fled and the townspeople happily raised Tancred's banner.

But this new force had not been sent as a reinforcement for Tancred. It was a quite separate expedition which had left the main Crusade under the command of Baldwin.

Baldwin and Godfrey had no intention of letting Bohemond and Tancred win control of the coast. Baldwin's expedition had come through the Gates in a blocking move, and now he peremptorily demanded that Tarsus be surrendered to him. Tancred, whose forces were much smaller, resentfully complied. When a further group of Bohemond's followers arrived a few days later, Baldwin refused to open the gates for them and they were massacred outside the city walls by the Turks. So much for solidarity.

Tancred now moved west to Adana, where the Turkish garrison fled, and then to Mamistra. Again the small force of Turkish occupiers withdrew and the Armenian population welcomed him in. Baldwin followed and the two Crusader forces actually fought each other before agreeing that they would both pull out.

Crossing the Anti-Taurus

eanwhile the main Crusade had been crossing the mountain range known as the Anti-Taurus. It had been unexpectedly horrific. The road was only capable of bearing a small, fit company and in the heavy rains of October the steep mountain paths disintegrated under the weight of tens of thousands of people and their baggage-trains. Sinking in the mud, weighed down by their arms and equipment, they endured a nightmare. Some tried to sell their armour, others simply threw it away. Entire baggage-trains slid over precipices.

When Baldwin rejoined the main army, after it had made its painful way down the other side of the Anti-Taurus, he found it was significantly smaller, and his own wife was dying. Godvere of Tosni was the daughter of one of the richest men in Normandy. With her death, Baldwin's one chance of inherited wealth disappeared. That settled matters. A few days later, with just a hundred knights, he set off to find an Armenian kingdom worth keeping. Bagrat rode with him. Their target was not a Moslem city but the Christian city of Edessa.

Left The capture of Antioch was a landmark in the success of the First Crusade. This fifteenth-century picture shows the key moment when Bohemond's men were let into the towers at night by a traitor. The massacre that followed is also faithfully recorded [*below left*]. The slaughter of 'infidels' — men, women and children — and the desecration of their tombs were clearly nothing to be ashamed of.

Above The moral purity of the Crusaders was considered to be an important factor in their military strength and defeats were often attributed to sexual indulgence. This fifteenth-century illustration shows women being expelled from the camp at Antioch at a time of crisis.

$\longleftarrow$ $\longrightarrow$

Baldwin Takes Edessa

Edessa, on the east side of the Euphrates, was the richest and most important of the Armenian towns. It was reputed to be the birthplace of Abraham and the locals told the story of how King Nimrod had captured Abraham and had him catapulted from the citadel rock into a blazing bonfire below. However, as Abraham was sailing through the air, God changed the flames to water and the logs to fish, so Abraham landed safe and sound in the pools of the town that still to this day bear his name.

Edessa was surrounded by rival Seljuk emirates who were keen to gobble it up. Its ruler was an Armenian Christian by the name of Thoros, who had managed to capture the city from the Turks two years before. He was now surviving only because his Turkish neighbours were too suspicious of each other to cooperate against him. He was most anxious for Baldwin's help.

The population were delighted to welcome Baldwin as their saviour, but Baldwin insisted that Thoros and his wife adopt him as their son and — more to the point — heir. This ceremony, which was designed for the adoption of infants, was rather curious. It involved Thoros putting on a doubly wide shirt. Baldwin, stripped, got in the shirt with Thoros and the two rubbed bare breasts together. Baldwin then had to go through the same process with Thoros's wife — much to the amusement of the onlookers.

This happy little family didn't last for long.

About four weeks later, by an extraordinary coincidence which Baldwin's friends insisted had absolutely nothing whatever to do with Baldwin, Thoros found himself faced by a popular revolt. When the old man was torn to pieces by a mob as he tried to escape from a palace window, Baldwin felt it was not his place to interfere. Thoros, it seems, had always been unpopular because he belonged to the Greek Orthodox Church, not the Armenian, and held a title from Alexius.

And so Baldwin became the sole ruler of Edessa. It was a pity that the Crusade's first independent conquest was taken from Christians rather than from Moslems, and it was a slight snag that it really belonged to Byzantium, but Baldwin was untroubled by such details. The new Count of Edessa found an immense treasure stacked away and used it to buy up the nearest emirate. He married an Armenian princess and so acquired control of a substantial principality around the city. Baldwin had his own state, rich, reasonably powerful, and to hell with his oath to the Emperor. What was more, he was protecting the west flank of the Crusade, which had now settled down to the long and painful business of besieging Antioch.

The Siege of Antioch

Antioch was almost as important as Constantinople in the symbolic Christian geography of the road to Jerusalem. It was here that the word 'Christian' was first used, when Saints Peter, Paul and Barnabus established the first Christian community. The Patriarch of Antioch was a rival in authority to the Patriarchs of Jerusalem and Constantinople. Even though the city had fallen to the Turks in 1084, its people were still Christian – Greek, Armenian and Syrian – and they still continued to worship as they always had.

And since Antioch controlled the route from Asia Minor into Syria, it was vital for the Crusaders to capture it.

The sight of the city must have staggered them. Its walls stretched over twenty-five miles, guarded by four hundred towers, and over such difficult terrain that they could never be fully surrounded. Its water supply was excellent. It had huge pasture areas within the walls. It was considered impregnable and had only fallen to the Turks through treachery. As a precaution, the Turkish Governor, Yaghi-Siyan, expelled the leading Greek and Armenian Christians, and imprisoned the Patriarch.

The siege dragged on. In the four months it had taken to reach Antioch, the expedition had only seen four days of fighting, but now they were subject to continuous sallies and ambushes as the garrison of Antioch tried to disperse them. It was not even possible to block all the gates of the city and prevent these attacks. And just to taunt the Christians, Yaghi-Siyan would from time to time have the Patriarch of Antioch dangled over the wall in a cage.

Yaghi-Siyan had survived by the same techniques as Thoros in Edessa – playing off the surrounding Seljuk rulers against each other. Now he had to appeal to them for help. The rulers of Damascus and Aleppo made attempts to break the siege, but were beaten off. As winter went on, the besiegers ran out of food even faster than the besieged. Foraging parties travelled up to fifty miles looking for supplies. Thousands – perhaps ten thousand of the poorest Crusaders – literally starved to death.

Stephen of Blois tried to put a brave face on it, writing home to his wife Adela: *'You may be very sure, dearest, that the messenger I sent with this letter left me outside Antioch safe and unharmed.'* But he could not disguise their sufferings through the winter: *'We have endured many sufferings and innumerable evils. Many have already spent all they have, and many would have died from starvation if the kindness of God had not saved them. We suffer from excessive cold and enormous amounts of rain.'*

Everyone on the expedition was self-financing, or was financed by their lord; food

had to be bought and as minor nobles ran out of cash, anyone who depended on them became destitute. The Crusade was blocked and dying, and more and more people began to desert. Peter the Hermit himself deserted, and had to be forcibly dragged back by Tancred.

Spirits somewhat rallied in the spring, when a fleet arrived carrying much needed supplies and building materials from Constantinople, shipped in by an exiled claim-ant to the English throne, Edgar Atheling. Edgar had commandeered an English fleet that was carrying Italian pilgrims to the Holy Land; it was quite clear to anyone who thought about it that pilgrimage was proceeding quite normally by sea and Jerusalem was perfectly accessible the whole time.

Then ambassadors arrived from the Vizier of Egypt. The Egyptians had lost control of Palestine to the Seljuks in the early 1070s and had been delighted to learn that Alexius was receiving help from the West to expel them. The Egyptian ambassadors explained that as the Christians were recapturing Byzantine lands, so Egypt would recapture its own lost territories from the Turks. Egyptian forces were poised to recover Palestine, including Jerusalem. Of course, the Vizier would be more than happy to restore free access to all Christians: *'We shall restore the holy city and the Tower of David and Mount Zion to the Christian people.'*

The Pope had called for an expedition to save Christians and their churches from the 'vile Turks'. Now the Egyptians were saying there was no need for them to conquer Jerusalem. But the Crusade had taken on a life of its own. The Crusaders had come too far, suffered too much, seen too many of their comrades perish.

From now on the Crusade assumed a new feeling – more fanatical, more savage, more visionary. The soldiers of Christ began to see themselves as the new Children of Israel, marching in the company of angels to the Promised Land. Their suffering was purgation. Even their horses were dead; they had nothing, but to bring on their millennial victory, they had only to be purified. The Bishops decreed that all immoral acts must cease, all profiteering end, and women be expelled from the camp; that way the Crusaders would deserve and be granted victory. But they could not afford to wait for it.

Adhemar, the Pope's legate, holds up the Holy Lance after the peasant, Peter Bartholomew, had dug it out of the floor of Antioch Cathedral following his dream. The miraculous 'discovery' was seen as an affirmation of divine approval and protection for the Crusade at its most desperate moment. From *Les Passages faits Outremer . . .* , c.1490.

← ———————————————————————————— →

The Capture of Antioch

Word reached the besiegers in May that Kerbogha, the mighty Emir of Mosul, was on the way to Antioch with an army of terrifying proportions — easily capable of crushing the Christians between itself and the defending garrison. The Crusaders' only hope was to get into the city before he arrived.

Tensions rose in the Christian camp, probably helped by Bohemond whose spies kept spreading rumours about the impossibility of the siege being successful. Faced with the certainty of extinction once Kerbogha arrived, more and more Crusaders were deserting, and Bohemond was probably hoping that his rivals amongst the leaders would be among their number. In the end, the only leader of note to desert was Stephen of Blois. On 2 June he abandoned the camp, taking with him a considerable number of Frenchmen. He chose his day badly. A few hours after he left the Crusaders captured Antioch.

As Yaghi-Siyan had always suspected, the only way Antioch could be taken was by treachery. Bohemond's spies had discovered that the guard in the Tower of the Two Sisters was not a happy man. Firouz was an Armenian armour-maker who had converted to Islam but who was now disenchanted with his position. His commanding officer had fined him for hoarding grain and, according to some reports, seduced his wife. Firouz was ready for revenge.

Bohemond had the key, but before he would turn it he insisted on his terms. He told the other leaders that he wanted to be left in control of Antioch. Then he instructed Firouz to let his men in through a window.

By that night there was not a Turk left alive in the city, nor a Frank left sober. Firouz had his revenge. But in their blood-lust the invaders killed many Christians too. The murderous rage that had marked Peter the Hermit's disastrous Crusade had taken over. The Crusaders were saving their souls not just by holy war, but by blood sacrifice.

Once in control of the city, however, the Crusaders discovered what a good job they had made of starving it out. There was practically no food left. Then Kerbogha's multitude arrived. The besiegers became the besieged — and starving! Soon a gold coin would buy a small loaf of bread. Two coins bought an egg. A chicken cost three gold coins. The only hope for the Crusaders was that the Emperor would come to their rescue with the imperial army. And sure enough he was on the way.

Unfortunately, before the Emperor had got very far, he bumped into the retreating Stephen of Blois, who regretfully explained that Antioch was lost and that the

Crusaders must surely all be dead by now – there was no point in continuing. Alexius agreed. Jerusalem had fallen to the Fatimids, who were his allies; the Turks had been defeated in western Anatolia; and since Antioch was not to be his, he turned round and went home.

But in Antioch twenty thousand half-crazed and starving survivors of the Crusade were pulling down heaven and wrenching a miracle out of it.

The Miracles at Antioch

On 10 June 1098 a shabby peasant with a reputation for drinking and womanizing demanded an interview with Count Raymond and the Bishop of Le Puy. When the two nobles reluctantly met this man, Peter Bartholomew, he claimed that St Andrew had come to him in a series of visions and revealed to him that the Holy Lance which had pierced Christ's side was buried in the Cathedral at Antioch. More visions were reported by others – saints, Christ himself and a meteor were seen. People who tried to desert by climbing down ropes over the wall were confronted by their dead comrades who told them to climb back in. They did.

Finally on 14 June an excavation was conducted in the Cathedral, but nothing was found. Everyone was just about to give up, when Peter Bartholomew leapt into the pit, clad only in his shirt, told everyone to pray and then triumphantly pulled out a length of iron. The Holy Lance had been found. God and his saints were with them.

The Pope's legate, the Bishop of Le Puy, ordered a three-day fast to begin on 24 June and then would do battle.

A fast was just what they needed. They had nothing to eat anyway; they were chewing leather and boiling tree-bark.

At dawn on 28 June the starving Crusaders attended mass, confessed their sins and opened the gates of Antioch. They stood no mortal chance. They had only two hundred living horses and had no strength. Only two hundred of them stayed behind to guard the city, under Raymond, who was too weak to walk.

They marched out behind the Holy Lance, and with white-clad priests bearing crosses praying aloud. But the miracles had not finished. As they stumbled towards the great Turkish army *'there appeared from the mountains a countless host of men on white horses, whose banners were all white,'* wrote the anonymous chronicler of the *Gesta Francorum*. *'When our men saw this, they did not understand what was happening.'* Battle was being joined by an army of ghosts – charging under the command of St George,

St Demetrius and St Mercury. *'Then we called upon the true and living God, and charged.'* The Turks saw — whatever they saw — and turned and fled.

It was a miracle. There could be no other explanation — although, of course, there was.

Kerbogha's mighty army was actually made up of levies from Baghdad and Persia, Palestine and Damascus, and the internal quarrels amongst the emirs took precedence over any unity against the Franks. The only thing that united his allies was a common fear of Kerbogha himself. The Emir of Damascus convinced the others that Kerbogha's real goal was the conquest of all their lands. If Antioch fell, he would be invincible. If it did not, well, who would suffer? The Byzantine Empire was simply recovering its own city from Yaghi-Siyan; so what?

The emirs decided to humble Kerbogha and they abandoned him at the critical moment. There was no miracle; just normal Turkish politics. But there were few Crusaders who now believed that the Holy Lance was a trick or who shared Bohemond's contempt for miracles. *'Let the cupidinous count Raymond and his foolish crowd assign the victory to the Lance,'* Bohemond declared.

They did.

And, miracle or not, Antioch was now well and truly in the hands of the Crusaders.

4

The March to Jerusalem

By the end of August 1098 Hugh of Vermandois, the first of the great lords to leave Europe, was already on his way home with his troops. The road to Jerusalem was open; the Egyptians had ejected the Turks from the Holy City, establishing their frontier just north of Beirut, and guaranteed free access to Christian holy sites. There was general confusion about what to do next.

The man who should have made the decisions was the Bishop of Le Puy, who had been appointed as the Pope's surrogate and leader of the expedition, but he had died, a victim of an epidemic that swept Antioch during July. With his death on 1 August, the influence of Rome over the Crusade ended. From now on, it was the Crusaders' own ideas of their purpose that would decide matters. But they lacked a commander.

Since it had been the Pope's intention to establish his own primacy at Jerusalem, the centre of the universe, the leaders invited him to come and do just that. They sent a letter to Rome early in September, explaining that they had *transferred the whole city of Antioch to the Roman religion and faith*' and the next move was up to him.

In the meantime the leaders of the Crusade were locked in dispute about who was to rule Antioch. Bohemond's claims were disputed by Raymond who insisted that, by right, the city should be handed over to the Emperor, in fulfilment of their vows.

But while the nobility argued and waited, there were plenty of lesser Crusaders who had a very clear idea of their next move. They declared that they were going to march to Jerusalem and if the great lords continued to squabble over Antioch, they would raze the walls to the ground.

Some Flemish followers of Peter the Hermit, having lost everything, had begun to behave as holy savages; they were known as 'Tafurs' (*Tafuria* is Arabic for 'penniless'), and were led by a mythical King Tafur. They became fanatical zealots, thinking of themselves as the men of pure motives. The Tafur fantasy was developed a few years afterwards in a popular tale, the *Chanson d'Antioch*: it was the poor who were destined to take Jerusalem as *'a sign to show clearly that the Lord God does not care for presumptuous and faithless men.'*

In the raiding parties that were organized to collect food, destroy Turks and keep the troops occupied, the Tafurs became notorious. *'Some of the poorest people in the crusading army,'* wrote Guibert of Nogent, *'always marched barefoot, bore no arms, themselves had absolutely no money but, entirely filthy in their nakedness and want, marched in advance of all the others and lived on the roots of plants.'* These holy madmen among the Crusaders became an increasingly powerful party in their own right, and it was partly to keep them quiet that an attack was organized on the strategically important town of Maarrat an-Numan.

It took two weeks to capture the town and once again the rivalries between Bohemond and Raymond dominated the assault. Raymond's men were the first to enter, but in an attempt to forestall him, Bohemond had it announced that he would grant amnesty to all inhabitants who assembled in a hall near the main gate. A lot of citizens were persuaded to surrender to him in this way. But Bohemond's promises were never worth staking your life on. The next day his troops entered the building and slaughtered everyone there who had accepted his protection.

Still the advance to Jerusalem was delayed. As at Antioch, the troops occupying the city found there was no food left. They got hungry . . . very hungry indeed, and in the end resorted to some radical cookery. Radulph of Caen, who was presumably told the tale by Tancred, reported that *'our troops boiled pagan adults in cooking pots; they impaled children on spits and devoured them grilled'*. The official excuse, offered in a letter to the Pope, was that they were hungry.

Those with religion but no brains now threatened to pull down the walls of Maarrat unless their leaders stopped bickering over Antioch and led them to battle at Jerusalem. Their object was not to rescue the Christians there, nor to free the holy

---

Jerusalem as portrayed in a French Book of Hours of
1270. This is obviously based on direct observation: the
Church of the Holy Sepulchre in the foreground is
immediately recognizable, and its details are accurately
drawn — even down to the right-hand door of the church
which is still blocked up to this day.

←――――――――――――――――――――――→

places – the Christians in Jerusalem did not need rescuing and the holy places were already open for business again – but to fight a mythic war against the 'Infidel'. Raymond was forced to concede that Bohemond, the man with brains but no religion, could keep Antioch and he, Raymond, would lead the Jerusalem forces. Tancred, who would have to keep an eye out for the family's interest in whatever was captured next, joined up with Raymond.

In January 1099, with the sixty-year-old Raymond in the lead as a barefoot pilgrim, some five thousand ardent Franks began walking south. They left Maarrat in flames. The Egyptian Vizier, baffled and disturbed, sent an urgent emissary to Alexius asking what his men were up to. Alexius replied that he had no control over them; he did not support what they were doing and he reaffirmed his alliance with Cairo. In fact the leaders of the Crusade themselves had no more control than Alexius. In the *Chanson d'Antioch* they are made to admit: *All of us together cannot tame King Tafur*.

Nothing could.

Advance on the Holy City

The Holy City now lay about three hundred miles ahead – a brisk two-week walk for pilgrims. The Crusaders took six months.

This was not because they were fighting for their lives. Most of the local rulers were only too anxious to hurry this dangerous throng on and out of their own territories as quickly as possible. The Emir of Shaizar, for example, provided them with guides and cheap provisions, and – for all anyone knows – probably wished them a pleasant onward trip. The Lord of Masyaf hastily drew up a treaty with them.

On the way to the coast, however, they fought what must be one of the most curious battles of all time. They besieged a castle that was defended entirely by sheep. The local inhabitants had driven their flocks into the disused fortress known as Hosn al-Akrad ('citadel of the Kurds'). When the Crusaders attacked, the peasants rather craftily released a few of the animals and the Christians – predictably – went chasing off in pursuit. This gave the locals a chance to slip away into the night, leaving their flocks behind them. When the Crusaders resumed the siege, they couldn't understand why no one was fighting back. They suspected it was yet another peasant ruse, whereas in fact it was the purely technical problem sheep have in mounting any sort of armed resistance.

The Crusaders, however, were eventually able to get the better of the sheep, and decided that this was a good spot in which to rest up for a few weeks. Raymond held court amidst the empty ruins, while the local emirs hurried to pay their respects and offer gifts to the invaders.

There is an Arab saying, 'Kiss any arm you cannot break — and pray to God to break it.'

The Emir of Tripoli rather overdid the friendliness. He invited the Crusaders to send emissaries to Tripoli to discuss a possible alliance. These emissaries were so dazzled by the prosperity and wealth of the city that the word 'alliance' was replaced in their minds by the word 'acquisition'. They duly reported back to Raymond and the Crusade lurched forwards towards the rich pickings.

So while the Emir of Tripoli was waiting for a response to his offer, he learnt that his proposed allies were at that moment besieging the second largest city of his realm — Arqa. Not that they wanted to capture it. Raymond was hoping that the Emir would give him a large sum of money to go away.

Within a couple of days the Crusaders had also captured the port of Tortosa. News of this got back to Antioch and persuaded Godfrey of Lorraine and Robert of Flanders that they ought to get a piece of the action. In the meantime, however, the siege of Arqa had turned out to be a pig's ear. Raymond had encountered a much more spirited defence than he had anticipated. He pleaded with Godfrey and Robert to join him. This was a mistake. The princes immediately started quarrelling again over the leadership of the Crusade, and of course the antagonism quickly spread through the ranks. Soon the Normans and the Provençals were — as usual — at loggerheads.

This time, however, the squabbles centred on Peter Bartholomew, who was still having visions by the dozen. Were they all a put-on or not? The Normans were convinced they were, because all the saints who appeared to Peter seemed to side with the Provençals against the Normans. Eventually the Normans publicly denounced Peter as a fraud and even called into question the authenticity of the Holy Lance, whereupon Peter indignantly demanded to be tested: he would undergo an ordeal by fire. God would enable him to walk through it unscathed.

A pile of logs was duly blessed by all the bishops and this was then set on fire in a narrow passage. Peter took the Holy Lance in his hand and dashed through the flames. What happened next depended on who was watching. Peter emerged into a scrum and fell, terribly burnt. The believers claimed he had been pushed back into the flames, the sceptics said he had been burnt in the ordeal. The only thing both sides could agree on was that twelve days later he was definitely dead.

Audience ratings for the Holy Lance slumped, never to recover.

Raymond was finally persuaded to abandon the siege of Arqa and the whole Crusade marched on Tripoli. There the terrified Emir hurried to release Christian prisoners, provided the Crusaders with horses and provisions, and even, it is said, offered to become a Christian himself.

The same sort of reception awaited them as they moved on down the coast into Fatimid territory, through Beirut and Acre. The real feelings of the locals, however, were exposed when a hawk killed a carrier pigeon flying over the Crusaders' camp. Tied to its leg was a message from the Governor of Acre (whose generosity they had just been enjoying) urging Moslems to rise up and destroy the invaders.

As they drew closer to the Holy City, envoys suddenly arrived from Bethlehem, whose Christian population requested instant deliverance from Moslem rule. Tancred was only too happy to oblige and made the detour to be welcomed as liberator. When he left to rejoin the main army the next day, his banner was flying above the birthplace of Christ. An eclipse of the moon added to the Crusaders' growing euphoria – the eclipse of the Crescent was imminent.

Finally they breasted the hill called Montjoie and caught their first sight of the place they had been dreaming and talking about for so long. They had been on the road for nearly three years. But there in the distance – finally – were the walls of Jerusalem. By the end of that day, 7 June 1099, they were encamped beneath the walls of the fabled city.

The Capture of Jerusalem

As the Egyptian Governor of Jerusalem, General Iftikhar al-Daula ('Pride of State'), watched the approach of the Crusaders he may not have felt too worried – the usual pre-battle butterflies in the tummy maybe, but not that dreadful sinking feeling of impending doom. He had captured the city from the Turks the year before, using a huge and well-equipped force, including forty rather effective siege-machines – large wooden catapults of the latest design, which could and did batter holes in the walls. Even so, it had taken six weeks. Now he had repaired and strengthened the

---

The siege of Jerusalem is here depicted as a physical assault on the Heavenly City, and scenes from Christ's Passion are shown in the background. The siege tower can be clearly seen in the front of the picture. From a fourteenth-century manuscript of William of Tyre's *History*.

walls and he knew that the Crusaders did not have such machines themselves. Nor could they build any – he had had the trees cut down for miles around.

There were not all that many attackers – no more than twenty thousand – and the city was strategically positioned with deep valleys on three sides. The Governor had stocked up vast quantities of provisions and poisoned all the wells around the city.

His biggest problem was manpower. Many people had fled from the Seljuk invaders in the early 1070s and the Seljuks had massacred a large part of the remaining Moslem population when they rebelled in 1076. Almost all the Jews had left. Iftikhar himself had killed or expelled the Turks and now he felt obliged to throw out the Christians in case they betrayed the city to the Crusaders. He was left with a few Jews (mostly belonging to a sect that believed they had to live in the Holy City), some Moslem civilians (also mostly there for religious reasons), his Arab cavalry and Sudanese archers. In a city that could house up to seventy thousand people, there were less than thirty thousand now. But he had informed his master, al-Afdal, the Vizier of Egypt, of the Crusaders' arrival and had been promised a relief force by the end of July.

His confidence must have been boosted even further over the next few days, by the extremely odd behaviour of the Crusaders. On 13 June the massed ranks of attackers suddenly flung themselves at the walls of the City without scaling ladders or siege-towers. What on earth had got into them? How could they hope to achieve anything like that?

In fact an aged hermit had promised instant success if they attacked at once – without any siege equipment. God's failure to fulfil his contractual obligation (as represented by the hermit) produced a profound depression amongst the Crusaders.

In the cold light of the next dawn they realized that their situation was not encouraging. It was characterized chiefly by the word 'lack'. They had a lack of siege equipment, a lack of wood to build such equipment, a lack of men, a lack of food, a lack of time (the Egyptian army was coming), a lack of faith (according to the aged hermit) and – perhaps worst of all – a lack of water. Conditions were becoming intolerable in the burning heat of summer and every effort to find water in unpolluted wells brought about fresh reports of casualties, as the Moslems sprang ambush after ambush. Morale plummeted.

One of the first cheering bits of news came as a result of the looseness of Tancred's bowels. Tancred had been suffering from dysentery for some time. Nevertheless he still went off at the head of a foraging party to find wood for siege towers. They were not having much success. His biographer Radulph writes:

⟵—————————————————————⟶

He had almost given up the search when the accustomed trouble struck again. So he pulled away from the others and dismounted. He hoped he would be able to avoid the gaze of his companions, but on looking back he saw that he had not done so. He therefore sought concealment further away, but again he could see a few men wandering about, so he changed his position a third and a fourth time, until in a deep recess beneath a hollow rock, surrounded by trees and bristling shade he found peace. Good gracious! Who but God? . . . For while Tancred was relieving himself there, he found himself facing a cave where four hundred timbers lay open to view.

The discovery of this cache of timber was followed by the arrival of six ships at Jaffa, bringing much needed provisions. Two of the ships were dismantled to provide more wood and the construction of the siege-towers got seriously under way — one under the auspices of Raymond and the other under Godfrey.

At this point the whole Crusade was boosted once again by a vision. The late Bishop Adhemar appeared to a priest and gave detailed instructions on how to capture Jerusalem. The Governor was baffled to see the attackers kick off their shoes and march barefoot round his city, singing hymns. His army gathered on the battlements and hurled ridicule and abuse at the procession as it made a circuit of the walls and then continued its way onto the Mount of Olives for a few rousing sermons. The late Bishop had guaranteed that if they did this, the city would fall within nine days.

Five days later the siege-towers had been completed and during the night the soldiers struggled to move them into position, fighting against a barrage of arrows and Greek Fire (the medieval equivalent of napalm). Godfrey's tower, topped with its golden cross, was in place by the morning of the 15th and by lunchtime his men had managed to get a bridge across from the top of the tower to the wall. Two Flemish brothers, Litold and Gilbert of Tournai, leapt across and the north wall of Jerusalem fell to the Crusaders.

The Massacre at Jerusalem

In later years Arabs would recall that when the Caliph Umar had captured Jerusalem from the Christians in 638, he had assured the Patriarch that Christian lives and property would be respected. He then requested a tour of the Christian holy sites.

Overleaf The Dome of the Rock, built *c.* AD 700, is a building of astonishing grace.
The Crusaders, after looting it, turned it into a church.

When invited to unroll his prayer mat in the Church of the Holy Sepulchre, he refused out of respect for the Christians, fearing that Moslems would want to appropriate the spot where the conqueror of Jerusalem had prayed. A treaty was then signed which precisely listed the legal rights of Christians: *'This peace ... guarantees them security for their lives, property, churches, and the crucifixes belonging to those who display and honour them ... There shall be no compulsion in matters of faith.'*

The Crusaders took a different approach. Fulcher of Chartres wrote:

> *Our Squires and footmen ... split open the bellies of those they had just slain in order to extract from the intestines the gold coins which the Saracens had gulped down their loathsome throats while alive ... With drawn swords our men ran through the city not sparing anyone, even those begging for mercy ... They entered the houses of the citizens, seizing whatever they found in them ... Whoever first entered a house, whether he was rich or poor ... was to occupy and own the house or palace and whatever he found in it as if it were entirely his own ... In this way many poor people became wealthy.*

It is impossible to know what was going through the minds of the Crusaders as they rampaged through the Holy City – but it certainly was not the Sermon on the Mount.

As the first wave of Crusaders swept down from the north wall, the Moslems fell back to the Temple area to seek refuge in the Dome of the Rock and the al-Aqsa Mosque, but in vain. Tancred and his men pursued them. He desecrated and pillaged the Dome of the Rock and bottled the Moslems up in the al-Aqsa Mosque and on its roof.

Raymond penetrated the south of the city and besieged General Iftikhar in the Tower of David. Unexpectedly, Raymond suddenly halted the attack and proposed a safe-conduct for the Egyptian Governor and his men if they would surrender the Tower. Fearing the worst but with little other choice, the General surrendered and the Franks, rather to the surprise of the Arabs, kept their word. Iftikhar and his men were the only Moslems in Jerusalem to escape with their lives.

The next day a band of Crusaders forced an entry into the al-Aqsa Mosque and – despite the protection of Tancred's banner flying above the building – slew everyone there, men, women and children, *'among them a large number of Imams* [religious leaders] *and Moslem scholars, devout and ascetic men who had left their homelands to live lives of pious seclusion in the Holy Place'.* At the same time the synagogue in which the Jews had sought shelter was set on fire and everyone in it was burned alive.

This was not the normal pillaging and looting of a conquering army – there were, for example, no reports of rape. It was a ritual slaughter. And then they gave thanks to God in the Church of the Holy Sepulchre. *'Oh day so ardently desired!'* wrote Fulcher of Chartres, *'Oh time of times the most memorable! Oh deed before all other deeds! … They desired that this place, so long contaminated by the superstition of the pagan inhabitants, should be cleansed from their contagion.'*

In the days that followed, one of the main problems was disposing of the corpses. One of the Frankish chronicles records a scene that has echoes of Auschwitz:

> *They also ordered that all the corpses of the Saracens should be thrown outside the city because of the fearful stench; for almost the whole city was full of their dead bodies. The Saracens who were still alive dragged the dead ones out in front of the gates, and made piles of them, as big as houses. Such a slaughter of pagans no one has ever seen or heard of; the pyres they made were like pyramids.*

The fanatical blood-lust of the Crusaders at Jerusalem would never be forgotten.

For the general public in Europe, the story was one of miraculous achievement. For the Emperor Alexius it was more problematic. A Frankish knight had set himself up as the ruler of Edessa. Another had seized Antioch. A band of bloodthirsty butchers had expelled his Fatimid allies from Jerusalem and done no good at all to the orthodox Christians there whom the Emperor regarded as his own subjects.

Pope Urban had no comment on the victorious outcome to the campaign of bloodshed that he had unleashed four years before. He died a few days before news of the capture of Jerusalem reached Rome.

The New Jerusalem

Most of the Crusaders, having done what they came for, went home. Less than three thousand Franks seem to have stayed on. Probably only three hundred of them were knights. Having killed almost the entire population, they were in possession of a large, empty city which was, of course, the biggest tourist centre in the world.

It had been in the hands of the Moslems for 461 years. Nonetheless, the majority of the population had remained Christian. During most of that time the Moslems had protected the rights of the Christians. Of course, the Moslems retained overall control – even today the key to the Church of the Holy Sepulchre remains entrusted to a Moslem. His name is Museba and his family has been responsible for locking and unlocking the most sacred Christian church in the world every day, according to their own account, since Moslems first captured the city.

With the triumph of the Latin Christians, however, things were going to change. They had come to rid Jerusalem of all other religions and to make it a purely Christian

Although this picture notionally depicts the sack of Jerusalem by Antiochus IV (who was attempting to eradicate Judaism and provoked the rising of the Maccabees) in 168 BC, it is clearly suggestive of the Crusaders looting of the city. The hint of criticism is made stronger by the fact that Antiochus did not sack the city – the episode has been invented. From a fifteenth-century French manuscript.

Jherusalem

city — and, what's more, Christian in their terms. The Orthodox Greek Christians, the Georgian Christians, the Armenian Christians, the Jacobite Christians and the Coptic Christians, who had been expelled in the lead-up to the siege, quickly discovered that victory had not been on their behalf. Their priests were banished from the Church of the Holy Sepulchre. They were not even allowed to hold services there. Meanwhile the ecclesiastical hierarchy of Jerusalem became exclusively Latin.

Most insufferable of all was the fact that the new Patriarch, Arnulf of Rhodes, proved himself to be quite capable of torturing his fellow Christians, in order to find out where they had hidden their portion of the True Cross. Torture appears to have loosened their tongues, but it also hardened attitudes between the Oriental and Western Churches. The Orthodox Christians learnt to hate the Latins with a deep and burning ferocity. Their feelings were still strong centuries later; in 1806 they held a religious procession carrying the bones of the boy-king Baldwin V, who had died when he was eight, to a gorge outside the city and hurled them down into it with solemn curses.

The Crusaders now voted on which of their leaders was to rule Jerusalem. The first vote went to Raymond, but he declared that he would not wear a crown in the very city where Christ had worn the crown of thorns. The next vote went to Godfrey of Lorraine, who accepted the post, but agreed that no-one should wear a crown in the Holy City. He therefore resorted to that most powerful of political weapons — the euphemism. He declined the rank of king and took instead the title Advocate (or Defender) of the Holy Sepulchre.

Godfrey's reign as almost-king was to last only a year, but in that time the fledgling state which was to become the Kingdom of Jerusalem took shape. As long as the princes could bury their differences they were more or less invincible, as was demonstrated when the combined forces of Raymond and Godfrey routed the Egyptian relief force that eventually turned up outside Ascalon. But such cohesion was the exception, not the rule.

Soon after Godfrey's election, the new papal legate — Urban's replacement for the Bishop of Le Puy — arrived from Rome to be appointed Patriarch. He was an ambitious Italian by the name of Daimbert, whose mission was to establish Urban's dream of ecclesiastical rule over the Holy Land. He was not, however, fool enough to imagine that God would grant him such pre-eminence without military backing. The de Hautevilles had backed Gregory VII and Urban II — they would back him.

Daimbert secured the support of Bohemond and Tancred. In return he recognized Bohemond as Prince of Antioch and Tancred as Prince of Galilee — both of whom in this way declared their independence of Godfrey. Since Antioch was clearly supposed to be returned to Alexius, it was also a declaration of hostility to Constantinople.

Godfrey was not strong enough to resist Daimbert's demands and by the time he died, he had even promised that the Patriarch should inherit control of both Jaffa and Jerusalem. The papal dream of theocratic rule was about to be realized. But Daimbert was outmanoeuvred by the laymen.

When Godfrey died, the Patriarch was off with Tancred attacking Haifa and word was secretly sent to Godfrey's brother, Baldwin of Edessa, to come to Jerusalem and take control. Baldwin was no friend of the church radicals. By the time Daimbert heard of Godfrey's demise, it was almost too late. In a panic he offered the government of Palestine (under his authority) to Bohemond. He instructed Bohemond to prevent Baldwin from marching on Jerusalem — by force if necessary. The Patriarch was prepared to stir two Christian princes to war against each other, to fulfil the ecclesiastical ambition of temporal power in the Holy Land. The letter, however, was intercepted and Bohemond never learnt of the generous offer until it was too late.

The dice were rolling in Baldwin's favour. Bohemond was captured by the Turks, while on an expedition, and Baldwin was able to march triumphantly into Jerusalem — grieving a little, his chaplain Fulcher of Chartres tells us, for the death of his brother, but rejoicing more at his inheritance.

Baldwin had no compunctions at all about being called king. On Christmas Day 1100, in the Church of the Nativity at Bethlehem, Daimbert gritted his teeth and crowned Baldwin King of Jerusalem. Three months later Tancred, who had been Baldwin's enemy since their confrontation at Tarsus, gave up his princedom in Galilee, and moved north to take over Antioch whose ruler, Bohemond, was still in a Turkish prison. The third Crusader state, Edessa, was given to Baldwin's young cousin, Baldwin of Le Bourg. Three young men who had come out with nothing — Baldwin, Tancred and Baldwin of Le Bourg — were now masters of the Levant.

The following year three armies of Europeans passed through Constantinople on their way to Jerusalem. Full of enthusiasm and inspired by the glorious example of the Crusade, they rode proudly into Anatolia. All three were destroyed there. The Crusade had not opened the pilgrim route; it had simply poisoned relations with Byzantium and left the Turks in control of central Anatolia as they had been.

But Europe now had three colonies in the Moslem East — Jerusalem, Antioch, Edessa. The question was — with so few Crusaders actually settling there — for how long?

Square in Baghdad. The city was the political and religious centre of Sunni
Islam, and its main communications lay northwards along
the Tigris-Euphrates valleys, and eastwards into
Persia. Palestine was a fringe region.

5

The Arab Response

As the Franks were still arguing over the booty, Moslem refugees began to arrive in Damascus during Ramadan, the month of fasting. Their tales of the hardships they had undergone and the horrors they had seen were so harrowing that they were allowed to break the fast.

In Baghdad, the centre of Islamic authority, nothing happened at all. The Iraqi poet, al-Muzaffar al-Abiwardi, did his best to whip up some sort of response:

> This is war, and the man who shuns the whirlpool to save his life shall grind his teeth in penitence.
> This is war, and the infidel's sword is naked in his hand, ready to be sheathed again in men's necks and skulls.

But there was nothing.

> I see my people slow to raise the lance against the enemy: I see Faith resting on feeble pillars.

In the best tradition of politicians throughout history when faced with an urgent problem, the Caliph, al-Mustazhir Billah, took the whole affair very seriously and appointed a committee of inquiry. And in the best traditions of committees of inquiry throughout history, the committee of inquiry produced no action at all. Baghdad was impotent.

Baghdad had once been the largest and most civilized city in the world. Before the Turkish invasions it had enjoyed free hospitals, public baths, a postal service, a water supply, a sewage system, as well as several banks – with branches in China. Under the rule of Caliph Harun al-Rashid three hundred years earlier, it had ruled over an Islamic empire that included North Africa, Palestine, Syria and Iraq, and beyond to Persia and Afghanistan, and to Azerbaijan and the southern shores of the Caspian Sea.

In those days Islamic culture had opened itself up to the influence of other civilizations. Ever since the days of Caliph al-Mamun (d. 833) Moslems had had the benefit of permanent endowments to support their cultural life, rather than the chance largesse of rulers. Al-Mamun had established colleges of translators who made the wealth of knowledge contained in Greek, Syriac, Persian and Sanskrit writing available in Arabic. He established the great Hall of Science with its library and astronomical laboratory in Baghdad.

Further north, in the city of Harran, a school of science had grown up which was centuries ahead of the West. By the time the Crusaders first achieved sword-contact with the Islamic world, one Harran scientist, Albatanius, had already correctly calculated the distance from the Earth to the Moon, while another, Jabir bin Hayyan, had suggested that if the atom could be divided it might release enough power to destroy a city the size of Baghdad!

Arab medicine was also highly developed. To practise medicine required a knowledge of surgery, anatomy and the circulation of the blood (four hundred years before Harvey). There were specialists in eye surgery, breast tumours, epilepsy, preventative medicine and — perhaps most important of all — hygiene. Arab doctors even used anaesthetic. A sponge was soaked in a mixture of hashish, opium, darnel and belladonna, and then left to dry in the sun. When it was needed, the sponge would be re-moistened and placed in the nostrils of the patient, who was — perhaps not surprisingly — plunged into a deep sleep.

Why was such a relatively sophisticated society so slow to respond to the Christian aggression from the West? How could two or three thousand Europeans maintain a hostile kingdom in the Middle East? This was a question that also haunted many Arabs at the time.

There were two big problems for Islam. The first was that the sense of outrage felt by those who suffered directly from the fall of Jerusalem was not, at first, widely shared. Invasions were commonplace. It would be a while before it was generally understood that the new occupiers of Jerusalem had a very different agenda from the Byzantines, Turks or Egyptians. The Crusaders had come not merely to exact tribute and taxes, but to impose their own civilization and their own Roman Christianity.

This was not simply an invasion; it was a colonizing war by one civilization against another. As this understanding grew, voices began demanding a concerted response by the entire Arab world. And this was the second great problem. There was no such thing as a united Arab world in the late eleventh century. North Africa had split away when the Fatimids came to power and the Seljuks had taken control of everything else. They, of course, were not Arabs at all.

The Divided Turks

Baghdad remained the notional centre of authority; it was still the home of the Caliph. But he, like all Arabs, had no place in politics in the Seljuk Empire. His Turkish overlord took the title Sultan. The Caliph was a religious figurehead. 'Men of the Turban' (religious and legal officers) and 'Men of the Pen' (administrators) might be Arab, but 'Men of the Sword', who were Turks (and usually illiterate), had all the power. And if they didn't, they fought each other for it. In the three years after the Christian capture of Jerusalem, Baghdad changed hands eight times, as the sons of Malik Shah fought for supremacy. The city was in chaos. The Turkish rulers were not prepared to take seriously the plight of Jerusalem and other towns on the western edge of the Seljuk world.

Away from the centre, each emir maintained his own independence and was terrified of his neighbour. The ruler of Damascus, Duqaq, was the brother of Ridwan of Aleppo. Ridwan had already killed three of his brothers and Duqaq was sure he was next on the list. As for Kerbogha in Mosul — they both knew he would have them from breakfast, given the chance. And in dozens of smaller emirates, politics was played by the rule 'My brother's enemy is my friend'. The emirs did not consider that the Franks were a greater enemy than any other individual emir amongst themselves. *'In former times almost every* [Middle Eastern] *city had its own ruler ...',* wrote William of Tyre. *'Those who feared their own allies not less than the Christians could not or would not readily unite to repulse the common danger or arm themselves for our destruction.'*

It would not have been hard to cut off Edessa and Antioch from Jerusalem, for example; Tripoli lay between them, unconquered, and it controlled the notorious pass of Nahr el-Kelb. When Baldwin was racing down from Edessa to Jerusalem to claim the kingdom on the death of his brother Godfrey, Duqaq, the ruler of Damascus, wisely decided to ambush him there. But the Emir of Tripoli, Fakhr al-Mulk, did not like the idea.

Fakhr al-Mulk had only enjoyed being Emir of Tripoli for a year and he had no intention of letting Duqaq gain a spectacular victory over the Franks and thereby — perhaps — impose himself over all Syria. So Fakhr al-Mulk did the obvious thing: he

Opposite The peaceful life of an Islamic village. Although it is widely believed in the West that the Koran forbids representational images, that is not strictly true. Iconoclasm only appears in the later Hadith (traditions) and was ignored in many periods of Islamic history. From an Arab manuscript of 1237.

Below The 'madrassah', or school, was a central element in Islamic life, and the teacher/doctor/religious leader was a leader of the community.

sent a messenger to Baldwin and warned him about the ambush. Baldwin lived to become perhaps the greatest king the Kingdom of Jerusalem ever had.

Nor did the story stop there.

A year later Duqaq took his revenge on the Emir of Tripoli. Raymond of Toulouse had turned up outside the walls of Tripoli with an absurdly small force of no more than three hundred men. The Emir sent word to Duqaq in Damascus and to the ruler of Homs that here was a chance to knock the Count out for the count (as it were). They duly turned up and surrounded Raymond – the Moslem forces outnumbering the Franks by as many as twenty to one.

And yet, when it came to battle, the men of Homs and the men of Damascus deliberately pulled out in order to give the victory to Raymond. This certainly gave Duqaq his revenge on Fakhr al-Mulk, but it paved the way for a fourth Crusader state – the Kingdom of Tripoli – and provided the vital bridge between the northern states and Jerusalem.

The Assassins

Nothing symbolizes the internal divisions of the Arab world more poignantly than the Assassins. Indeed without the Assassins' murder of Nizam al-Mulk, the Crusades might not have got as far as they did in the first place.

The Assassins were an extremist Shi'ite sect which had been founded – only five years before Pope Urban preached the First Crusade – as a reaction to Sultan Malik Shah's devotion to Sunni Islam.

The Sunni/Shi'a split has its roots in a civil war soon after Mohammed's death. The Prophet's son-in-law, Ali, who had become the fourth Caliph or 'successor', was murdered; so were his sons and grandson. The Shi'ites (Shiat' Ali means 'the party of Ali') hold that Ali was the first true successor to the Prophet and they regarded the Sunni Caliphate in Baghdad as corrupt and based on the shedding of sacred blood.

The 'Assassins' were Ismailis – mystic Shi'ites who believe in the divinity of the seventh Imam, Ismail ibn Jafar, and who traditionally maintain that it is the duty of the community to share its wealth evenly. The word 'Assassin', however, is an invention of the West's. It was supposedly coined because of the hashish with which its adherents – the hashishi – were thought to be drugged when executing their kamikaze missions.

This militant arm of the Ismaili movement was founded by a cultivated man of poetry and science, Hasan as-Sabah, who had been born in 1048, and had seen Shi'a-dominated Persia overrun by the Sunni Seljuk Turks. Hasan as-Sabah resolved to turn his world back to the path of Shi'a, so in about 1071 he fled to Egypt. Fatimid Egypt had its own Shi'ite Caliph; that was the basis of its split from the Sunni Caliph of Baghdad. Hasan quickly discovered that the real power in Egypt did not lie in the hands of the Caliph but in those of his Armenian Vizier. But at least Cairo was full of like-minded militants and Hasan helped to forge a new revolutionary movement.

The plan was to be set in motion the moment the old Caliph died. His son, Nizar, was to seize power from the Vizier, attack the Seljuks and bring the entire Moslem world back into the Shi'ite fold. In the meantime Hasan was to return to the areas now dominated by the Seljuks and prepare a 'fifth column' that could spring into action the moment Nizar took command in Egypt.

This Hasan did. He created one of the most effective terrorist organizations in history. His weapon was political murder. These murders had to be carried out against the most public figures possible in the most public way possible (usually after Friday prayers at the mosque). The Assassin had therefore to expect to be cut down himself. Each mission was a suicide mission.

Such a murder removed a dangerous enemy of the sect, it intimidated other enemies of the sect, and it demonstrated the determination and fanaticism of the sect's adherents.

The Assassins scored a spectacular success with their first murder. They killed Malik Shah's Vizier, Nizam al-Mulk. Malik Shah died immediately afterwards and his Empire shattered into countless fragments. Nizam was the only man who could have held the Empire together – the way was clear for a Shi'ite revival.

But events did not unfold as they were supposed to. In Cairo, instead of Nizar inheriting the Caliphate from his father, it was the ruthless al-Afdal who inherited the Vizierate from *his*. And al-Afdal was not the sort of chap who was going to wait around for an insurrection to happen. He knew exactly who the trouble-makers were likely to be and he had them liquidated. Nizar himself, by way of an example, was buried alive.

Hasan as-Sabah thus found himself with a fully paid-up organization of kamikaze commandoes raring to go and demonstrate their dedication, self-sacrifice and ferocity, but with no immediate political agenda. His ultimate objective was still the destruction of the Sunni Caliphate and so Hasan set about doing everything he could to make that likely. He gave up on Cairo and began acting on his own account, undermining and destabilizing Sunni Islam wherever and whenever he could.

Because he was now estranged from the Fatimids (who were still nominally the heads of the Shi'ite movement) Hasan found that he was now not only the enemy of the Sunni Caliph but also of the Shi'ite Caliph. He was thus pitted against the entire Islamic establishment and discovered that his natural allies were more often than not the invading Christians.

For the next half century, the Sunni world had this counterforce eating it away from the inside. From his stronghold near the Caspian Sea, Hasan, now known as the 'Old Man of the Mountains', actively stirred up dissension amongst the emirs of Syria, helping to keep emir against emir and brother against brother. And wherever and whenever it suited his purpose he became an active ally of the Franks.

The Beginnings of Jihad

At the end of the first decade of the twelfth century calamity seemed about to engulf the Moslems of North Syria. In July 1109, the Franks finally sacked Tripoli after a siege that had dragged on for over five years. That elegant, affluent city of learning and craftsmanship was destroyed. The great library, the Dar al-Ilm, was pillaged and its hundred thousand books burned — their contents lost to posterity for ever. The inhabitants were sold into slavery or simply kicked out of their homes.

Then, in May 1110, Beirut, the place where St George was fabled to have slain the dragon, was overrun by the Franks and its inhabitants massacred in revenge for their stubborn defence. Terrified by this example, the city of Sidon capitulated. In eighteen months, three of the most famous cities of the Arab world had fallen to the invading Christians. Imad ed-Din quoted a survivor:

> I do not know whether it is pasture for wild animals or my house, my birthplace, I turn to it, my voice full of tears, my heart torn with suffering and love, and ask: House, why did destiny pronounce such an unjust sentence on us?

Damascus and Aleppo were filled with refugees who had lost everything. People were evacuating whole towns ahead of the Franks; when Tripoli fell, some Aleppans fled before they too were conquered.

The citadel at Aleppo. This magnificent entrance was built
after the Crusades, but the defences were robust enough to prevent
the Crusaders ever capturing the strongpoint. Had they done so,
they would have transformed their prospects of survival.

←——————————————————→

'*I know nothing but weeping*'.

The streets of Moslem cities in Syria were filled with desperate people not knowing what to do. One refugee from Maarrat wrote: '*I come from a town which God has condemned, my friend, to be demolished. All the inhabitants perished. They passed their blades through old men and children.*'

A few Moslems, Arabs rather than Turks, saw these events in a wider context. Less than four hundred years earlier their ancestors – their own families, in the case of many refugees – had taken these lands from Byzantine Christian rulers in the *jihad*, the Holy War for Islam. In many places, lands which had been granted to warriors of the *jihad* had been held in trust by the same Arab clans ever since. Now the Christians were recovering by war what had been taken away by war. There must surely now be a new *jihad*, a war of defence, led by the successor to the Prophet, the Caliph of Baghdad, and his Sultan.

One of the most persistent promoters of this idea was a *qadi*, or judge, in Aleppo. His name was Abu al-Fadl ibn al-Khashshab and he was the most prominent Arab citizen of Aleppo. He was the *ra'is*, a position with functions rather like a mayor. He represented the interests of the merchants, commanded the militia and, most important of all, represented the people to their Turkish ruler, Ridwan.

Ridwan had decided to adopt a conciliatory attitude to the Franks. This stuck in the throats of his Arab subjects – a fact which Ibn al-Khashshab never tired of pointing out to him. When Tancred had forced Ridwan to attach a crucifix to the minaret of the great mosque in Aleppo, Ibn al-Khashshab had organized a riot to have it removed. Now Tancred had imposed a treaty upon the Aleppans, by which they had to pay him twenty thousand dinars a year. Ridwan had even agreed to hand over his ten finest horses. What is more, all the trade routes to the Mediterranean were now under the control of the Franks and profits were suffering. The situation was intolerable.

Once again, Ibn al-Khashshab turned up at Ridwan's citadel to recite the complaints and demand a delegation be sent to Baghdad to get help from the Sultan. This was the sort of help Ridwan needed like he needed a dose of dysentery. To tell the truth he was even more scared of the ambitions of his cousin the Sultan than he was of the Franks. But he had to keep his *qadi* quiet somehow, and in any case previous delegations to Baghdad had never achieved anything, so he reluctantly agreed.

Ibn al-Khashshab set off for Baghdad with a band of Sufis – Moslem ascetics – merchants and lawyers. He had a secret agenda which he had neglected to tell Ridwan about. He had no intention of relying solely on words to persuade the Sultan. Once in Baghdad, the worthy *qadi* set about organizing a full-scale riot in favour of action against the Franks.

On Friday, 17 February 1111, he and his companions burst into the Sultan's mosque, forced the preacher to descend from the minbar and then proceeded to smash it to pieces. *'They wept and groaned for the disaster that had befallen Islam with the arrival of the Franks,'* wrote Ibn al-Qalanisi, *'for the men who had died and the women and children who had been sold into slavery.'* To keep them quiet (because they were interrupting prayers) the religious officials who were present made various promises *'on the Caliph's behalf, that troops would be sent to support Islam against the infidel'*. But, of course, nothing happened. And the following Friday the same thing was acted out again – this time in the mosque of the Caliph.

The Caliph was furious and wanted to punish the offenders, but what could he do? He was only sovereign in name. The real power lay with the Turkish Sultan and it suited him to espouse the rioters' cause, as a means of restoring Baghdad's power. He had a first-class military commander in his general, Mawdud, who was prepared to reassert control over the independent emirs of Syria. Mawdud had captured Mosul for him and was now its governor. The Sultan ordered the army to prepare for 'Holy War against the infidel enemies of God' and sent Mawdud to the 'rescue' of his cousin Ridwan in Aleppo.

Ridwan must have heard the news of his rescue with a sinking heart. He had no doubt that this was a campaign as much against him as against the Franks. He did not dare resist at first. In fact he asked Mawdud to hurry to his aid. Once Ridwan saw that Mawdud's forces were reasonably small, however, he barricaded the gates of Aleppo, arrested Ibn al-Khashshab and his colleagues, and told Mawdud to go away. Mawdud's troops did what they could to ravage the environs of Aleppo and then broke up without striking a single blow against the Franks. Nothing, it appeared, was going to prevent the onward march of the Christian soldiers.

The Great Fear of the Franks

Of course, if you were on the other side of the fence things looked somewhat different. The Franks were very few in numbers, surrounded by enemies and very far from home. Fulcher of Chartres vividly captures 'The Great Fear Which Then Possessed Everyone':

> *At that time it was impossible, because of the snares of the enemy, for a messenger sent by any of us to venture forth to the king nor one from him to come through to any of our cities,*

<———————————————————————————>

Hence it was not known by the towns what the king was doing, nor could they tell him what they were doing.

> *In many fields the ripened harvest withered*
> *And no one went into the fields to gather it* [Matthew 9:37]

For none dared to do so.

The Franks were weak, but the Sultan could not deliver a knock-out punch. He assembled another army under Mawdud. This time Mawdud arrived not at Aleppo but Damascus; he was not an altogether welcome guest here either. Still, the Emir of Damascus was being attacked by King Baldwin and needed help. He did his best to pretend to be firmly behind Mawdud and his mission. One day, however, while the General was leaving the great mosque in the centre of Damascus, an Assassin leapt out and stabbed him twice just above the navel. *'Mawdud never lost his head. He walked as far as the north gate of the mosque and then collapsed.'*

Mawdud's assassination at the very moment he was about to wage *jihad* against the Franks gave Baldwin a golden opportunity to indulge in an enjoyable bit of Moslem-baiting. He sent a message to the Emir of Damascus informing him that a nation that kills its leader in the house of its God deserves to be annihilated. Fulcher of Chartres heaved a sigh of relief at the disappearance of so able a foe: *'The Lord permitted him to scourge us for a while but afterwards willed that he should die a vile death and by the hand of an insignificant man.'*

Clearly Sultan Mohammed had to establish his authority over the Emirs of Syria before he could attack the Franks. In 1115 he despatched yet another army into Syria, under the command of the picturesquely named Bursuq ibn Bursuq. This time its purpose was unequivocal; to bring the squabbling emirs to heel. Bursuq arrived to find his army confronted by the whole power of Syria – the troops of Damascus and Aleppo in alliance with the Franks of Jerusalem, Antioch and Tripoli! Confronted by the might of Baghdad, the emirs of Syria and the Franks of Syria had simply closed ranks.

In effect, a new regional identity was being born. It was not going to be possible to organize *jihad* against the Franks from Baghdad; the Turkish rulers of Syria valued their independence too much. It was clear that the Franks had settled in; they were part of the structure of Syria. The massacres of their original conquest were now in the past; the troops were under better control, and no longer burned with ferocity against the infidel. They had got used to things. And they were learning about their new home.

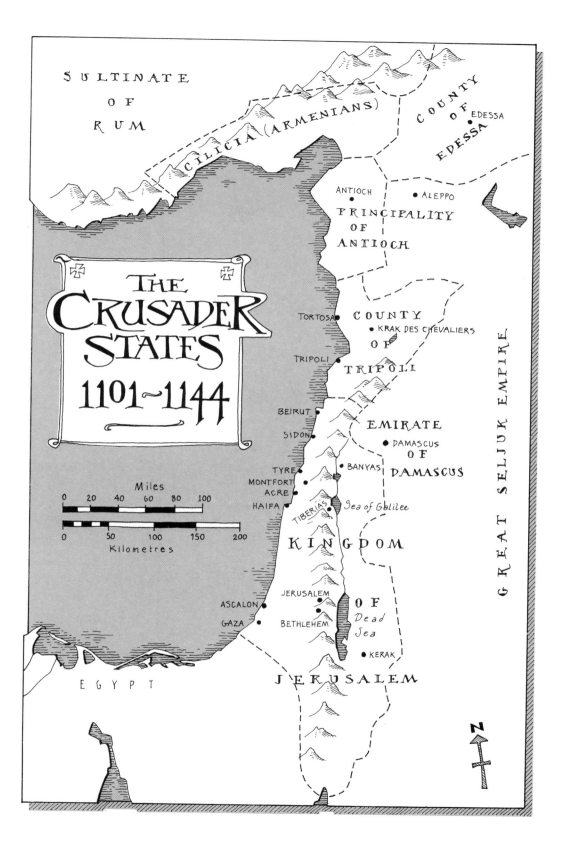

SULTINATE OF RUM

CILICIA (ARMENIANS)

COUNTY OF EDESSA

EDESSA

ANTIOCH

ALEPPO

PRINCIPALITY OF ANTIOCH

THE CRUSADER STATES

1101~1144

TORTOSA

KRAK DES CHEVALIERS

COUNTY OF TRIPOLI

TRIPOLI

BEIRUT

EMIRATE

SIDON

DAMASCUS

OF

TYRE

BANYAS

DAMASCUS

MONTFORT

ACRE

HAIFA

TIBERIAS

Sea of Galilee

KINGDOM

GREAT SELJUK EMPIRE

JERUSALEM

OF

Dead Sea

ASCALON

GAZA

BETHLEHEM

KERAK

EGYPT

JERUSALEM

Miles
0 20 40 60 80 100

0 50 100 150 200
Kilometres

N

The very next year King Baldwin took his troops on a holiday to the seaside *'to see what he had not seen and perchance to find something on the way that he might want.'* They returned from their trip to the Red Sea in high spirits and with lots of sea-shells to show off! *'When they told us what they had seen,'* writes Fulcher of Chartres, *'we were as delighted with their tales as by the sea shells and certain precious stones which they brought and showed us.'*

The New Franks of the East

It really seemed as though the Franks were becoming a permanent part of the landscape. About 1125 Fulcher of Chartres, who had been at Clermont when the Crusade was announced, wrote, *'We who were Occidentals have now become Orientals. He who was a Roman or a Frank has in this land been made into a Galilean or a Palestinian ... We have already forgotten the places of our birth ... He who was born an alien has become as a native.'*

In 1118 King Baldwin of Jerusalem died. His successor was his cousin Baldwin of Le Bourg, the ruler of Edessa. Baldwin II inherited a feudal kingdom like any in Europe; he had tenants-in-chief, who held lands on condition that they supplied knights to their king. But there was one crucial difference between this kingdom and any in Europe. The rulers were Latin Christians from Europe. Their subjects were not.

There were always at least seven times as many natives as Franks in the kingdom and probably never more than two thousand Frankish knights. The Frankish overlords did not farm the land themselves; they stayed in the towns and left the land to the native Christians and Moslems. Europeans were desperately needed to swell the population and every effort was made to encourage peasants to come and settle in manors in the countryside. The kingdom was always very conscious of its weakness. Edessa, Tripoli and Antioch were especially vulnerable; they did not attract the steady flow of armed pilgrims who came to visit Jerusalem.

But now a new generation was growing up: Franks who had been born and brought up in this land. They were called *'pulani'* – 'chickens' – and they could never regard themselves as aliens. Syrian manners were becoming the norm; bathing was a regular habit, men sometimes even wore turbans, and they lived in palatial homes of a kind which did not exist in Europe. Amongst the established Frankish families, the hatred of Moslems that had inspired the first Crusaders had died away, but there was still a constant flow of newcomers with a less sophisticated view of Islam. They were usually shocked by the extent to which the old-timers had gone native and did all they could to revive the xenophobia of the past.

A Syrian nobleman, Usama, who had friends among the knights of Jerusalem, once described what happened when he was praying on the Temple Mount in a spot set aside for the purpose. He was on his knees, praying towards Mecca, when a Frank picked him up bodily and turned him to face East, insisting that this was the correct direction for prayer. Usama's friends rushed over and apologized, explaining that this ruffian had newly arrived in the East and had never seen anyone praying in any other direction before.

However much the Franks believed they were in Syria to stay, they were still regarded by the Moslems as aliens and usurpers.

The Search for a Leader

Arabs who wanted *jihad* to be waged against the Frankish settlers would have to stop looking towards Baghdad and find a leader within Syria. That was clearly the conclusion drawn by the *qadi* Ibn al-Khashshab in Aleppo. The death of Ridwan at the end of 1113 gave him the chance. He installed Ridwan's sixteen-year-old son, Alp Arslan, as the new ruler and appeared to have him firmly under his influence.

But it quickly became apparent that the new ruler had a few disturbing quirks. Having beheaded most of his father's supporters, Alp Arslan appeared to develop a taste for that sort of thing. He executed two of his brothers and then started on the domestic staff and anybody else who didn't take his fancy. Soon no-one dared to go near the Emir except for his eunuch Lulu (Pearls) and even he had had enough after ten months. In September 1114, Lulu killed his master and tried to take over the government himself. Within three years, Lulu was himself murdered and Aleppo plunged into turmoil.

Ibn al-Khashshab assembled the worthies of the city. They needed a strong ruler to rescue them from the current mess and also to fight the Franks. They had to forget about Baghdad; their fate was in their own hands. The most likely candidate was the Emir of Damascus, but such was the hatred and distrust between the two cities that he was out of the question. Ibn al-Khashshab therefore made a most unlikely proposition.

This picture of a Christian and a Moslem playing chess (a game which originated in Persia – 'checkmate' was originally 'Shah mate' meaning 'The Shah is dead') beautifully illustrates the kind of integration which appalled newly-arrived Crusaders. The Moslem, playing Black, appears to have the game sewn up. The Christian has a resigned look and is signalling 'pax' while his opponent seems to be indicating it is time for a drink.

←→

Ilghazi

Ilghazi, the Turkish Emir of Mardin (to the east of Aleppo), was a drunkard who had supported the Frankish alliance against the Sultan Mohammed's attempt at *jihad*. There would have been a few raised eyebrows when the *qadi* suggested Ilghazi as the new Emir of Aleppo. But these were desperate times. Ilghazi was a fine general (despite his penchant for the bottle) and, most important, he had the will to fight. So Ilghazi was invited to take over Aleppo and – by implication – the struggle against the Franks. Within the year this unlikely policy had produced a spectacular result.

At the start of the summer of 1119 Ilghazi combined with the Emir of Damascus and assembled a huge army. They then marched towards Antioch. Both Tancred and Bohemond had died of fever and Antioch was now ruled by Tancred's nephew Roger. King Baldwin told Roger to wait for him while he collected the army of Jerusalem. The Franks clearly took the threat very seriously for Baldwin even armed his force with a portion of the True Cross.

But Roger decided not to wait for reinforcements. He marched the entire army of Antioch out towards Aleppo and there prepared to encounter the Moslems. He realized his mistake only when it was too late. On Saturday, 28 June, the Franks awoke to find their camp surrounded and outnumbered by a vast Moslem army. Roger and his men must have known their number was up, and there are echoes of Custer's Last Stand as the Archbishop of Apamea confessed the entire army before the hopeless battle.

The Moslems charged with the *qadi* Ibn al-Khashshab riding at their head. According to Ibn al-Qalanisi, who was in his mid-forties at the time, *'in less than an hour, the Franks were all lying dead . . . horses bristling like hedgehogs with the arrows sticking out of them.'* According to Kemal ad-Din, the historian of Aleppo, only twenty Moslems were killed and only twenty Franks escaped. Amongst the dead was the reckless Roger himself, crumpled at the foot of his jewelled cross with his head cleaved through to his nose.

The Frankish prisoners who were left alive were then dragged across the plain in chains and then tortured and killed by the Turcoman troops. The entire Norman knighthood of the Latin East was wiped out. The battle was remembered ever after in the Frankish Kingdom as 'the Field of Blood'.

News of the disaster electrified Antioch. With Roger dead, the Patriarch took control and began to arm the merchants and even the clergy, in preparation for the onslaught that must surely follow.

Nothing happened.

Ilghazi distributed the booty to his men and then retired back to Aleppo to celebrate. There was plenty to celebrate. After all the uncertainty and doom-mongering of the previous years, Aleppo went wild. Ilghazi was the hero of the hour: *'After God it is you whom we trust'*, sang the poets in the city streets. The celebrations went on for days. The trouble was that when the city finally stopped celebrating, their hero just went on and on and on . . . when he finally stopped celebrating it was only because he was too ill.

Three years later, Ilghazi died, his health broken by alcohol, without having achieved another such decisive stroke. But from now on Syrians would not look to Baghdad for leadership against the Latin invasion.

Balak — the Raging Dragon

In the meantime, however, another star had appeared in the Moslem firmament. This was Ilghazi's nephew Balak — a sober man, just turned forty and a brilliant general. In his brief career, his name lit up the hopes of Moslems and spelt terror to the Franks. For a surprising number of pages, 'Belek' dominates the nightmares of Fulcher of Chartres.

Balak's reputation had started to swell when he captured King Baldwin II's cousin Joscelin in 1122. It swelled even more the following year when he also made a prisoner of King Baldwin himself. In 1124 Balak succeeded in making himself ruler of Aleppo and from there he began what appeared to be a steady reconquest of Frankish outposts in the north.

When a slight hiccup occurred in this triumphal progress, Balak acted with ruthless determination. In August, Joscelin and Baldwin managed to become masters of the fortress in which they were imprisoned. Joscelin then escaped through enemy territory, crossing the Euphrates with the aid of two inflated wine-skins (he was a non-swimmer), and eventually got the news of their adventure to Jerusalem.

But before a rescue could be mounted, Balak stormed the fortress and recaptured it. Balak's harem had been in the castle and it had probably been broken into. He was taking no chances. Everyone who had defended the castle against him — whether Frank or Armenian, man or woman, was flung off the battlements. Only Baldwin and two others were spared.

In 1124 Balak received an urgent call for help from the people of Tyre, who were holding out against a Frankish siege. Balak was himself besieging a castle called

Manbij, but he immediately decided to go to the rescue. As he was making a last tour of inspection of the siege arrangements at Manbij, however, a chance arrow struck him in the chest. He wrenched the shaft out of himself and, spitting in the air, murmured, *'That blow will be fatal for all the Muslims.'* Then he fell dead.

Balak could well have been the great leader of *jihad* that Ibn al-Khashshab had been praying for. Certainly when *'the raging dragon'* bows out of the pages of Fulcher of Chartres' chronicle, the historian makes no secret of the relief amongst the Franks: *'And we all praised God because Belek, the raging dragon who had oppressed and trampled on Christianity was suffocated at last.'*

With Balak gone, Tyre capitulated. The Franks now held the whole coast from Egypt to Antioch. Aleppo floundered under the inept rule of Timurtash, Ilghazi's nineteen year-old son, whose only contribution to the Holy War was to release King Baldwin for a ransom of twenty thousand dinars, and thus rekindle the energies of the Franks.

A year later an even more deadly blow was dealt to the cause of *jihad*, not by the Franks but by the enemy within – the Assassins. The man who had tried hardest to kindle the flame of Holy War amongst the Moslems, Ibn al-Khashshab, was no friend of the secretive sect of the Assassins. For him their collusion with the Franks was rank treason. Ridwan had allowed Assassins to settle in Aleppo and Ibn al-Khashshab had shown them no mercy after Ridwan's death. It was inevitable that the organization would take its revenge. One day in the summer of 1125 he was assassinated while leaving the mosque.

During the next few years the Assassins set about undermining almost the whole of Moslem Syria, murdering the new emirs of Mosul and Aleppo, establishing themselves firmly in Damascus and all the time forging closer and closer links with the Franks in Jerusalem. It was the blackest of times for the Arab world, but salvation was at hand. *'Syria would have been left completely at the mercy of the Franks,'* wrote Ibn al-Athir, *'with no one to defend its inhabitants; but God in His mercy to the Moslems was pleased to raise to power Imad ed-Din.'* This was Zengi, the leader they had been praying for.

6

The Fight Back Begins

In many ways, Imad ed-Din Zengi was an unlikely champion of Islam. His first decisive act, in 1126, was to put down an uprising in Baghdad organized by the leader of the Islamic world – the Caliph, who wanted to free himself of his Seljuk overlords. But Zengi was to be hailed as the man who set the Islamic world on the road to recovery of its shattered pride. *'Before he came to power the absence of strong rulers to impose justice, and the presence of the Franks close at hand, had made the country a wilderness, but he made it flower again,'* wrote Ibn al-Athir.

Zengi seems to have a been a simple, austere man, who could be found sleeping on a straw mat in his tent more often than in one of the many palaces at his command. He was a heavy drinker, but he imposed the strictest discipline on his troops. The Arab chroniclers are unanimous in their praise for the way in which Zengi protected civilians from the sort of depredations that were normally inflicted by armies.

Kemal ed-Din, the historian of Aleppo, records how, when Zengi's troops were leaving Aleppo, they were under strict orders not to trample on any of the crops, and they obeyed so conscientiously that *'they seemed to be walking between two ropes'*.

Zengi clearly inspired fear in even the most important of his followers. Ibn al-Athir tells the story of an emir who had billeted himself on a Jew in the city of Daquqa, which he held from Zengi as a fief. The Jew didn't enjoy the Emir's company that much and appealed to Zengi, who thought he had a point. Zengi didn't need to reason with the unwanted lodger – *'He had only to give the Emir a look to make him pack his bags and move'*.

Zengi's rise to the top had begun soon after he suppressed the Caliph's revolt. The Sultan of Baghdad rewarded him with control of Mosul and then acquiesced in his seizure of Aleppo. This was a strong base from which to challenge the Franks, but it was nine years before Zengi attacked the Crusader kingdom.

In 1131, King Baldwin II of Jerusalem died. His successor was his son-in-law, Count Fulk of Anjou. In 1137 Zengi ambushed Fulk's army, and the King and his bodyguard took refuge in a fortress north-east of Tripoli. They were surrounded and soon ran out of provisions. They had been reduced to eating their own horses when Zengi offered them terms of surrender. Hardly daring to believe their luck, they paid him 50 000 dinars and were allowed to leave unmolested.

It was not long, however, before the Franks were kicking themselves, for a huge relief force under the command of the Emperor of Byzantium was close at hand. If they had held out just a bit longer, Zengi would have had to raise the siege. It was a great victory for the Moslem leader, and one which enabled him to bring back prosperity to the region.

With his prestige on the rise, Zengi's eyes inevitably began to stray towards Damascus. The Frankish chronicler William of Tyre was very sniffy about such ambitions: '*Zengi, mightily puffed up by his successes, like an ever-restless worm, dared to aspire to conquer the kingdom of Damascus.*'

Nor were the people of Damascus themselves over-enthusiastic about his attentions. They didn't trust Zengi one inch.

Their fears were not assuaged when Zengi captured the nearby town of Baalbek from them. Having sworn on the Koran that he would spare the lives of the defending garrison if they surrendered, Zengi proceeded to crucify thirty-seven of them and had the commander burnt alive. If he wished to offer the good citizens of Damascus his protection, it was a kind of protection they thought they could well do without.

In fact the Governor of Damascus, Unur, was so unenthusiastic that he sent an envoy to King Fulk of Jerusalem proposing an alliance against Zengi, whom he dubbed '*this cruel enemy, equally dangerous to both kingdoms*'. Unur's overtures were welcomed by the Franks and the astounded world witnessed the extraordinary sight of a large Frankish army, under the King of Jerusalem, riding to the aid of its Moslem neighbours in Damascus.

Zengi beat a retreat and the Frankish army joined forces with the Damascenes to recapture the fortress of Banyas, which had gone over to Zengi's side and which Unur had promised to hand over to the Franks in return for their help. '*Then might have been witnessed a strange and novel sight,*' wrote William of Tyre, '*a hostile people encouraging their enemy to the fiercest warfare, and as an ally, actually in arms for the destruction of a common foe ... Christians and Damascenes were equal in courage and united in purpose.*'

Banyas eventually surrendered and was duly presented to the Franks in an unusually civilized and orderly fashion. There was no massacre of civilians, no pillaging, and the ex-Emir of Banyas was even granted a pension from the revenues of the public baths and orchards to live on in his retirement!

Zengi Captures Edessa

To win Damascus, Zengi would have to undermine its allies, the Franks. So he now set his sights on what he saw as the weakest Christian outpost, Edessa. In 1144, after King Fulk's death, Joscelin of Edessa fell out with his neighbour and overlord, Raymond of Antioch, to the point that *'each rejoiced in the distress of the other and exulted over any untoward mischance.'* That helped. Towards the end of 1144 Zengi lured Joscelin away by attacking another Turkish prince with whom Joscelin had just signed a treaty of alliance. As soon as Joscelin and his army marched off to defend their new ally, Zengi turned round and started to besiege Edessa.

The defences of Edessa were not what they had been. The previous lords of Edessa had actually lived in the city and made sure that it was well supplied with everything necessary for any possible siege. Joscelin, however, had taken up residence at Turbessel *'far from the disturbances caused by his enemies'*, says William of Tyre disapprovingly.

The native inhabitants of Edessa, continues the chronicler, *'were utterly ignorant of the use of arms and familiar only with the business of trading ... The protection of the city was entirely in the hands of mercenaries.'* What was more, these mercenaries were not being paid and their numbers were therefore dwindling. William of Tyre blamed not only Joscelin but also the Archbishop of Edessa, the Very Reverend Hugo: *'Although he was said to have amassed great riches, which he might have used to pay troops for defending the city, he preferred, like a miser, to store up his wealth rather than to consider his perishing people.'* All of which was probably well known to Zengi, for he had his network of spies everywhere.

The walls of Edessa were massive and protected by lofty towers. But, as William of Tyre puts it, *'walls, towers, and ramparts avail but little if there are none to man them.'* For four weeks Zengi threw everything he had at the city. Finally, on Christmas Eve 1144, Zengi himself personally went into the tunnels that the miners had dug under the great walls. His inspection complete, he gave the orders to set fire to the wooden props and beams that supported the tunnels. Once the fire had taken hold, the wooden supports collapsed, bringing down with them the walls of Edessa. Zengi's troops poured in.

Under the first onslaught, the desperate citizens rushed for the shelter of the citadel. But a horrible shock awaited them. Archbishop Hugo had ordered the gates of the citadel to be closed against them. In the panic that followed, thousands of men, women and children were trampled to death. The rest, including the Archbishop himself, were slaughtered by Zengi's troops. Many at the time blamed the Archbishop. *'An unsavoury reputation will ever attend his memory'*, mutters William of Tyre. *'For terrible are the words of Scripture concerning men of his sort: "Thy money perish with thee".'*

Zengi finally stopped the massacre of citizens. He slew the Frankish men and sold their women into slavery, but he protected the native Christians. He also destroyed the Latin churches but left the Armenian, Jacobite and Greek churches unmolested. He made it quite clear that his *jihad* was against the Franks – not against all Christians. He even showed favour to the Syrian bishop, Basil, who, when questioned about his future loyalty, proudly replied that his loyalty to the Franks showed how capable he was of loyalty.

Zengi basked in unparalleled glory. He was the toast of the Arab nations and he accumulated titles by the score, as the chronicler Ibn al-Qalanisi recorded:

> *The Emir, the general, the great, the just, the aid of God, the triumphant, the unique, the pillar of religion, the cornerstone of Islam, ornament of Islam, protector of God's creatures, associate of the dynasty, auxiliary of doctrine, grandeur of the nation, honour of kings, supporter of Sultans, victor over the infidels, rebels and atheists, commander of the Moslem armies, the victorious king, the king of princes, the sun of the deserving . . . .*

And so on and so on.

In fact Ibn al-Qalanisi apologizes for not using all Zengi's correct titles every time he mentions him, on account of the fact that if he did, he wouldn't have room for anything else.

The taking of Edessa raised spirits and morale throughout the Moslem world. The first conquest of the Crusaders had been wrested back from them. The others, it seemed, were sure to follow. And from the ranks of the refugees new voices were heard proclaiming that the *jihad* was not just a war of defence, but a counter-crusade: a Holy War to drive the Franks from the Holy Land and restore Jerusalem to Islam.

But it would not be Zengi who did that.

Two years after capturing Edessa he was sleeping in his tent after a particularly heavy bout of drinking, *'gorged with wine and unusually drunk'*, sniffs William of Tyre. He woke up to see one of his eunuchs drinking from his own goblet. Zengi muttered a few drunken threats about what he would do to the fellow and then fell fast asleep again. The eunuch was so terrified that as soon as he was certain that the great man was safely snoring again, he snatched up a knife and stabbed him all over in a frenzied attack. The assailant then fled.

'And yet he slumbered amidst a proud army, ringed by his braves with their swords. He perished, neither riches nor power of use to him,' wrote Ibn al-Qalanisi.

Nur ed-Din — the Saint-king

The discipline that Zengi had enforced with such an iron hand dissolved like starch out of a stiff collar. His treasury was plundered and his enemies suddenly came out of the woodwork. *'His treasures now became the prey of others, dismembered by his sons and adversaries',* recorded Ibn al-Qalanisi. *'At his death his enemies rode forth, brandishing the swords they dared not brandish while he lived.'* Towns and fortresses were seized back by those from whom Zengi had taken them and the Franks began raiding across the borders again as his eldest son, Saif ed-Din, rushed to Mosul to claim his inheritance in the east.

His second son, however, paused amidst the uproar in the camp to make a symbolic gesture which would grow in significance as the years went by. He strode into the tent where his father's body still lay, took Zengi's signet ring off his finger and placed it upon his own. Then he sped to Aleppo, accompanied by his faithful general, Shirkuh, to take over.

'Nur ed-Din was a tall, swarthy man with a beard but no moustache,' Ibn al-Athir wrote in his eulogy. He had *'a fine forehead and a pleasant appearance enhanced by beautiful, melting eyes.'* More significantly, he was the Turkish equivalent of a *pulan*: he belonged to a new generation of Turks who were much more Arabized than their fathers.

Being Arabized meant entering more fully into the world of religion. Nur ed-Din held scholars and men of religion in high esteem and would even go as far as to *'rise to his feet in their presence and invite them to sit next to him'*. *'He studied many religious books . . . applied himself assiduously to prayer . . . ardently desired to do good.'*

Where Zengi had been cruel and unscrupulous, Nur ed-Din believed he should appear upright and just. Where Zengi had no qualms about hitting the bottle, Nur ed-Din disapproved of alcohol and in 1148 he banned the use of wine in his camp. He even stopped his troops listening to music, and proscribed instruments such as *'the tambourine, the flute and other objects displeasing to God'*. Nur ed-Din was, in short, an Islamic fundamentalist.

'I have read the lives of the kings of old,' writes Ibn al-Athir, *'and after the right-guided Caliphs and Umar II* [the ideal rulers of orthodox Sunni tradition] *I have not found one*

The technique of undermining a castle wall – in this case under the cover
of a wheeled canopy or *mantelet*, onto which the defenders are
throwing boulders and 'Greek fire'.

more upright or a sterner advocate of justice ... Among his virtues were austerity, piety and a knowledge of theology.' He turned his back on extravagance and presented an image of poverty and humility. Nur ed-Din's wife once complained about this excessive austerity,

> *and so he allotted to her, from his private property, three shops in Homs that would bring her in about twenty dinar a year. When she objected that this was not much, he said: 'I have no more. Of all the wealth I have at my disposal, I am but the custodian for the Moslem community, and I do not intend to deceive them over this or to cast myself into hell-fire for your sake.'*

Kemal ad-Din adds: *'Nur ed-Din abandoned luxurious garments and instead covered himself with rough cloth.'* He even insisted on calling himself not Nur ed-Din ('Light of Religion') but plain *'Mahmud'*. Before battle he would pray: *'O God, grant victory to Islam and not to Mahmud. Who is this dog Mahmud to merit victory?'*

The only snag about all this humility and piety was that they were also good politics and his enemies did not hesitate to accuse him of hypocrisy. What is more, Nur ed-Din himself exploited them for all they were worth. He constructed a vast propaganda machine, a network of scholars and writers, who poured out speeches, sermons, poems, books, circulars, letters and inscriptions. In short, he propagated the image of himself that he wished people to believe.

So one has to view the eulogies of court writers like Ibn al-Athir with a certain circumspection, and yet, for all that, there does seem to have been something quite remarkable about this twenty-nine-year-old man who took over the front line against the Franks in 1146, and few would call his sincerity into doubt. Even his Frankish enemies confirmed his statesmanship and piety. *'Nureddin ... was a wise and prudent man, and, according to the superstitious traditions of his people, one who feared God,'* wrote William of Tyre.

The goals that Nur ed-Din had set – from the very moment he came to power – were expressed in the slogan *'jihad and unity'*. 'Unity', of course, meant 'unity beneath the banner of Aleppo'. This was why the Governor of Damascus was less than enthusiastic about the cause. *Jihad* meant all-out war and the restoration of Jerusalem (whose importance as an Islamic shrine was now being emphasized more than it had been in the past). Nur ed-Din even had a pulpit built in Aleppo, ready and waiting to be installed in the al-Aqsa Mosque in Jerusalem when the great day arrived.

Now it might seem obvious that any leader who was prepared to declare *jihad* in this way would receive the unbounded support of all men of religion. But this was not actually the case. The men of religion in the Islamic world had shown no particular enthusiasm for *jihad* over the previous half century of Frankish occupation. There were exceptions like al-Harawi in Damascus and al-Khashshab in Aleppo, but in the main the energies and enthusiasms of the religious establishment were focused on the internal struggle against co-religionists who held slightly different views — particularly the Shi'ites. The battle against unorthodoxy seemed far more important to most Sunni Islamic leaders than the threat of the Western Christians.

It was also important to Nur ed-Din himself. In 1149 he banned Shi'ites from Aleppo and by 1157 he was even prepared to put down a Shi'ite rebellion in his capital by brute force. Nur ed-Din fused the concept of *jihad* with Sunni orthodoxy. The two became so inextricably linked that the Sunni religious leaders became his most enthusiastic supporters.

Nur ed-Din also had fewer distractions than did Zengi. Zengi had been master of Mosul as well as Aleppo; Mosul was far to the east and Zengi had had to take as much notice of the problems of Baghdad as of the Frankish frontier. That Iraqi side of the inheritance, though, passed into the hands of Nur ed-Din's brother, Saif ed-Din. Wonder of wonders, these two brothers actually helped and supported each other, so that Nur ed-Din was able to concentrate on his western neighbours.

The Loss and Recapture of Edessa

As soon as Nur ed-Din took over the reins of power, he was in control. Joscelin, the ex-lord of Edessa, tried to reclaim his old city and — with the connivance of the Armenian Christian inhabitants — established himself back in the town. Nur ed-Din acted with such promptness and determination that it took everybody by surprise, especially the languid and pleasure-loving Joscelin, '*a lazy, idle man, given over to low and dissolute pleasures*', as William of Tyre fondly remembered him.

Within fewer days than anyone would have thought possible, Nur ed-Din had

---

Overleaf
The Pools of Abraham, Edessa (modern Sanli
Urfa in southern Turkey), outside one of the several
reputed birthplaces of Abraham. Legend has it that
when Nebuchadnezzar fired Abraham from a catapult
from the citadel high above into a bonfire below, God
turned the bonfire into this pool so that Abraham
landed wet but unscathed.

surrounded Edessa. There was panic amongst the Christians. Joscelin and his collaborators, who had had no time to construct defences, ran around like headless chickens. Eventually they decided on that time-honoured military manoeuvre known as 'making a run for it'.

The Armenian civilians who had assisted them were also left with no choice but to flee with the Frankish troops; otherwise they faced reprisals as traitors. The gates were flung open and chaos ensued as *'a great multitude of all ranks and classes'* scrambled to get out while, at the same time, the Turks tried to get in. Writes William of Tyre:

> *There might have been seen a most piteous spectacle. A helpless throng of unwarlike citizens, old men and sick people, matrons and tender maidens, aged women and little ones, even babes at the breast, all crowded together in the narrow gateway. Some were trodden under the feet of the horses; others, crushed by the on-pressing multitude, were stifled to death; while still others fell under the merciless sword of the Turks.*

Eventually the panic of those trying to leave prevailed. The Franks cut a way through the besieging troops *'and our people spread out over the plain,'* says William. But to no purpose. Nur ed-Din pursued them and cut them down.

This was a crucial triumph for Nur ed-Din. Edessa was the symbol of his father's glory and thus vital to his prestige. The speed with which he accomplished this impressed friend and foe alike. It certainly impressed Unur, the Governor of Damascus, with the need to keep on the right side of the new master of Aleppo. He hurriedly offered his daughter's hand in marriage to Zengi's son. And, of course, it suited Nur ed-Din to accept.

It did not follow, however, that Unur now trusted his new son-in-law. On the contrary, the Governor of Damascus still preferred an alliance with the infidels. It would take an extraordinary man to persuade Unur to tear up his alliance with the Franks and throw in his lot with the Emir of Aleppo. And yet that is what was soon to happen. The man responsible was not even a Moslem. He was a Christian monk living some three thousand miles away. His name was Bernard.

7

St Bernard's Dogs

The news of the loss of Edessa to Zengi had spread through the West like wildfire. Pope Eugenius III immediately called for a second Crusade, but without a great deal of response. In France, King Louis summoned his bishops and nobles for the usual Christmas thrash and took the opportunity to present them with his scheme for rescuing the Holy Land. But the suggestion went down with the members of the court like a lump of left-over Christmas pudding.

Enter Bernard, Abbot of Clairvaux! Almost single-handedly he swung the whole thing around.

Bernard was one of the most powerful men in Europe at this time. He had helped establish Pope Innocent II back in 1130 and the present Pope had been his pupil. Bernard was a charismatic orator. He had such power to sway men's souls – even to persuade them to give up everything they possessed – that it was said that when Bernard was around *'mothers hid their sons and wives hid their husbands'*.

Bernard was not exactly an intellectual – in fact he was more of an anti-intellectual. There was no room for 'reason' in Bernard's style of religion. His interest was 'the heart' – the passion of belief. This was to prove fatal to the people whom Bernard persuaded to journey east.

On 31 March 1146, Bernard mounted a stage in a field outside the town of Vézelay and delivered his first Crusade sermon. It was the medieval equivalent of a pop concert. Massed crowds, too big for any building, gathered for a day out in the open, with a world-famous figure to entertain them. Bernard was not the sort of rock 'n roller to disappoint them. The crowd went wild. After the performance, so many mobbed the stage to take the Cross that Bernard ran out of ready-made ones and – in

Louis VII taking the Cross at
Vézelay in 1146 in the presence of the
Bishop of Versailles and St Bernard
of Clairvaux. From *Les Passages faits
Outremer . . . , c.* 1490.

what must have been a moment of pure theatre — tore off his own garments and cut them up into crosses for the crowd.

Everywhere Bernard went he was a sensation. Crusade fever swept across Europe. Bernard promised would-be Crusaders not just the Earth, but Heaven too! God will *'award to those fighting for him wages: the remission of their sins and everlasting glory'.* And he had no qualms about appealing to his audience's mercenary instincts: *'If you are a prudent merchant, if you are a man fond of acquiring this world's goods, I am showing you certain great markets; make sure not to let the chance pass you by ...'* Don't miss this golden opportunity, folks! Instant Salvation Guaranteed! Available only for a limited time! Hurry! Hurry!

For Bernard, the fall of Edessa was not a set-back, but an unrepeatable, once-in-a-lifetime opportunity, provided exclusively for You, by God, to atone for your sins and win His grace! *'This is a plan not made by man, but coming from heaven and proceeding from the heart of divine love.'*

As usual, this particular manifestation of divine love sparked off massacres of Jews throughout Germany. Bernard was asked to come and restore order. He had opposed a rival Pope who had Jewish origins with the slogan: *'It would be an insult to Christ if the offspring of a Jew occupied the throne of St Peter.'* But he was not, by the standards of his day, a fanatical anti-Semite. Bernard ordered the monk who had been inspiring the massacres back to his monastery and started to preach the Crusade in Germany himself.

The German Crusaders

Even though his sermons were having to be delivered via a German interpreter, Bernard was a wow. *'I opened my mouth,'* Bernard wrote with some complacency to the Pope, *'I spoke; and at once the Crusaders have multiplied to infinity. Villages and towns are now deserted. You will scarcely find one man for every seven women. Everywhere you see widows whose husbands are still alive.'* No wonder mothers hid their children and wives their husbands whenever Bernard the Abbot was around!

The King of Germany himself broke down under one of Bernard's harangues. Bernard turned upon the great man and, taking on the voice of Christ himself, thundered in his ear: *'Man, what ought I to do for you that I have not done?'* Stumped for an answer, Conrad is reported to have burst into tears and taken the Cross then and there.

The German Crusade set off in May 1146, followed by the French in June.

Ibn al-Qalanisi confirms the sense of foreboding that permeated the Arab world at this time:

> *Reports kept coming in – from Constantinople, from the territory of the Franks, and from neighbouring lands too – that the kings of the Franks were on their way from their countries to attack the land of Islam. They had emptied their own provinces, leaving them devoid of defenders, and had brought with them riches, treasures, and immeasurable material. They numbered, it was said, as many as a million foot-soldiers and cavalry, perhaps even more.*

Of course there were nothing like a million – but there were tens of thousands.

The Germans made their way through Hungary without too much incident. Once they got into Byzantine territory, however, Conrad's control began to slip. At Philippopolis a local juggler tried to earn an honest penny by displaying his talents to the Crusaders. He was so convincing that some of the Germans accused him of witchcraft. A riot developed and the suburbs of the town were burnt to the ground.

At Constantinople Emperor Manuel, like his grandfather Alexius, considered one crusading army at a time quite enough to deal with and persuaded Conrad to move on, without waiting for the French. When he reached Nicaea, Conrad split his forces in two, sending the non-combatants by the coast road while he and the main army took the shorter, more dangerous route straight across Anatolia. William of Tyre relates how the Greek guides led them by unfrequented ways into a wilderness and then suddenly deserted them. True or not, his analysis of why it happened illustrates Latin feelings about the Greeks:

> *It was common talk, and probably quite true, that these perilous wanderings were devised with the knowledge and at the command of the Greek Emperor, who has always envied the successful advance of the Christians. For it is well known that the Greeks have always looked with distrust on all increase of power by the western nations (as they still do), especially by that of the Teutonic nations, as rivals of the empire. They take it ill that the king of the Teutons calls himself the Emperor of the Romans. For thereby he seems to detract too much from the prestige of their own Emperor.*

Near Dorylaeum they were suddenly ambushed by a large Turkish army, led by the son of Kilij Arslan, come to revenge his father's defeat by the Crusaders in this very spot fifty years before. The Christians were weary and thirsty and taken completely by surprise. Weighed down with their armour, they were unable to engage the Turks in close combat. After a short battle *'these great Christian princes, whose arms and strength, courage and numbers had seemed incomparable, suddenly collapsed.'* Barely one tenth of that great expedition escaped. Conrad himself just made it back to Nicaea.

The Frankish Expedition

$\mathfrak{H}$ere the remnants of the German army joined up with the Franks under King Louis VII, and together they decided to take the coast road on which the non-combatants had been sent. Conrad, however, took a boat back to Byzantium. He was ill, although William of Tyre suspected another motive: *'perchance he found the arrogance of the Franks unendurable'.*

And so they moved on in the worsening winter conditions. Provisions began to get low and discipline went to the wind. Even when they arrived at the port of Attalia

St Bernard, portrayed here in his Abbey of Clairvaux, stoutly resisting the devil. From a French manuscript *c.* 1445.

(modern Antalya) they found that food was in short supply, since the surrounding countryside was in the possession of the Turks and the people of Attalia relied on supplies arriving by sea. Worse still, the fleet provided by the Emperor of Byzantium to take them the rest of the way turned out to be far too small. The situation became even more acute as the food shortage began to take its toll; *'in fact'*, says William of Tyre, *'the survivors of the army, and above all the poor, nearly perished of famine'*.

They were unable to get away, and yet they were unable to stay where they were. In this crisis the King of France showed the mettle of a true aristocrat. He packed the available ships with his own household and what cavalry he could, and cleared off —

abandoning the foot-soldiers and the unarmed pilgrims under his protection to their fate. He did leave 500 marks with the Governor of Attalia, for provisioning them, but the Governor refused to keep them within the safety of the city walls. Outside, they had little chance of surviving the Turkish archers and so these wretched creatures, starving, leaderless and unprotected by knights, limped along the road towards Antioch. Less than half of them made it.

King Louis at Antioch

King Louis arrived at Antioch amidst pomp and *'the greatest magnificence'.* Prince Raymond of Antioch feasted the new arrivals, gave them the best accommodation, distributed gifts and generally made them feel glad to be in such a civilized place. It was spring. The sap was rising. The air was full of optimism, camaraderie and romance.

It was not to last.

Prince Raymond was particularly relieved to see even the reduced force that arrived; he was desperate to smash the rising power of Nur ed-Din. He *felt a lively hope that with the assistance of the king and his troops he would be able to subjugate the neighbouring cities, namely, Aleppo, Shaizar, and several others . . . For the arrival of King Louis had brought such fear to our enemies that now they not only distrusted their own strength but even despaired of life itself.'*

But Raymond did not know Louis. The King was still under the spell of the Abbot Bernard. His heart was fixed on Jerusalem. Besides, he felt his own force alone was too small to rescue Edessa and Conrad had already sailed on to Acre. Relations between the two men soured. Neither was the situation helped by the flowering relationship between the dashing Prince Raymond and Louis's wife, the famous, the glamorous, the clever, the cultured, the incredibly wealthy Eleanor of Aquitaine.

Eleanor had already complained that when she married Louis she thought she had married a man but found she had married a monk. She cannot have been encouraged by Louis's determination to lead a religious life for the duration of the Crusade, which, presumably, involved very little in the way of sexual recreation. Whether this is so or not, there were soon rumours flying round Antioch that the fair Eleanor (aged twenty-six) had found an admirable substitute in her uncle Raymond (aged forty-nine). King Louis found his honour in jeopardy and himself in danger of becoming a laughing stock.

What made matters worse was the fact that Eleanor made no secret of her support

Nur ed-Din's Warriors

Nur ed-Din's army was unusually committed to the idea of Holy War. It was an unusual army. Most Turkish rulers relied on Turkish soldiers; Turcoman tribesmen and Mameluks who came from the regions north of Persia. Turcomen were usually new converts to Islam; Mameluks were children bought as slaves from pagan tribes on the steppes and reared as soldiers. When Nur ed-Din had lost the Iraqi section of his father's domain to his brother, he had also lost a large part of the army. In their place, he recruited Kurdish warriors.

The Kurds had been Moslems for centuries and lived in Armenia, Georgia, Northern Iraq and Eastern Anatolia. In the early twelfth century thousands of Kurds were driven out of these regions by a new Christian power in Georgia. The Georgian Christians were waging a crusade of their own, in a manner copied from the Latins. Armies led by priests and bishops, and with knights wearing the cross, were creating a new Eastern Christian empire. Nur ed-Din's Kurdish troops were refugees who had been forcibly educated in the concept of Holy War.

---

for her uncle's plan and her utter contempt for Louis's decision to do nothing until he had visited the holy shrines of Jerusalem. Finally, when Louis publicly announced his intention of leaving for Jerusalem, the spirited Eleanor announced her intention of staying in Antioch and of seeking a divorce. Louis's response was effective but ignominious. He kidnapped his wife, had her dragged to the ship by force and set sail for Acre.

In Jerusalem, however, there was general relief that Louis had not stayed in Antioch. A council was held at the court at Acre to consider how *'they might endeavour to enlarge the kingdom and add to the glory of the Christian name'.* Never had so many stars of court, church and battlefield gathered for such a glittering occasion in the short history of the Kingdom of Jerusalem.

After a thorough discussion, the leaders, counsellors, advisers and wise men of the Franks, the Germans and the Kingdom of Jerusalem came to the unanimous decision that the most sensible thing would be to attack their only Moslem ally. To the newcomers, it must have looked obvious. Aleppo did not mean anything to them, but Damascus was a name they knew from the Bible. It was Moslem, it was strategically

The conference at Acre and the subsequent
abortive siege of Damascus, from a
manuscript made *c.* 1280. It illustrates
William of Tyre's *History* in which he
confesses himself baffled by the conduct of
the siege.

important, and it would put Nur ed-Din on the defensive. But those who had been there longer should have known better.

On 25 May 1148 the combined Christian armies set out for the attack on Damascus. The ruler of Damascus, Unur, had by this time plenty of warning of the approaching armies. He blocked off water-holes, strengthened his fortifications and sent off pleas for help to his Moslem rivals, including Nur ed-Din.

The spirit of St Bernard hovered in the air. It was Bernard who had fired the people of Europe with the idea of the Crusade. It was Bernard who had given the Crusade its highly religious profile. He had not been there to take the decision to attack Damascus, of course, but it had been taken in his spirit – putting religious conviction before reason and common sense. Having said that, one can excuse the Frankish military planners for not knowing one thing. They could have had little idea of the effect that Nur ed-Din's propaganda war was already having upon the Damascenes.

Débâcle at Damascus

Damascus at this time was surrounded by orchards and the Crusaders decided that, if they captured these first, the city would be a piece of cake. These orchards, however, were not simply pretty little groves of fruit trees, they formed a quite formidable defence for the city, as William of Tyre describes:

> ... the orchards stretched out five miles or more in the direction of Lebanon and, like a dense, gloomy forest, encircled the city far and wide. To indicate the limits of each orchard and also to prevent trespassers entering at will, these groves are enclosed by walls of mud .... These orchards are of the greatest protection to the city. The vast number of trees planted close together and the narrow paths made it difficult – in fact, well nigh impossible – for anyone to approach Damascus from that side. Yet, from the very first, our leaders had determined to lead the army through the orchards and in this way open an approach to the city.

It must have been a pretty nerve-racking business to be in that first wave of attackers. There were high towers spaced out amongst the orchards from which defenders constantly rained down arrows. As the Franks made their way down the narrow mud-walled paths, at any moment they might be stabbed by a lance thrust through a peep-hole in the walls. Many died in this way.

On the first day of attack the Damascenes came out of the city to fight. The Arab chroniclers record that the regular militia of the city was supported by 'volunteers fighting for the faith'. Hatred of the Franks was at grass-root level. Striding ahead of the

Turkish soldiers and Arab enthusiasts was an elderly lawyer by the name of al-Findalawi. Unur rushed up to him and told him he was far too old to fight the Franks and that he should leave it to others. But al-Findalawi turned and, referring to a passage in the Koran, said: *'I have offered myself for sale and He has bought me. By God, I neither agreed nor asked that the contract should be annulled!'* The old man continued on into the battle and fought until he was cut down. Al-Findalawi's sacrifice was to be long remembered. His grave became a place of pilgrimage; the *jihad* had found one of its first martyrs.

For all their enthusiasm, however, the Damascenes were driven back into the city and the Franks took possession of the orchards. During the engagement Conrad is supposed to have slain a courageous Turkish knight in a remarkable way: *'With one blow of the sword, he severed from the body of his enemy the head and neck, the left shoulder with the arm attached, and also a part of the side.'*

The citizens were in desperate straits, but then the situation changed. Reinforcements began to pour into Damascus from the north and the attackers were held at bay for several days. The Crusaders then made a fatal error. They decided to abandon their hard-won position in the orchards and establish themselves on a more open plain to the east of the city. The Moslems reoccupied the orchards immediately. The Crusaders found their new site was without water and also faced the strongest section of city wall. It was completely untenable and the opportunity of taking Damascus evaporated before their eyes in the pitiless heat and dust of the Syrian July.

At dawn the next day, the Crusaders bowed to the inevitable, packed up their bags and slunk away *'in miserable confusion and disorder'*. Harassed by the Damascene archers every step of the way, their route became littered with corpses of men and their 'splendid mounts' — *'the bodies stinking so powerfully,'* says the Damascus chronicler, *'that the birds almost fell out of the sky!'*.

St Bernard's Crusade ended in fiasco. The post-mortem and the recriminations were not long in following.

The Post-Mortem

For a start, how on earth did the leaders come to evacuate the orchards and take up an indefensible position? William of Tyre wrote that he *'often interviewed wise men and those whose memory of those times is still fresh'*, but he could never get to the bottom of the matter. He was certain of one thing, however: it was the local barons who had provided the bad advice — but what were their motives?

One view was that the old hands of the Kingdom of Jerusalem were getting their own back on the new boys from Europe. The local barons had assumed that Damascus was to be an addition to their own kingdom. They had been astonished to discover that the newly-arrived Kings of France and Germany were intending to hand the city over to one of their own cronies – the already wealthy Count Thierry of Flanders! *'They preferred that the Damascenes should keep their city rather than to see it given to the count.'*

Others ascribed the action of the local lords to the baleful influence of Raymond of Antioch, still itching to get even with Louis. Still more put the treachery down to a deal between the local Franks and Unur. Money had undoubtedly changed hands at some stage, although it was later discovered to have been counterfeit.

Back in Europe, most of the opprobrium inevitably fell on the instigator of the whole enterprise – Abbot Bernard of Clairvaux – he who had promised so much on behalf of God. Had he not proclaimed that the Crusade was planned in heaven? That it could not fail? A German monk in Wurzburg condemned it all as the work of the devil and, pointing his pen at Bernard, denounced the *'pseudo-prophets, sons of Belial and witnesses of Anti-Christ, who by stupid words misled the Christians and by empty preaching induced all sorts of men to go'.* Bernard himself was as bewildered as anybody and could only complain to the Pope that it seemed *'to point an end almost to existence itself'.* His only comfort was that it was probably all the fault of those iniquitous Greeks.

But if the causes of the disaster were debatable, there was little doubt about the results. The Kingdom was permanently weakened. From that time on, the nobility who had come in such numbers from the West to aid the Kingdom of Jerusalem *'looked askance at the ways of our leaders',* said William of Tyre.

> They justly declined all their plans as treacherous and showed utter indifference about the affairs of the kingdom . . . their influence caused others who had not been present there to slacken in love towards the kingdom. As a result, fewer people, and those less fervent in spirit, undertook this pilgrimage thereafter. Moreover, even to the present day, those who come fear lest they be caught in the same toils . . . From this time on, the condition of the Latins in the East became visibly worse.

The Franks had turned Damascus into an enemy and given Nur ed-Din's career the very boost it needed.

8

Arab Unity

In 1150 Nur ed-Din camped outside Damascus with his army, but he made no attempt to attack it. This was psychological warfare, and he sent a letter to Abaq, the prince of Damascus:

> *I have no intention, in camping here, of waging war against you nor of besieging you. I am only driven to act thus because of the numerous complaints by Moslems . . . for the country people have been despoiled of their goods and separated from their wives and children by the Franks, and there is no one to defend them . . . Having been given the power that God has granted me to help the Moslems and to wage* jihad *against the polytheists I may not abandon them.*

He bombarded the city with poems and official letters, while at the same time carrying out a clandestine correspondence with the military.

By chance, Nur ed-Din's right-hand man, Shirkuh, had a brother called Ayub who just happened to be a high-ranking officer in the Damascene army. Shirkuh managed to persuade him to assist the cause from within. Since Ayub's activities were covert, we don't know exactly what he did to help Nur ed-Din, but judging from the generosity with which Nur ed-Din later rewarded him, his contribution must have been significant.

Faced with this propaganda onslaught, the rulers of Damascus failed to find any

---

Nur ed-Din brought a golden age to Damascus, building schools, hospitals, courts of justice and even 'a palace for the poor'. A number of his buildings still stand to this day – such as this bathhouse which is still in use. Its profits were used to support the Great Mosque.

adequate countermeasure. They certainly managed to do exactly the wrong thing — sullenly reiterating their reliance on the Franks. *'Between you and us,'* they wrote to Nur ed-Din, *'there is henceforth nothing but the sword. Some Franks will come to our aid if you besiege us'.* They were simply playing into his hands. Especially when, shortly after Nur ed-Din's arrival outside the city, the spring rains broke a long winter drought and the citizens cheerfully attributed it to: *'the goodness, the justice and the piety'* of the sovereign of Aleppo.

Four times in four years Nur ed-Din returned, building up the pressure each time. When the rulers of the city did call in the Franks for protection, it *'plunged upright citizens and men of religion into anguish and led them to deplore even more this disastrous and abominable situation'.* In April 1154 Nur ed-Din surrounded Damascus for the last time. When the Aleppan war-cry echoed through the city, both troops and civilians opened the gates and welcomed the besiegers. The ripe plum fell into Nur ed-Din's lap just as he always knew it would.

Zengi's son had finally achieved, without bloodshed, what his father had failed to achieve. Moreover, Nur ed-Din proved himself to be the kind of conqueror you dream of being conquered by. He assembled all the city worthies and assured them their lives and property would be safe. At the same time he provided food-stocks for the hungry populace. Over the next few years, Nur ed-Din reduced and abolished taxes; he founded schools, hospitals, mosques, convents, public baths and palaces of justice. Damascus found itself launched on a golden age. Its citizens never regretted their change of allegiance to the Emir of Aleppo.

For the first time since the Franks had appeared upon the scene, Damascus and Aleppo were joined under a single ruler. The power of a united Syria could at last be turned against the invaders. Their first battleground was Egypt.

The Struggle for Egypt

Egypt was still an enormously wealthy country, but its government had fallen into disrepute. The nominal head was the Fatimid Caliph, the religious leader, who claimed descent from the Prophet's daughter, Fatima. But for many years the Caliph had been no more than a puppet and the real power had lain in the hands of his chief adviser and manipulator, the Vizier.

Now being Vizier of Egypt was in many ways a great job: enormously well paid, more perks than a baseball player, a great palace to live in and unlimited power. The only snag was that it was not what you could call a *secure* career. In fact, of the last fifteen Viziers only one had left office alive. And don't imagine that the others had died of old age. They had been poisoned, stabbed, hanged, crucified, beheaded, lynched by mobs and variously done away with, either by their rivals or by their nearest and dearest. To be Vizier was to take part in a bloody game of musical chairs which always seemed to end in tears.

In 1163 Shawar, the latest ex-Vizier of Egypt, who unusually had managed to escape with his life, turned up at the court of Nur ed-Din begging for help to win back his so briefly held kingdom. By way of inducement he was able to offer substantial money, land and one third of the grain revenues of Egypt! Nur ed-Din refused to be rushed into a decision. To get to Egypt meant a march through Frankish territory. It would be pointless to send a small army, but sending a large one would expose the rest of Syria.

Eventually Nur ed-Din opened up a copy of the Koran at random and consulted it. He then called in his chief adviser and general, a short, fat, one-eyed man, by the name of Shirkuh. Shirkuh was a rather surprising character for the Saint-King's closest confidant. He was a Kurd of lowly origin who had risen to high rank through his own merits. But he was no saint. He was often drunk, occasionally violent and recklessly generous. But he was beloved by his men and he was a general of genius.

Before the end of May 1164 he had reinstalled Shawar as Vizier in Cairo. The usurper was killed and his body thrown to the dogs in the street by order of the Caliph. *'For it is a matter of indifference to a supreme ruler,'* explains William of Tyre, *'whether one rival claimant or the other wins, as long as there is someone who will devote himself slavishly to the care of his lord's personal affairs and to those of the realm.'*

Having gained his objective, Shawar showed his gratitude by reneging on his promises to Nur ed-Din and telling Shirkuh to clear off out of his country. When Nur ed-Din's General showed no sign of moving, Shawar took his doomsday option. He invited the Franks to come and defend him! The King of the Franks didn't need much persuading. Ever since he had taken over the throne of Jerusalem in 1162, King Amalric had had his eye on Egypt. In fact he had already invaded once and besieged the very town in which Shirkuh was now holed up.

Amalric was a curious figure. He *'was excessively fat'*, William of Tyre informs us, *'with breasts like those of a woman, hanging down to his waist'*. But he was otherwise good-looking, with sparkling eyes and blond, though slightly receding hair. He had the bearing of a prince, but a strange way of laughing so that his whole body was convulsed, and he was not an easy conversationalist — perhaps because of a slight stutter.

In the third week of July 1164 a combined force of the two former enemies, Egyptian and Frankish, besieged Shirkuh in the city of Bilbeis. *'What a marvel!'* exclaimed al-Qadi al-Fadil in a panegyric to Shawar. *'You oppose one enemy with the help of another! . . . The crosses serve to help Islam!'* Nur ed-Din, however, had no intention of losing his best general. So he tried to draw Amalric out of Egypt by attacking a Frankish stronghold near Antioch. The Frankish troops who had remained within the kingdom hurried to the siege, but Nur ed-Din was soon able to lure them into a trap, in which many were massacred and the leaders captured.

Syrian confidence must have soared at the spectacle of so many proud Frankish princes shuffling into Aleppo chained together *'like the lowest slaves'*. Amongst them were the Prince of Antioch, the Count of Tripoli, the Governor of Cilicia, and the Count of Edessa. *'They were cast into prison and became the sport of infidels.'* Nur ed-Din then sent a sackful of Frankish scalps and banners to Shirkuh with instructions to be sure to display them on the ramparts for the Franks to see. Amalric took the hint and came to terms with Shirkuh. Each side agreed to leave Egypt and return to their homes. In Shirkuh's case it took another bribe of 30 000 dinars from the Vizier to help him on his way.

Two years later, news leaked out that Nur ed-Din's chief general was once again busy planning another visit to Egypt – this time with the clear intention of staying. The Vizier immediately implored Amalric to come to his aid again, and the race for the Nile started all over again.

Saladin

'**M**y uncle Shirkuh turned to me and said: "Yusuf, pack your things, we're going." When I heard this order, I felt as if my heart had been pierced by a dagger, and I answered, "In God's name, even were I granted the entire kingdom of Egypt, I would not go."' This is how Saladin recalled the beginning of his great adventure in later years. And he concluded with admirable brevity: 'In the end I did go with my uncle. He conquered Egypt, then died. God then

---

In 1149 Nur ed-Din trapped Raymond of Antioch's army
near the Fountain of Murad and destroyed it. Raymond was
killed and thus paid the ultimate penalty for failing to persuade
the leaders of the Second Crusade to attack Nur ed-Din
and Aleppo. From *Les Passages faits Outremer . . . , c.* 1490.

placed in my hands power that I had never expected.' The first hardship Saladin would have had to endure was a sandstorm while crossing the Sinai:

> *The men dared not open their mouths to speak to one another, nor could they keep their eyes open. Dismounting from their horses, they lay prostrate clinging to the ground, their hands pressed into the sand as far as possible, lest they be swept aloft by the violence of the whirlwind and again be dashed to the ground. For in that desert waves of sand like those of the sea are wont to rise and fall as in a tempest.*

Nevertheless, Shirkuh still managed to take the Frankish-Egyptian forces by surprise. Instead of showing up outside Cairo in the south, as expected, he and his huge army suddenly appeared from behind the pyramids of Giza on the other side of the Nile, beyond their reach.

He could not get at them either. But nor could he get at Cairo. It was stalemate. The Franks showed their admirable spirit of free enterprise by threatening to return home unless the Vizier payed them a lot more money. Nur ed-Din's general also had a proposal for his fellow Moslem in Cairo: *'The Frankish enemy is at our mercy, cut off from their bases. Let us unite our forces and exterminate them. The time is ripe; the opportunity may not arise again.'*

But Shawar was not in the business of *jihad*. He had Shirkuh's messenger executed, dutifully reported the contents of the message to the Franks and ratified his agreement with Amalric. The annual tribute was to be increased. A sum of four thousand gold pieces was to be handed over to the Franks and Amalric was to *'guarantee with his own hand, in good faith, without fraud or evil intent, that he would not depart from the land of Egypt until Shirkuh and his entire army should be utterly destroyed or entirely driven from the territories thereof'*.

But Shirkuh was not easily to be destroyed. He set off across Egypt at an extra-ordinary rate, with Amalric and Shawar in pursuit. Only when he found a battle-ground that suited him, at Babain, did Shirkuh pause to give battle, and there he was able to inflict casualties out of all proportion to the size of his army. The young Saladin commanded the centre battalion.

Shirkuh then established himself in Alexandria, whose Sunni population wel-comed him. But the city was immediately besieged by the Franco-Egyptian army. Shirkuh tried to draw them off by breaking out, but they simply let him go, leaving Saladin to cope with the problems of a starving city under siege.

Eventually Shirkuh was forced to do a deal with the Franks: *'We are wasting our time here, and the days are passing without result. Many duties await us at home.'* Amalric, who was indeed getting nervous about the situation back in the Kingdom of Jerusalem, agreed. There was a strange truce before they all went home; Amalric flew his standard from the Pharos lighthouse and Saladin recuperated in the Frankish camp. He was given a bodyguard, made friends with many Franks and was generally treated with great respect. It was even rumoured that he was knighted by the Constable, Humphrey of Toron.

But Shirkuh and Saladin must have returned to Damascus disappointed men. It was beginning to look as if the conquest of Egypt was beyond their reach – certainly as long as Shawar could call in the protection of the Franks. Nur ed-Din told Shirkuh: *'You have exerted yourself twice, but have not achieved what you sought'* and put him in charge of the town of Homs. Saladin is reported as saying: *'I suffered such hardships at Alexandria as I shall never forget.'* Neither could have imagined that within a year and a half each in turn would have become lord of Egypt.

The Fall of Egypt

The surprise move came from Amalric. At the beginning of November 1168 he suddenly appeared before the walls of Bilbeis, broke in and massacred the inhabitants, regardless of age, sex or religion. William of Tyre was clearly deeply troubled by this treacherous breach of an alliance. The reason some gave for the attack was that Shawar was plotting with Nur ed-Din against the Franks. But others, he says, *'claim that all these charges were false, that the Sultan Shawar was quite innocent and, far from deserving such treatment, had in good faith kept the treaty ... They assert that the war made against him was unjust and contrary to divine law; that it was merely a pretext invented to defend an outrageous enterprise.'*

It was an adventure that could not lead anywhere; even though Amalric besieged Cairo, he could not hope to rule Egypt. There simply were not enough Latins in the east to do it. He pulled out. But in the meantime Shawar had applied to Nur ed-Din for help. Shirkuh must have been hardly able to believe his luck. Here he was being

---

Overleaf
Nur ed-Din's army was essentially a form of feudal levy, composed of semi-independent Emirs who brought their own men for relatively brief periods of service. It was supplemented by slave-soldiers (Mameluks), Kurdish mercenaries and volunteer enthusiasts. From a French manuscript.

actually invited to enter the city he had coveted for so long. He was on his way in a matter of weeks.

On 8 January 1169 Shirkuh finally and triumphantly entered Cairo. Two days later he had an interview with the Caliph. And a week after that, Vizier Shawar was killed. The dirty work was entrusted to Saladin and some other emirs. They unhorsed the Vizier and dragged him off to a tent, where he was kept in suspense until the order came from the Caliph to behead him. *'Thus strong through the power of the sword, Shirkuh became master of all Egypt.'* But he was not to enjoy his dream for long. Three months later he was dead. The office then fell on his chief lieutenant, his nephew Saladin.

9

Saladin the Upstart

'Upon the death of Shirkuh, the advisers of the Caliph al-Adid suggested that he name Yusuf the new Vizier, because he was the youngest, and seemingly the most inexperienced and weakest, of the emirs of the army.' This is how Ibn al-Athir interpreted Saladin's rise to power. In fact, at the risk of spoiling a good story, the idea that Saladin was a shy, retiring nobody who had suddenly been forced into the limelight is not really tenable. He had killed Shawar and put his uncle Shirkuh into power. He had demonstrated ability in the invasions of Egypt and proved himself in battle.

Even before the Egyptian campaign, the young Saladin must have shown promise for his uncle to have chosen him as his aide-de-camp in preference to Shirkuh's own sons. Before that, Nur ed-Din had himself appointed Saladin as chief of police in Damascus, a job in which Saladin was supposed to have levied a tax off the earnings of prostitutes. At any rate he seems to have earned a reputation for being pretty tough – a contemporary poet warns the thieves of Syria to 'go softly', for this Yusuf is prepared to cut off their hands.

There is a touch of Prince Hal in some of the Arab accounts of Saladin's assumption of power. They report that, on his appointment, he repented of 'wine-drinking and turned away from frivolity' so that he might in the future 'assume the dress of religion'.

There was certainly nothing uncertain, weak or inexperienced in the way Saladin handled his new situation. He was unexpectedly running an alien country of which he had little experience, amongst strangers, strange customs, and in the most dangerous job in a court celebrated for its intrigues and conspiracies. Some people might have come unstuck. Not Saladin. He immediately set about winning over the population by spending the money that his uncle had collected. He started moving Fatimid troops out of Cairo and the moment he got wind of a palace conspiracy, he acted ruthlessly and effectively.

One of his colleagues is supposed to have become suspicious of a ragged man carrying a new pair of shoes. On examination the shoes were discovered to contain a letter from a group of Egyptian emirs, headed by one of the palace eunuchs, requesting the Franks to come back and help destroy the Syrian interloper. This story is probably just an example of Saladin's propaganda, but however he learnt of the plot and whether or not there was a plot, Saladin had the eunuch killed.

This seems to have been the signal for a revolt by the Black Regiment of the Fatimids. Trouble had been brewing amongst them for some time, and they had made and broken Viziers. *'They thought that all white men were pieces of fat and that all black men were coals.'* On the day after the eunuch's murder, the Black Regiment gathered in the main square and a pitched battle raged for the next two days. They were finally forced back to their own quarter and when this was burnt down, they sued for mercy. They were allowed to escape to Giza, presumably disarmed, and here they were set upon by Turanshah, Saladin's brother, and massacred virtually to a man.

The Rift between Saladin and Nur ed-Din

By the end of 1169 Saladin was the unchallenged master of Egypt. His wealth was vast. He gave his father and brother control of territories that brought them one million dinars a year. No matter how many times Saladin swore allegiance to Nur ed-Din, there was no disguising the situation: the former protégé was now in a position of almost equal power to his old master, and of greater wealth. This is not something that Nur ed-Din could have relished.

According to some accounts, Saladin's independence of action got up Nur ed-Din's nose. But the chronicler Abu Shama reports that Nur ed-Din was most irritated by the way that Saladin spent money without asking for his advice; the whole point of conquering Egypt was that it was rich and Nur ed-Din had good use for the money.

Nur ed-Din was also impatient for Saladin to abolish the Shi'ite Caliphate. But Saladin knew he could not move too fast without risking a popular revolt. In May 1170 he dismissed all Shi'ite judges and replaced them with orthodox *qadis*, but the circumspection of his efforts in this direction and his refusal to deal with the Fatimid Caliphate itself led Nur ed-Din *'to suspect and revile him'*.

Finally, in June 1171, Nur ed-Din wrote to Saladin ordering him to remove the

Saladiñ rex Ægypti

'Saladin King of Egypt' became a stock figure in the European
line-up of legendary heroes. This representation comes from a
fifteenth-century Italian manuscript.

Caliph. Saladin still hesitated, but since this was a direct order he would have to obey or openly revoke his allegiance to Nur ed-Din. It was at this point that Saladin's amazing luck came to his rescue. The Caliph died. The timing was so perfect that it's hard to believe that poison was not involved, and yet only one source mentions such a possibility. Perhaps it's easier to believe it was just Saladin's luck.

The Caliph of Baghdad was now officially recognized in Egypt. Sunni orthodoxy had triumphed. But this did not smooth relations between Cairo and Damascus. On the contrary, the removal of the Fatimid Caliphate meant that Saladin simply became more independent. He was now absolute ruler of a state that was even larger and richer than Syria. Tensions with Nur ed-Din were bound to get even worse. For the next few years, Saladin was to execute an elaborate ballet in order to avoid confronting his 'master' head-on.

Egypt and Syria were separated by the Frankish fief of Transjordan. Shortly after the death of al-Adid, Saladin dutifully acted on a promise he had given Nur ed-Din that he would help capture this vital link. He boldly marched into southern Jordan and laid siege to the fortress of Kerak. After a few days, however, 'convinced that it was impregnable, Saladin gave the order to depart and returned to Egypt by the desert route'.

Ibn al-Athir says that the fortress was actually on the point of surrendering and that the real reason for Saladin's sudden departure was the imminent arrival of Nur ed-Din. The last thing Saladin wanted was a face-to-face meeting with his master, in which he would inevitably have to revert to being the subordinate. What if Nur ed-Din ordered him back to Damascus? It was safer to keep at a distance and maintain the fiction of submission whilst pursuing a policy of independence.

Another reason, says Ibn al-Athir, was that Saladin had no intention of removing the Franks from Palestine. A combined attack by the Syrians from the east and the Egyptians from the west might well annihilate the Frankish kingdom, but that would increase Nur ed-Din's power and, what is worse, remove the buffer between Cairo and Damascus. So Saladin pretended that he had to rush back to Egypt to suppress a Fatimid revolt. 'Nur ed-Din did not accept the excuse.'

Indeed, Nur ed-Din was furious and threatened to invade Egypt. Saladin hastily summoned a family council. His nephew, Taki ed-Din, was all for war, but his father, Ayub, is quoted as telling Saladin, 'I am your father and if there is anyone here who loves you and wishes you well it is I. But know this: if Nur ed-Din came, nothing could ever prevent me from bowing down before him and kissing the ground at his feet. If he ordered me to lop off your head with my sabre, I would do it. For this land is his.'

However, the story goes that when the council was over, Ayub told his son privately that if Nur ed-Din came he would not be allowed to touch a single sugar cane. But why provoke a confrontation? If Saladin continued to show submission and deference towards Nur ed-Din, his old master would have no excuse for invading. Saladin accepted the advice, and he continued to refer to himself, in their correspondence, as 'the servant' and to Nur ed-Din as 'the master'. He maintained the fiction that everything he did was in Nur ed-Din's name — whether it was ruling Egypt or annexing the Yemen.

Nur ed-Din, on the other hand, was expecting something a little more concrete: *'since the time when Egypt was taken Nur ed-Din had wanted an agreed sum of money to be contributed which would help him meet the expenses of the Holy War ... He was waiting for Saladin to suggest this on his own account and did not ask him for it.'* Eventually Saladin sent him a gift, consisting of some of the Fatimid family treasures (confiscated after the death of al-Adid): 60 000 dinars, some 'manufactured goods', an ass and an elephant.

Nur ed-Din seems to have taken this present as a calculated insult. He was expecting the revenue due from his new state of Egypt and instead all he was being offered was a 'gift' from the nephew of his former lieutenant who now clearly regarded himself as his equal. *'We did not need this money ... ,'* he retorted proudly, *'he [Saladin] knows that we did not spend money on the conquest of Egypt out of a need for [more] money'.*

But of course he needed the money badly. To assert his rights, Nur ed-Din ordered an audit of his newly acquired province. In fact his disenchantment with Saladin had become so bitter that no one in his court dared to mention Saladin's name any more. He was only referred to as 'the upstart', 'the disloyal', 'the ingrate' or 'the insolent'.

But before the auditor could make his report to Damascus, Nur ed-Din was dead — probably of a heart attack. Saladin's luck was infallible. The great atabeg had been out riding with one of his emirs who happened to say: *'God knows if we shall meet here again in a year's time,'* to which Nur ed-Din replied, *'who knows whether we shall meet here in a month's time?'* According to Ibn al-Athir, Nur ed-Din was actually in the midst of preparations to invade Egypt and take it from Saladin, when *'there came a command from God that he could not disobey'.*

Master of Damascus

Nur ed-Din left behind his ten year-old son, al-Salih, as his heir, with the inevitable result that there was a vicious scramble for power — for control of the boy — amongst the emirs. The Governor of Aleppo declared himself the boy's regent, but neither he nor any other Turk had the backing of the emirs of Damascus. They

ويحمل القفص والجمالة والقبس والآلة بالله انها اضغت على الله بالله فأضاعت بعض من زبرجها

وتنشد من زبرجها فلما قمت أنسى قمت بالرقعة درهما وقطعة وقلت لها ان رغبت في المستوف المعلم

اشترى لي الدرهم فوجي بالسر المذهب وان ابنا ان نرجى في خبزي القطعة وابرزكن

ثانك الى استخلاص البدر التم والابلج الهم وقالت دع جدالك بما عن بدلك فاسطك

طلع الشيخ ولدته والشعر وانسج بردته فقالت ان الشيخ من أهل يروج وهو الدبي وشتى

discussed their vulnerability to the Franks and decided that, like it or not, the only man who could successfully defend them was The Upstart. In one of the great U-turns in history Saladin *'was secretly summoned by the important men of Damascus'.*

In late October Saladin made his way across 'the desert wastes of Syria' and arrived at Damascus with a small army; the gates were thrown open to him. Saladin remembered the occasion in a roseate glow: *'We dawned on the people like light in darkness,'* he wrote. *'The people rushed to us both before and after we had entered the city in joy at the [coming of] our rule.'* In actual fact he had been met outside the gates by a not inconsiderable part of the Damascene army, over whom the emirs had lost control, but they had put up no serious resistance and dispersed without fighting. *'They knew that chaff is winnowed by the wind,'* as one of his *qadis* put it.

The take-over had been bloodless and Saladin immediately reassured the people of his good intentions towards them. He was anxious that his actions should be seen as legitimate by a population that had committed itself to Nur ed-Din. He cut taxes and claimed that he had taken the city as a step on the road to the conquest of Jerusalem. Everything he did was ostensibly for the Caliph in Baghdad and for the cause of *jihad*. He put himself forward as the only possible leader of the *jihad* — the only true *mujahid*. The unity of Syria under him was a simple necessity if the Franks were to be driven out.

'This Saladin . . . a man of humble antecedents and lowly station, now holds under his control all these kingdoms, for fortune has smiled too graciously upon him.' It is hardly surprising that Nur ed-Din should have looked upon Saladin as an upstart, but it is curious that the Frankish historian William of Tyre should see him in exactly the same light. William continues: *'Saladin, in defiance of the laws of humanity, wholly regardless of his lowly condition, and ungrateful for the benefits that had been showered upon him by the father of that boy king, had risen against his rightful lord.'*

Within a couple of hundred years, Saladin's lowly birth was reckoned to be a point in his favour. *'Saladin was . . . a man of humble enough birth,'* wrote Boccaccio, *'but of great and loftiest spirit and highly trained in deeds of war . . . He was munificent in giving and of his*

This illustration of the Caliph of Baghdad's
standard bearers indicates his essentially
ceremonial role. The Caliph was not
a military figure.

magnificence one cannot say enough. He was a pious man and he marvellously loved and honoured good men.'

But as he installed himself in Damascus in that October of 1174, his enemies in Aleppo saw Nur ed-Din's son as his true successor and Saladin as nothing but an ambitious adventurer who had betrayed his master: *'You go too far, Yusuf, you overstep all limits. You are but a servant of Nur ed-Din, and now you seek to grasp power for yourself alone? But make no mistake, for we who have raised you out of nothingness shall be able to return you to it.'*

The people of Damascus, on the other hand, were ready for a new leader. The combination of Nur ed-Din's Holy War propaganda and the continuing flow of refugees from Frankish lands had created a hotbed of religious fervour which was in a way similar to the energy that had launched the Crusades in Europe eighty years earlier.

Jihad Fever in Damascus

The centre of religious energy in Damascus was a suburb that had been founded by refugees from the Christian occupation in Palestine. In the region of Nablus, the Frankish overlord, Baldwin of Mirabel, had managed to generate an entire Islamic fundamentalist movement by himself.

Baldwin had been strapped for cash. A power struggle in Jerusalem between the forceful Queen Mother, Melisende, and her son, the boy-king Baldwin III, had resulted in her setting up a luxurious but powerless shadow-court on Baldwin of Mirabel's doorstep. It was to be paid for out of income from the royal estate lands around it. Baldwin must have suddenly found himself being ordered to find large cash sums for the King's mother out of his own pocket, because his lands were part of that royal estate.

Desperately squeezed, he quadrupled the poll tax on his peasants. As this led to increased crime, he imposed draconian penalties; when people tried to run away, he ordered that they lose a foot. The peasants protested by attending religious services instead of working. There had been less Moslem emigration from this region than most, so the population was overwhelmingly Moslem. Every Friday became the equivalent of a strike day; fields emptied as peasants flocked to the village of Jama'il to listen to the midday Friday sermon of a religious teacher called Ahmad ibn Muhammad ibn Qudama.

Ibn Qudama was a strict orthodox firebrand who raged against the oppression taking place. In 1156 Baldwin decided to deal with him. That gentleman heard what was in store for him and organized a mass flight of over 130 families from Jama'il and the surrounding villages under cover of a pretended onion-planting expedition. They managed to get safely over the Jordan to Damascus, where they settled outside the walls. There the refugees founded a community dedicated to extreme religious orthodoxy and the vigorous teaching of *jihad*. Mosques and madrassas (schools) were founded and the suburb that resulted is to this day still called al-Salihiyya – 'Purity'.

Saladin against his Fellow-Moslems

Saladin's rhetoric may have been full of allegiance to the cause of *jihad*, but he actually spent most of the next ten years fighting Moslems rather than Franks. His first objective was Aleppo, where his nominal master and Nur ed-Din's rightful heir, al-Salih, was being kept under close guard by the emirs. Saladin was initially quite confident. When he wrote to his nephew he allowed himself a pun on the Arabic name for Aleppo, Halab, which means milk: *'We have only to do the milking and Aleppo will be ours.'* It was not that easy.

The moment Saladin first brought his army up to the walls of Aleppo, the thirteen year-old al-Salih appeared in the market place and made an impassioned appeal to the Aleppans. *'Behold this unjust and ungrateful man who wishes to take my country from me without regard to God or man! I am an orphan, and I rely upon you to defend me, in memory of my father who so loved you.'*

Never act with dogs or children, said W. C. Fields, and the same was true in medieval politics. After al-Salih's screen-stealing performance, it was difficult for Saladin to maintain the image of the faithful servant dutifully coming to the rescue of his master's son. The Aleppans were certainly not having any of it and decided to put a halt to the whole performance by calling in the services of the Assassins. Even while Saladin was encamped outside Aleppo, Assassins made a bold attempt on his life. One of his emirs was killed in the attack.

Overleaf
Caravans were essential to the operation of Middle
Eastern civilization. They often consisted of thousands
of pack-animals (especially camels, of course), and were
temporary travelling cities. The destruction of a caravan was a
social and economic catastrophe.

←————————————————————————————→

The next year Saladin defeated a combined Aleppan-Mosuli army just outside Aleppo. He gave the Lord of Mosul's tent to his nephew, and its contents were recorded by one of the chroniclers. It's rather extraordinary what a Syrian war-lord in the twelfth century took with him into battle: treasure-chests, wine, musical instruments, singing girls and a collection of birds including doves, nightingales and parrots. Saladin returned the latter to the Lord of Mosul with the note: *'Tell him to go back to playing with these birds, for they are safe and will not bring him into dangerous situations.'*

Saladin then turned to besiege Aleppo again and, once again, the Assassins struck. This time four of them actually managed to get right up to his tent. There was a violent struggle in which Saladin's cheek was gashed. Perhaps his life was saved by the fact that he had taken to wearing a mail coif under his head-dress. The Assassins were cut down and two of Saladin's protectors died.

Saladin himself retired a shaken man, blood streaming from his face. From then on he became understandably paranoid. His tent was henceforth surrounded by a stockade and he would not talk to anybody he did not recognize. Some say that he took to sleeping fully armed in a cage. In fact fear spread throughout the entire army and everyone became afraid of everyone else.

It was a situation that could not be allowed to continue. Saladin's answer was to go to the heart of the matter. In August of 1176 he set about besieging Masyaf – the Syrian stronghold of the Assassin's sect, and which is still to this day a centre of the Ismailis. But within a few days he had called the siege off. The reason why still remains a mystery.

The Assassins' own story was that Rashid ed-Din Sinan, 'the Old Man of the Mountains', was returning to his castle when Saladin's agents tried to capture him. As they approached him, however, a mysterious force suddenly rendered their limbs useless and the Old Man told them to tell Saladin he wished to see him in private. The agents rushed back and told Saladin, who was so frightened that he could hardly sleep. Nevertheless he woke up in the middle of the night to find some hot cakes of a type only baked by the Assassins on his pillow and a poisoned dagger to which was attached an insulting and threatening verse. Saladin lifted the siege the next day.

The more likely version is that Rashid al-Din Sinan had sent letters to Saladin's uncle, threatening to kill off members of the Ayub family, and it was this that persuaded Saladin to raise the siege. What is certain is that he never threatened them again.

In 1181 Nur ed-Din's heir, al-Salih, died. It was, of course, yet another staggering example of Saladin's amazing luck that al-Salih should have taken ill and died at such an early age – he was only nineteen; *'one of the most handsome of men'* and very popular in Aleppo. Of course there was talk of poison, but no one was able to prove anything. It might have been noticed, however, that one of the suspects later did very well for himself in Saladin's service.

Saladin certainly had his army all ready to move into Aleppo, but the lord of Mosul got there first. Saladin therefore redoubled his propaganda campaign, and claimed that he had been given Aleppo by the previous Caliph and had only left al-Salih in charge out of respect for his father – all of which was, of course, total eyewash.

During the next year Saladin stepped up his attacks east of the Euphrates and made an unsuccessful assault on Mosul. He still claimed, of course, that he was acting on behalf of the Caliph in Baghdad, even though the Caliph refused to legitimize his claims. He made some useful gains in the area that effectively reduced the power of Mosul. When he finally turned back to settle the score with Aleppo, in June 1183, the Governor realized the game was up and surrendered.

Saladin ensured that the take-over was bloodless; he needed to have the support of the Aleppans. For Saladin, Aleppo was *'the eye of Syria and its citadel was the pupil'*. Nor was the significance of its falling into Saladin's hands lost on William of Tyre: *'Redoubled fear took hold of our people on hearing this news, for the result most dreaded by them had come to pass. From the first it had been apparent to the Christians that if Saladin should succeed in adding Aleppo to his principality our territory would be as completely encompassed by his power and strength as if it were in a state of siege.'*

So perhaps Saladin's claims that his anti-Moslem campaigns were all part of *jihad* were not quite so ludicrous as his enemies would have us believe. His propaganda machine certainly went to work to emphasize the connection between his annexation of Aleppo and *jihad*. In letter after letter he stressed that the conquest of Aleppo was merely a milestone on the road to victory in the Holy War. Once he controlled Aleppo, Damascus and Egypt, he had the Franks in an unprecedented vice, and could attack as no-one had done before.

And – to do him justice – he did.

10

The Fall of Jerusalem

As Saladin moved his army down to Damascus in preparation for the attack on the Kingdom of Jerusalem, the Frankish King and his barons were *'in a perpetual state of anxiety and suspense'*, trying to guess where and when Saladin was going to strike. For they were quite certain now that strike he would.

It was unfortunate for the Kingdom that the twenty-one-year-old King Baldwin IV was a leper. In recent years his terrible disease had become so bad that he had been persuaded to hand over the reins of the Kingdom to his sister Sibylla's husband, Guy de Lusignan — a man *'unequal to the burden both in force and wisdom'* in the rather jaundiced view of William of Tyre. When Saladin eventually confronted the Frankish army near the Pools of Goliath, it was Guy who was in charge. Saladin tried to tempt the Franks into battle by feigning a withdrawal, but Guy refused to advance. He just waited for Saladin to go home. This was, militarily, the most sensible thing to do, and exactly what was advised by Guy's chief rival at court — Raymond of Tripoli.

Saladin's army was made up of knights whose income was drawn from lands which they had themselves to supervise. They were not full-time professional soldiers who could stay in the field of battle throughout the year. Saladin had to achieve a quick decisive victory against the Franks and then retire. The easiest way for the Franks to defeat Saladin was by avoiding battle, because the Christians had a permanent military force that would still be there when Saladin's army had disbanded. In addition to the normal knight-service of a feudal lord, which was temporary, the King of Jerusalem could call on the Knights of the Order of the Temple and the Knights of the Order of St John's Hospital.

Eventually Saladin had to turn tail and return to Damascus with nothing to show for his costly expedition. It was actually a great success for the Franks, but it was not a very heroic way to win. For Guy's enemies within the Frankish court, it offered a

← →

The Military Orders

The Military Orders – the Order of the Temple and the Order of St John's hospital – had begun as gentle religious charities to assist pilgrims, but twenty years after the conquest of Jerusalem they became organizations of monk‑knights.

Although both Orders still had some purely pacific brothers – the Hospitallers, for example, ran the great Hospital in Jerusalem (a hostel and clinic for poor pilgrims) – these were organizations dedicated to fighting as an act of charitable love for Christ. They maintained their own networks of castles, with all the equipment and horses needed for war, and paid troops of mercenaries who dressed in the distinctive tunics of their Orders. They had their own independent finance, from huge donations, large estates in Europe and from managing the finances of the Crusades. Their castles, such as the extraordinary Krak des Chevaliers (which belonged to the Hospitallers), were the major defensive walls of the Kingdom.

propaganda opportunity not to be missed. *'Plain people who were with the army and who had no part in the wickedness of the Christian leaders wondered why it was that when such an opportunity offered, no engagement with the enemy occurred, nor was anything done about a fight,'* wrote William of Tyre, who belonged to Count Raymond's faction.

Raymond's party now openly accused Guy of cowardice in refusing to fight – regardless of the fact that Guy had, of course, been following Raymond's own advice! Guy's enemies were so successful in tarnishing his reputation that a short time later they were able to persuade the dying King to depose Guy from the Regency and reinstate Raymond.

The fact was that the Kingdom had become as riddled with intrigue as the young king was with leprosy. There were so few knights, there was such a high mortality, there was so little new blood, that it had become an incestuous hot‑house of bitter faction‑fighting.

These factions revolved, to some extent, around the two women that Baldwin IV's father, King Amalric, had married. He had been forced to annul his marriage to his first wife, the voluptuous Agnes de Courtenay, but only on condition that their two children, the leprous Baldwin and his sister Sibylla, should be next in line to the throne. This was, of course, resented by Amalric's second wife, the beautiful Greek, Maria Comnena, who had her own child by him – Isabella. The two women naturally detested each other.

Maria, now Queen Mother and a powerful woman, married Balian of Ibelin, who supported the ambitious Count Raymond of Tripoli. Raymond spoke Arabic and understood the Moslems, but he coveted not only the Regency but also – in all probability – the Kingship itself. This party was backed by the Knights Hospitaller.

Agnes's faction, which included the Commander of the Knights Templar, tended to consist of men whom she found attractive, such as Eraclius, the Patriarch of Jerusalem, and Guy de Lusignan, whom she married to her daughter Sibylla, plus her brother Joscelin, the powerful Seneschal of Jerusalem.

A key figure in this party was one of the most remarkable characters in the Kingdom – the famous, the infamous, the loathed, the loved, the devilish, the dashing, the crazy, the intrepid, the brutal, the rash – the quite extraordinary Reynald de Châtillon.

Reynald de Châtillon – Enter the Villain?

Reynald de Châtillon was the one man in the Frankish Kingdom whom Saladin would swear to kill with his own hands.

Reynald had arrived in the Kingdom of Jerusalem with King Louis on the Second Crusade. He was a high-born nobleman but a younger son. He had therefore come to the East in search of the fortune that he did not have at home. Of all the nobles who joined King Baldwin at the siege of Ascalon in 1153 only two served for pay. Reynald was one of them. He was a bit of a manic aggressive.

He was a man of charm and – quite clearly – very attractive to ladies. Reynald had already caught the fancy of one of the most powerful women in the Latin East, the twenty-eight-year-old Constance, Princess Regnant of Antioch. *Lady Constance, widow of Prince Raymond of Antioch, who after the fashion of women, had refused many distinguished nobles, secretly chose as her husband Reynald de Châtillon, a knight in the pay of the king ...'* tut-tuts William of Tyre from the opposite court faction. *'Many there were, however, who marvelled that a woman so eminent, so distinguished and powerful, who had been the wife of a very illustrious man, should stoop to marry an ordinary knight.'*

The new Prince of Antioch, however, was anything but an 'ordinary knight'. His lucky marriage might be disapproved of in courtly circles from Constantinople to Jerusalem, but he didn't give a fig.

←――――――――――――――――――――――――――――――→

The Patriarch Aimery of Antioch himself disapproved – and yet when, in 1156, Reynald attacked Cyprus, Aimery became his financial backer.

Cyprus was prosperous, peaceful and had been extremely friendly to the Crusaders. Of course it was not a Moslem land – it was orthodox Christian – so Reynald's adventure was not exactly a Crusade. But to demonstrate that religion was close to his heart, he invited the wealthy Aimery to finance the expedition. When the Patriarch declined, Reynald realized he would have to resort to his subtlest powers of persuasion. He therefore arrested Aimery, smeared his bare head with honey and forced him to sit all day in the blazing sun like a sort of human fly-paper.

After a day of these sort of arguments, the venerable Patriarch was duly convinced and stumped up the required cash. Reynald was thus able to sail off to Cyprus, financed by the coffers of the Church, and devastate the place to his heart's content. William of Tyre says:

> He then completely overran the island without meeting any opposition, destroyed cities and wrecked fortresses. He broke into monasteries of men and women alike and shamefully abused nuns and tender maidens. Although the precious vestments and the amount of gold and silver which he carried off were great, yet the loss of these was regarded as nothing in comparison with the violence done to chastity.

And just to show the Emperor of Byzantium (to whom Cyprus belonged) that he was not forgetting the priesthood, Reynald had their noses cut off. It was a great triumph that left Cyprus vulnerable to Moslem pirates and no longer at all friendly. The island that had helped save the First Crusaders from starvation, by sending food parcels, no longer had the inclination nor the ability to help the Kingdom of the Franks.

King Baldwin was furious when he heard of Reynald's escapade and fell over himself to make it up with the Emperor. The Emperor, however, was quite capable

―――――――――――――――――

Overleaf
Krak des Chevaliers, the Hospitallers' great stronghold, is a
masterpiece of castle design. Castle-building was much more
advanced in the East than in Europe at the time of the First Crusade,
but with so few settlers (there were only a thousand fief-knights in
Outremer, far fewer than in England) the Crusaders quickly learned
the new techniques in order to survive.

of sorting Reynald out for himself. Three years later, he descended on Antioch at the head of a huge army. Reynald had not expected to bring down the entire might of the Roman Empire on himself. He was terrified. After quick discussion with his staff as to the best course of action, he decided on total abject grovelling as the only way out.

Toad of Toad Hall could not have done it better. He dressed himself in a woollen tunic with short sleeves, put a rope around his neck, held a naked sword by the point and appeared barefoot before the Emperor. There he surrendered his sword. Then, according to William of Tyre, *'he threw himself on the ground at the emperor's feet, where he lay prostrate till all were disgusted and the glory of the Latins was turned to shame; for he was a man of violent impulses, both in sinning and in repenting'.*

The next year, the irrepressible Reynald was out again, raiding Christian farmers, when the Governor of Aleppo caught him at it. Reynald spent the next sixteen years in a dungeon in Aleppo.

Reynald Released

On his release in 1176 Reynald found that his wife Constance was long dead and he was no longer Prince of Antioch. He quickly began hunting for another rich widow and found Stephanie, who held Transjordan and was mistress of the powerful desert castle of Kerak. From this base, Reynald set about doing what he enjoyed doing best – fighting Moslems.

In 1180 King Baldwin negotiated a peace treaty with Saladin, guaranteeing the free movement of goods around the region. But seeing the rich caravans slowly lumbering along the road past Kerak was more than Reynald could bear and in 1181, truce or no truce, he captured one on its way to Mecca. Saladin demanded restitution under the terms of the treaty, but Baldwin left Reynald alone. It was very useful to have a dangerous man in Transjordan, astride the route linking Syria and Egypt.

Reynald had no trouble justifying his growing reputation amongst the Arabs as the man they loved to hate. He spent two years constructing ships in sections so they could be carried by camel. At the beginning of 1183 Reynald made his way down to the Red Sea and launched his prefabricated boats in a series of piratical raids against merchant ships, pilgrims and ports. The Moslem world was taken by surprise and horrified – it was rumoured that he intended to attack Mecca itself and even carry off the body of the Prophet so that Moslems would have to make their pilgrimage into Frankish territory!

The raiders were stopped; Reynald himself got safely back to Kerak, but the others were eventually captured. A couple were taken to Mecca to be publicly executed there, and some to Cairo. In Alexandria, the traveller and diarist Ibn Jubayr saw some of them being led into the city mounted backwards on donkeys and accompanied by trumpets and drums. Saladin was determined to kill the prisoners because they had penetrated into the secret parts of Islam and it was essential that no Franks should know that road, otherwise *'the enemy would flood into the sacred territory'*. It seems likely that Saladin's particular animosity towards Reynald dates from this raid.

The Wedding at Kerak

While Jerusalem was split between the two court factions, and Guy was being denounced as incompetent, Saladin turned up at Kerak with a huge army. It was the worst possible moment. There was a wedding going on.

Reynald's stepson, the seventeen-year-old Humphrey of Toron, was being married to the Princess Isabella.

It was a marriage that was supposed to heal the rift in the Kingdom; Isabella was the daughter of Reynald's personal enemy, Queen Maria Comnena. In fact it simply provided the opportunity for Maria and her faction, led by Raymond of Tripoli and the Ibelin family, to oust Guy.

While the bridegroom's father and friends had gathered at Kerak, the bride's family had rushed to Jerusalem and pressed the sick King to strip Guy of his position. Raymond of Tripoli was made Regent instead and Balian of Ibelin carried the child of Guy and Sibylla to be crowned as the future Baldwin v. Maria's faction was triumphant.

Meanwhile, at Kerak, the wedding was not going very well. Reynald had brought in entertainers, actors, musicians, cooks, servants and all the townspeople and country-folk from miles around. They had not expected Saladin to gatecrash with siege engines and begin assaulting the castle. William of Tyre writes:

> Great crowds of helpless people of every description and of both sexes filled the castle within, a burden rather than a help to the besieged. There were many actors and performers on the flute and psaltery and other people who had flocked thither from all over the country for the festivities attending the wedding . . . Moreover, many Syrians with their wives and children had come in from the surrounding country. The place was filled with them so that those who wished to pass back and forth could not do so freely on account of the dense crowds. Thus these too became a hindrance . . . to those who were trying to defend the place.

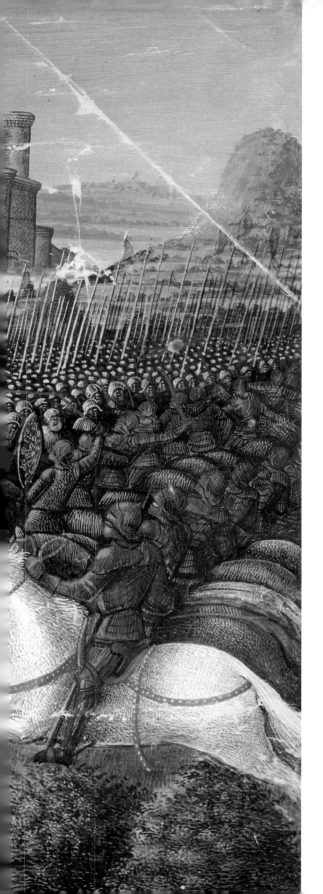

Left In this elegant and highly formalized version of the Battle of Hattin, from the fifteenth-century *Les Passages faits Outremer . . .* , 'the fountain' or spring of Sephoria is depicted as a real fountain. The battlefield appears to be very well watered, and both sides are fighting with equal gusto. In fact the battle site was waterless and the Christian infantry, dehydrated and demoralized, retreated up to the two hills known as the Horns of Hattin rather than fight.

Above Saladin ordering captives to be chained after the Battle of Hattin. In fact his generosity towards many of his prisoners (except the Military Orders and Reynald de Châtillon) was held by many to be his biggest mistake. From a fourteenth-century French manuscript.

But Lady Stephanie was determined that nobody was going to say she couldn't throw a good party. In the midst of the siege she had some of the wedding feast sent down to Saladin in his camp outside. It must have been the most dangerous act of waitressing ever attempted.

Saladin, in response, enquired in which tower the happy couple would be spending the night and then ordered his siege engine not to bombard that tower. Elsewhere, however, he kept up a constant barrage of missiles so that *'even those who had fled to the innermost apartments, the most retired seclusion, shrank with terror before the crash and roar of the oncoming missiles. It seemed to them like thunder and, ever in suspense lest the building be shattered and fall upon them, they momentarily awaited the stroke of the bolt.'*

The nightmare wedding went on for about a month. King Baldwin took his time before coming to the rescue. When he eventually made his move across the Jordan, Saladin backed off into Syria.

A Coup in Jerusalem

In March 1185 King Baldwin IV died, aged twenty-four, leaving the eight-year-old Baldwin V on the throne, and the division in the Kingdom as bitter as ever. For the time being Prince Raymond of Tripoli was Regent and his faction held sway. A four-year truce was negotiated with Saladin, under which Palestine began to prosper once again. But not for long. At the end of August 1186 the boy-king died.

Agnes's party moved fast. Her brother Joscelin put troops into Beirut and Tyre, and proclaimed Sibylla as Queen. Raymond of Tripoli hurriedly summoned all the barons to a High Court at Nablus, where Balian of Ibelin, his wife Maria and Isabella were waiting. They were determined to put Isabella and Humphrey on the throne.

But it was too late.

In Jerusalem a dramatic coronation was already taking place. It was agreed there that Sibylla should take the throne if she divorced Guy and, according to one account, she had consented on condition that she could freely choose her next husband. Once she was crowned, however, Sibylla – who seems to have been a remarkably spunky lady – took the crown and turned to Guy of Lusignan, saying:

> I, Sibylla, choose as king and husband my husband, Guy of Lusignan, who is my husband. I know him to be a man of prowess and honour, well able with God's aid to rule his people. I know too that while he is alive I can have no other husband, for as the scripture says: 'those whom God has joined together let no man put asunder'.

Raymond and his faction had been hopelessly outmanoeuvred. Reynald, Guy and

Sibylla were in the ascendant and the country was on the edge of civil war. The only thing that could hold it together was another attack by Saladin. Reynald de Châtillon made sure that it came sooner rather than later, forcing the Kingdom into an unwilling unity. Within weeks Reynald swooped down on another rich caravan on its way from Cairo. *'He broke the truce to attack it, ill-treating and torturing the men and imprisoning them in narrow dungeons. When they invoked the truce his only reply was: "Call on your Mahomet to save you!"'*

When this was reported to Saladin, he swore that if Reynald should ever fall into his power *'he would kill him with his own hand'*. In the meantime he demanded restitution under the terms of the truce. Neither Reynald nor Guy responded. Raymond of Tripoli, who could see what was coming, made his own personal deal with Saladin immediately from his castle at Tiberias. King Guy was only dissuaded at the last minute from attacking Tiberias!

The Battle of Hattin

Saladin now assembled the greatest army he had ever put together. It probably consisted of at least thirty thousand regulars plus an unknown number of volunteers. He boasted in a letter to the Caliph that the widest plain was too narrow for such an army and that the dust that it raised on the move would darken the eye of the sun. In the Palestinian al-Salihiyya quarter of Damascus, Ibn Qudama's son and nephew took the lead in becoming *fedayeen*, warriors of the *jihad*.

Saladin desperately needed a decisive victory against the Franks, for there were still many who accused him of preferring to attack Moslems rather than Christians. On Wednesday, 1 July 1187, he led a huge force over the Jordan and into Tiberias. Resistance lasted for one nominal hour. Guy called a council at Acre; most people advised him to do nothing, but the Grand Master of the Temple and Reynald de Châtillon demanded action. Guy ordered that the army move towards Tiberias. They camped some miles off.

Had they done nothing more, Saladin would have been forced to withdraw, as he had done at the Pools of Goliath. But when a message came to them from the Countess of Tripoli asking to be rescued, chivalry demanded that something be done, even though her husband Raymond maintained that it made more sense to ransom her. He would rather lose wife and city, he said, than lose the Kingdom.

When Guy had accepted Raymond's advice at the Pools of Goliath, he had held his army back and been called a wimp; he was never going to be called a wimp again.

He announced that they would march at dawn. They camped on 3 July at a well under a double hill called the Horns of Hattin. The well was dry. Raymond announced that they were all dead men, and the Kingdom was finished.

That night Saladin's army set fire to the scrub around the camp, and made a continuous racket. In the morning the Christian army was encircled, and desperately thirsty. Down the slope they could see the lake, but it was impossible to break through. The Moslems charged and charged again; the July heat was ferocious and the knights were dehydrating in their armour. Raymond led a charge and the Moslem lines simply opened up and let him through. The gap which he had left was filled immediately by Moslem forces, cutting off the infantry from the knights. Raymond rode two hundred miles to Tripoli, unmolested, while behind him the slaughter went on.

The King's tent was moved to the summit of the hill. Saladin's son remembered afterwards saying to his father, *'We have routed them'*, and his father saying, *'Be quiet. We have not beaten them so long as that tent stands there.'* At that moment it fell. So did the Kingdom.

The entire fighting force of Jerusalem was destroyed in one day on the Horns of Hattin.

After the battle Saladin had King Guy and Reynald brought to his tent. Both were exhausted, terrified and half dead from thirst. Saladin offered Guy a drink of iced rose-water. When he had slaked his thirst the King passed the goblet to Reynald, but Saladin stopped him. He pointed out that Guy had given Reynald the drink, *'not I'*. For, under the rules of Arab hospitality, once a visitor has been offered something, he is under the host's protection.

Saladin went outside, paced around, came back and sliced off Reynald's head. Guy was trembling with terror, but Saladin reassured him. The only other prisoners who were to be killed were the Templars and Hospitallers, the carriers of the Crusade ideology. They were given to the Sufis to kill. Sufis were holy miracle-workers, the kind of religious figures popular with many ordinary folk but disapproved of by serious religious philosophers. It was a great joke to watch them trying to kill people.

The haul of prisoners sent to Damascus was prodigious. Saladin had even captured the piece of the True Cross which the army of Jerusalem carried into battle as though the knights were the Children of Israel marching into battle with the Ark of the Covenant.

Saladin Recaptures Jerusalem

Saladin's army now moved through the defenceless realm. Acre, the economic heart of the Kingdom, surrendered at the beginning of August. Its inhabitants emigrated. Galilee was occupied; Jaffa resisted and its population were enslaved. Tyre resisted and was left for a while; Beirut did not. By the end of August there was not much left. But Saladin took his time getting to Jerusalem.

Before he attacked, he allowed Balian of Ibelin to enter Jerusalem to rescue his wife, the ex-Queen Maria, and their children. Balian had to promise to spend only one night in the city and not to bear arms. Balian, however, found the city preparing its defence and he was not 'allowed' to leave. He wrote to Saladin explaining that he would have to violate his oath, and Saladin not only accepted that but sent an escort to take Balian's wife and children to Tyre. Strangely, Saladin explained that since Balian had violated his oath, he (Saladin) was released from his own oath to take the city by fire and sword.

Queen Sibylla was in the city and she and the Patriarch were likely, left to their own devices, to mount a desperate defence. Saladin did not want Jerusalem damaged; it was worth more to him intact. He may have hoped that Balian would take a

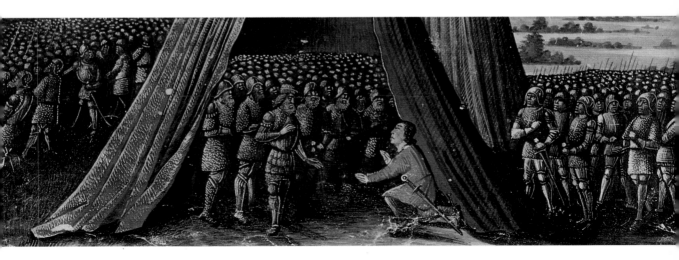

Balian of Ibelin surrendering the city of Jerusalem to Saladin,
from *Les Passages faits Outremer . . . , c.* 1490.

more rational approach. On his arrival Balian had demanded that the Patriarch immediately recognize him as the Lord of Jerusalem and, once he had received that homage, he began minting coins at high speed, supposedly to pay for the defence of the city. The coins omitted the name of any king. Balian did attempt to defend the city, but not suicidally, and after a thirteen-day siege, he surrendered.

There was no massacre.

Saladin entered the city on the anniversary of Mohammed's journey to heaven from the Foundation Stone. In a very deliberate contrast to the way the Crusaders had taken it eighty-eight years earlier, not a building was looted and no person was harmed.

The terms were that a ransom would be paid of 10 dinars for every man, 5 for every woman and 1 for every child; 30 000 dinars could be put down as a lump sum for seven thousand of the poor. Anyone who could not pay would be taken into slavery. The Latin Patriarch shocked the Moslems by paying his 10 dinars and departing with cartloads of treasure leaving the poor to be led off into slavery. Saladin's brother, al-Adil, distressed by the number of captives, asked for a gift of a thousand; he freed them all. The Patriarch, seeing a chance to do the right thing at no loss to his pocket, asked if he too could be given some and was granted seven hundred. Balian was given five hundred. Saladin then released all old people, all captive husbands of freed wives, and gave gifts to widows and orphans.

It was a deeply moving event. Then he set about cleansing the city; the al-Aqsa Mosque had been the Templars' headquarters and the Dome of the Rock had been turned into a church. They were restored. His advisers urged him to demolish the Church of the Holy Sepulchre, but it was simply closed for three days and then was open to pilgrims again – for a fee. Jerusalem's only trade was pilgrimage and the money was needed.

The Holy Places were open to pilgrims of all religions, but the Latin Kingdom of Jerusalem was finished. That was what everyone believed.

11

To the Rescue

Conrad of Montferrat was an able and vigorous fighter, the kind of man to get into trouble. He had set off to follow his father to Jerusalem in 1185, but his fondness for trouble got him stuck in Constantinople. He got on rather well there, in fact he married the Emperor's sister, but trouble would not go away. When the relatives of a man he had killed announced that they would blind him, he decided that it was time to go. He slipped away in a ship one July night with a company of Flemish knights.

Others say he was looking for trouble; he knew that Saladin was threatening to invade Outremer.

He had a nose for trouble. When his ship sailed into Acre, he realized that something was up. The port bell did not ring. Instead of mooring, the ship just put down one cautious anchor. When the port officer's boat came alongside, Conrad said he was a merchant and asked what was happening. That was how he learned that the Kingdom had fallen and that Saladin had taken the port four days earlier. The great man was now about to receive the surrender of Tyre.

The anchor came up and Conrad was off. By the time he reached Tyre the surrender negotiations were almost complete. The city was filled with refugees from the ruined Kingdom, preparing to take ship for a Europe most of them had never seen. Saladin had already sent in his banners to be flown over the citadel. Conrad announced that no-one was leaving; he was taking over and Saladin could stuff his peace terms. The banners went into the moat. That was the thing about Conrad. He just loved a good fight.

Saladin turned up with Conrad's father, who was a prisoner from Hattin, and paraded him outside the walls, saying he would be killed if Conrad did not pack it

These many-oared vessels being loaded with supplies give some idea of the preparations for shipping an army across the Mediterranean. From a fourteenth-century French manuscript.

in. Conrad said the old man was not worth a single stone. Saladin, who was not into killing old men, drifted off to capture Ascalon instead.

By November the mopping up was almost complete. Saladin's troops were weary and needed to go home, and he had no reason to argue. All that remained were a few outposts up in the north. Antioch was still in Latin hands, with its port of Saint Symeon; so was Tripoli, a hundred miles further south. Apart from that, the Latin Kingdom of Jerusalem had been reduced to three castles – Marqab, Tortosa and the isolated fortress of Krak.

Nothing else, except for Tyre. Saladin had every reason to suppose that these details could be dealt with reasonably easily. He suggested that his next step should probably be to conquer Europe. Saladin, however, had reckoned without the power of free enterprise. The profit motive was going to achieve what religious zeal could not.

The Commerce of Crusading

Acre had become big money, especially for the merchant aristocrats of Venice, Pisa and Genoa. These three cities competed ferociously for the Mediterranean trade, trying to obtain monopoly rights in ports everywhere.

At the time of the First Crusade, Venice was the dominant power and had been rather sniffy about getting involved; there did not seem to be much profit in it. The Genoese, however, had run supplies and equipment to the siege of Antioch and as soon as the town was captured they were granted their own market there. Suddenly the potential for making money out of the Crusade became obvious. The Pisans quickly sent their own ships to help. The Venetians eventually launched an immense Crusade fleet and it went straight to war – to sink the Pisan fleet, taking four thousand prisoners.

Job done, it went home.

By the time of Saladin's victory these three Italian cities were heavily dependent on their income from Outremer. They had their own quarters in the major ports, with the rights to run their own markets and use their own weights and measures, and they had complete control of all transport between Christendom and Syria.

Conrad knew how important all this was to the Italian merchant states and how desperate they were to get back into Acre, which had become the main centre for Oriental trade. Conrad was a most unusual knight – he understood about business. He had no doubt that the Italian merchants would help.

Pisa and Genoa were actually at war when Jerusalem fell, but they had agreed that this was an emergency that demanded a truce – especially when it became clear that the Sicilians were sending ships to help Conrad and might reap the reward. Conrad proceeded to hold Tyre together with the help of only two hundred knights and the Sicilian fleet. Saladin, however, realized he was going to be a tough nut to crack, and decided to utilize the Europeans' innate gift for in-fighting. To help things along, he allowed most of the Franks who surrendered to him to go to Tyre or Tripoli.

Even King Guy was released, on the promise that he would go overseas and never take up arms again against Saladin. Guy must have had that vow annulled by a cleric at once. Saladin can have expected nothing less and, sure enough, the squabbling got under way. Guy took his supporters from Tripoli and marched to Tyre – where Conrad, determined not to lose control, refused to let him in.

So far, from Saladin's point of view, so good.

A Pisan fleet arrived in Tyre early in 1189 and, having failed to get what they wanted from Conrad, the Pisans did a deal with Guy. They assisted him in moving to Acre and set him up with a small force to besiege it. Soon the Pisans and Genoese were being offered ever-increasing chunks of the Kingdom as Guy and Conrad competed for their support – and the siege works of Acre became formidable. Saladin besieged the besiegers, but could not shift them. And new armies were coming from the West, led by the greatest heroes of their time.

The Forces against Saladin

Europe had changed greatly since the days of the original Crusade. Life had become altogether more ordered and stable; trade had expanded greatly, roads were being developed, great fairs and markets in France and Flanders handled an ever-expanding commerce, above all in textiles. The age of rural brigands was drawing to a close; the fairs of Champagne, the cloth industry of France and Bruges, the English wool trade and the German Hanse (an association of traders) were becoming too important to be messed about. The new class of wealthy merchants were always likely to support civil authorities that could provide a secure legal framework for peaceful business.

England, having been wholly conquered by the Normans, was the easiest country to stabilize. Henry II, who was King of England when Jerusalem fell, ruled a highly ordered state (by the standards of the time). It was a sign of the importance of his court in running the realm that the English were subject to the highest taxes in Europe.

France was more fragmented: The whole of western France, including Rouen and Tours, belonged to Henry of England, most of the south belonged to Henry's wife, Eleanor of Aquitaine, and everything to the east of Lyons belonged to the Holy Roman Empire. But young King Philip Augustus had considerable wealth at his disposal from Champagne, west Flanders, Paris and Burgundy, and he was ambitious to be a new Charlemagne.

The Holy Roman Emperor, Frederick Barbarossa, was proud of being an old Charlemagne, descended from the original article. He held sway as King of Germany over an area that stretched from Brussels to Brandenburg and from Denmark to the Tyrol. The imperial crown gave him lordship over Bohemia, Silesia and north Italy. Although the Italian cities fiercely defended their rights of self-government, the trade which flowed through them gave him wealth to match that of Henry II.

Now all three of these mighty rulers, Henry, Philip and Frederick, turned their gaze towards Saladin and announced that they would destroy him.

The New Crusading Zeal

It was not easy for a European king to go on a Crusade – in fact it was a great nuisance, taking a lot of time and a phenomenal amount of money. It also meant abandoning his kingdom, in an age when rule was an extremely personal business. There had to be a very good reason for bothering. That reason was clearly not direct financial profit – any booty obtained would be more than consumed by the cost of the army – and no European leader could consider himself directly threatened by Saladin. Nor was it a matter of personal religious conviction. Although all three rulers had their religious moments, these certainly did not govern their political lives.

There had been little enthusiasm for crusading for fifty years, since the horrible mess of the Second Crusade. But the fall of Jerusalem sent a shock-wave through Europe. Pope Urban III was so startled that his heart stopped beating. His successor, Gregory VIII, issued an appeal for action which began, *'We and our brothers were*

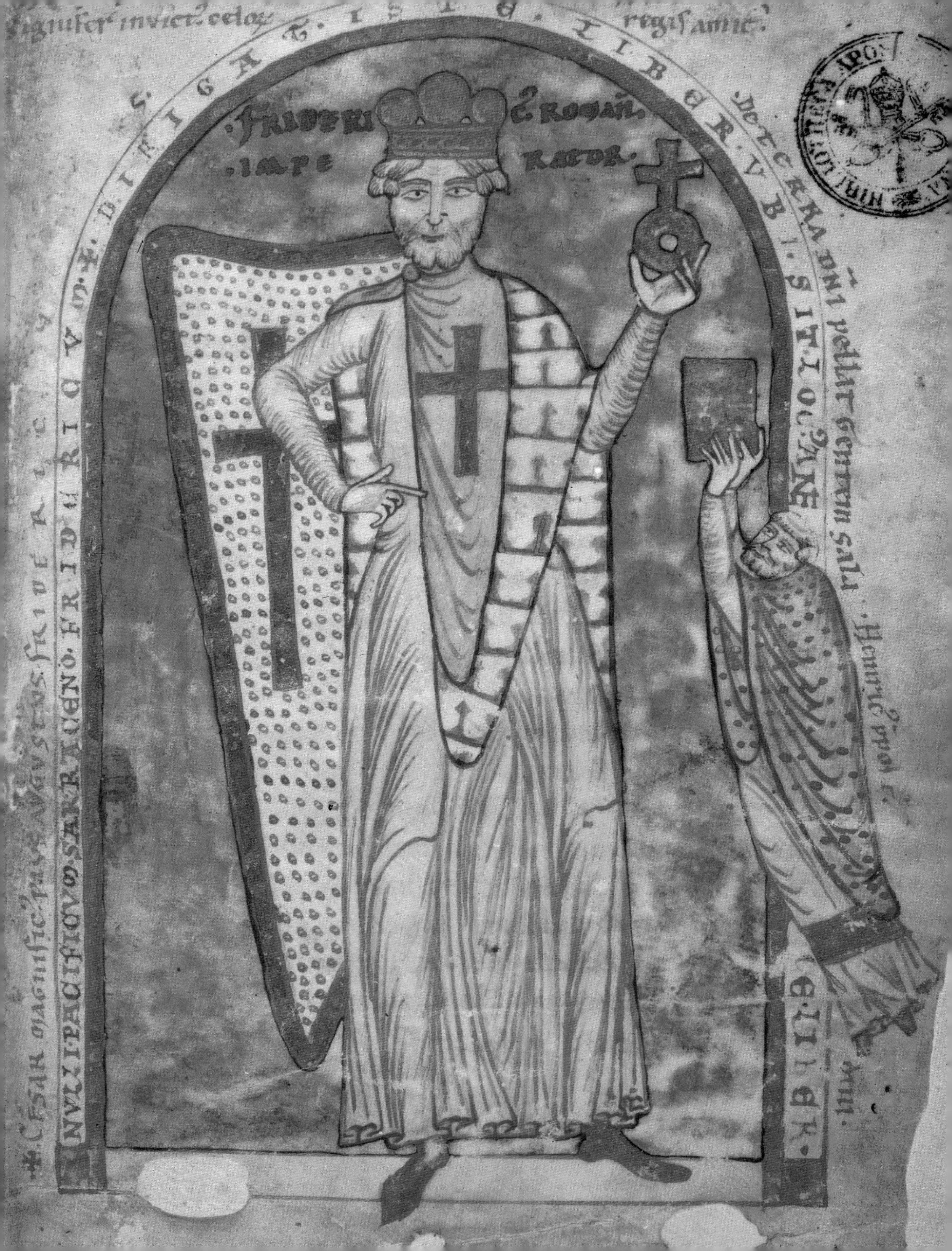
FRIDERI C. ROMAN.
IMPE RATOR

thrown into confusion and buffeted by such a depth of horror and grief that it was not clear what we ought to do.'

But some knew exactly what to do. Volunteers began arriving in Tyre and Tripoli by the boatload: knights from Flanders, France, Germany, Hungary, Denmark — even a flotilla of Londoners — all acting in concert with a flood of public feeling that was reinforced by a barrage of poems and songs lamenting the loss of the Holy Land.

Even the Arab chronicler, Ibn al-Athir, who was twenty-seven years old when Saladin took Jerusalem, was deeply struck by the force of this emotion: *'A Frankish prisoner told me that he was his mother's only son, and their house was their sole possession, but she had sold it and used the money obtained from it to equip him to go and free Jerusalem. There he had been taken prisoner. Such were the religious and personal motives that drove the Franks on.'*

Public opinion demanded that the Kings of England and France stop fighting each other and go to the rescue of Jerusalem, and that feeling was so strong that they had to respect it. Henry and Philip met, agreed to take the Cross together and drew up elaborate rules for their Crusade. Saladin's success was generally held to be a divine punishment, so this had to be a clean-living expedition. No swearing, gambling or women were allowed (*'except perhaps a washerwoman on foot, to be above suspicion'*), everyone would dress neatly and simply, and eat only two dishes a day. The French would wear red crosses and the English white ones. They also established a new tax, the 'Saladin Tithe', to pay for the enterprise. But they were soon squabbling again and Henry's own son, Richard, was fighting with Philip against his father.

The Crusade of Frederick Barbarossa

In the meantime the Holy Roman Emperor, Frederick Barbarossa (Frederick Red-Beard), had already set out for the Holy Land, on 11 May 1189. He was sixty-seven years old and this was to be the crowning act of a great career. *'No-one in all Germany … was considered to be of any manly steadfastness at all, who was seen without the saving sign, and who would not join the comradeship of the Crusaders.'*

It was certainly one of the largest crusading armies ever to leave Europe. It was

---

Frederick Barbarossa, the Holy Roman Emperor, who sought to crown his career by taking Charlemagne's supposed route to Jerusalem and recapturing the city. His expedition came to an abrupt end when he was drowned while swimming in southern Turkey.

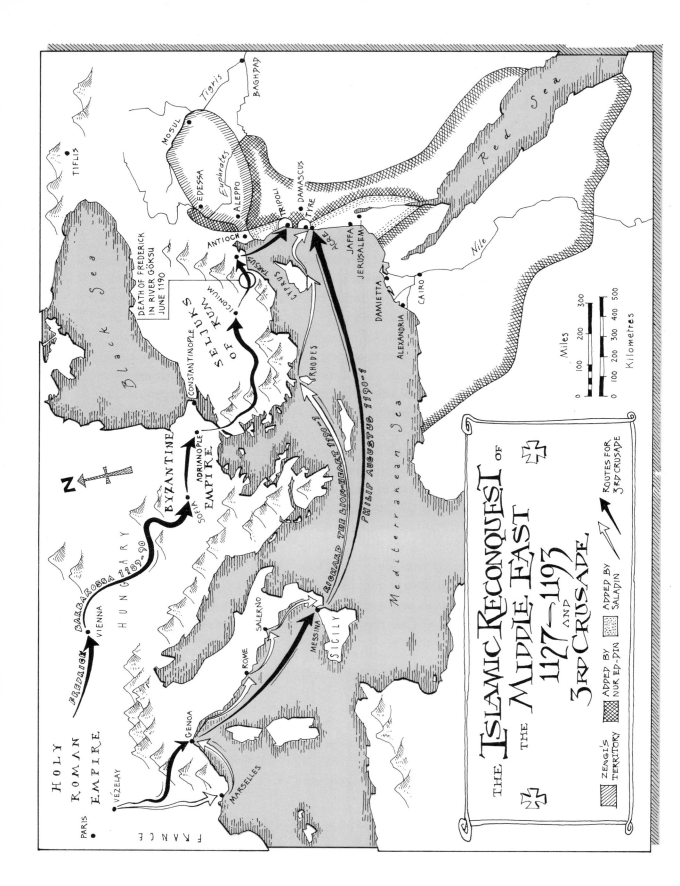

THE ISLAMIC RECONQUEST OF THE MIDDLE EAST 1127–1193 AND 3RD CRUSADE

ZENGI'S TERRITORY

ADDED BY NUR ED-DIN

ADDED BY SALADIN

ROUTES FOR 3RD CRUSADE

also the best equipped and the best disciplined and the best organized. It must have looked invincible. It sent Saladin into a frenzy of diplomacy, trying to patch together a general Islamic alliance to meet such a threat.

Frederick's army was so large that there were not enough ships to transport it, and it had to march overland, by the route that no army had successfully negotiated since the First Crusade.

His army was not welcome in the Byzantine Empire and was given a hard time. It crossed the Dardanelles into Asia in March (avoiding Constantinople) and in May inflicted a series of serious defeats on the Turks of Armenia – but it suffered horribly from thirst, hunger and ambushes. The soldiers were desperate, even chewing horse manure in search of moisture. Men grew so weak on the march that they simply lay down to die, and there were many desertions.

The survivors made it through to the Taurus mountains, and crossed a pass that brought them down into the valley of the Göksu, a fast-flowing river that winds through canyons that open out occasionally into wooded meadows. In the ferocious heat of July, Barbarossa could not resist plunging into the cold, refreshing water. To the stunned disbelief of his troops, he drowned.

It was the last straw. Frederick's Crusade ended there, on 10 June 1190. More than half of the army had already perished on the road. Some of the survivors simply caught the nearest ship back to Europe. Frederick's son did what he could to hold the remains of the expedition together, but it was no use. He even fished his father's body out of the water and had it pickled in vinegar. He then had it carried in a barrel so that the old man could at least complete his vow and reach Jerusalem. But at Antioch, where they suffered a terrible epidemic, the Crusaders realized that the vinegar had failed, and the corpse was rotting. It had to be quickly buried.

In October the wreckage of Frederick's great army arrived at Acre to support the siege. The whole Moslem world heaved a sigh of relief. *Thus did God spare us the maleficence of the Germans.'*

Richard the Lion-heart

King Henry of England too was dead. He had fallen sick during the fighting against Philip of France. His son, Richard, had become King of England while Frederick and his mighty force were marching east. Richard, who was dubbed a knight by King Louis of France, had learned the arts of war fighting against his own father. When Louis died and Philip became King of France in 1180, Philip had encouraged Richard to go on with this family feuding. It offered the best hope of destroying Henry's Empire in France.

Richard had spent as short a time as possible in England. He detested a country which he found wet, boring, spoke a foreign language – English; he, of course, was a Frenchman – and had nothing to offer if you did not enjoy the company of sheep. Apart from money. Better, though, to take the money and run. In his own words, '*I would sell London if I could find a buyer.*'

His father had even banned tournaments, because they were disturbing to public order. England was a dead loss. There was not even anybody to fight against.

Now Richard had a new reason for detesting England. During his coronation the usual pre-Crusade anti-Jewish riots broke out in London and then spread like a contagion, culminating in a horrific massacre at York in March 1190. Jews were under the King's special protection. That was because they were a very important source of royal money. The English were stupid as well as boring. Richard was furious.

Philip and Richard would have to go on Crusade together, not because they were such good friends, but because they were now enemies. So long as the King of England ruled half of France, they had to be enemies. If only one went, the other would attack.

Richard was the very image of a romantic warrior: tall, strong, handsome, with flaming red hair and the gracious manners he had learned at his mother's court. Philip, on the other hand, was austere, poorly educated, not keen on physical risks and his looks were marred by having lost an eye. Philip was not a hero, but public opinion was forcing him to go on Crusade.

One month after Frederick's death – one year after his own accession – Richard met Philip at Vézelay. Their armies were assembled. They were ready to rescue the Holy Land. The plan was to go via Sicily. It was a plan that had been agreed with King William II of Sicily, who was married to Richard's sister Joan, and who had been intending to join the Crusade. But he too had died, four months after Henry. Sicily was now ruled by William's illegitimate cousin, who rejoiced in the famous name of Tancred. Tancred had locked up Joan, kept her dowry and also kept a large legacy that should have gone to Richard. He cannot have been looking forward to Richard's visit.

Richard the Lion-heart depicted as a warrior king, from a fourteenth-century Chronology of the Kings of England.

Philip marched his army to Genoa, where ships had been contracted. Richard took his to Marseilles, where it was supposed to be picked up by an English fleet. The fleet was late and he left the army to wait for it while he coasted down Italy. He spent five days at Salerno, visiting the great medical school. From there he went south to cross to Sicily.

Just before crossing, he confiscated a hawk from a peasant. Hawks were for hunting, and hunting was for nobles, not for peasants. It was dangerous arrogance; since he only had one companion he quickly found himself in the centre of an angry mob. In the heat of the moment he hit a man with the flat of his sword. The sword broke. Richard had to fight his way out, throwing everything he could get his hands on at his pursuers.

The Crusaders in Sicily

Southern Italy was where the cultures of east and west came together; the medical centre at Salerno was said to have been founded by a Latin, a Greek, a Jew and an Arab, and the knowledge of all four traditions was available there. In Sicily, Norman rulers issued their decrees in Latin, Greek and Arabic. In 1186 the Moslem traveller Ibn Jubayr, who visited Sicily, was struck by the Orientalism of the island; the King kept black slaves and his chamberlains were eunuchs.

For Richard's army, lodged outside Messina, it was hard to come to terms with the situation. They were, after all, on their way to fight the Saracens and now Saracens were all round them. Even worse, the island was full of Greeks and they hated Greeks. Relations between the visitors and the locals quickly broke down. An Anglo-Norman Crusader, Ambroise, wrote a rhyming account of his experiences:

> For townsfolk rabble and the scum
> of the city, bastard Greeks were some,
> and some of them Saracen born
> did heap upon our pilgrims scorn.
> Fingers to eyes they mocked at us
> calling us dogs malodorous.
> They did us foulness every day;
> Sometimes our pilgrims they did slay.
> And the corpses in the privies threw
> and this were proven to be true.

Swords and Damascus Steel

Since swords are at the very heart of crusading, it may seem startling that a royal sword should snap in two at the critical moment. It was brittle. European bladesmiths had stopped making the highly wrought swords of their ancestors, which had given smiths their reputation for magical powers. Those swords had been made by endlessly plaiting wires of impure iron; reforging, hammering and plaiting until the molecules of the iron aligned themselves to form a steel. The quality of the steel depended on the impurities added to the mix, and each smith produced his own unique metal. The result was strong, sharp and flexible — but pretty useless at cutting through armour.

By Richard's day, a knight wore mail over his whole body; to the old hauberk had been added leggings, sleeves and gloves of mail, and lately a plate-metal helmet. Even the horses wore mail coats. What was needed now was not a sharp, flexible, slicing blade, but a rigid, pointed, metal bar that would pierce. If the sword flexed, it would not penetrate armour. The down side, as Richard was reminded, was that modern swords were not meant for fencing or for swiping. If you did that, they broke.

The old arts of the bladesmith had survived in the East, where armour was used much less. Metal twisted and retwisted was used to create swords which had a beautiful watery surface, showing the ripples of up to a million layers of wafer-thin metal. Brought by merchants for distribution through Damascus, this became known as 'Damascus steel'; not only was it super-sharp, but the structure of the metal meant that as particles came off the edge (through hitting something, for example), a new edge formed. The Islamic sword was self-sharpening. Hence the apocryphal story in which Richard demonstrated that with sheer might he could smash his rigid sword through a table (obviously *not* using the flat of his sword), while Saladin demonstrated that his fine Islamic blade could slice though silk floating in the air.

Overleaf
The extraordinary confidence trickster, Isaac Comnenus,
established himself in the stronghold of St Hilarion
in northern Cyprus. It was taken by Richard in a
campaign of breathtaking speed and daring which also
happened to be his honeymoon.

Even worse, they began overcharging the Crusaders for supplies. Soon there was armed conflict between the soldiers and the townsfolk; Richard settled it by launching a full assault on the city and sacking it. Whereupon Tancred released Joan, paid over her dowry money and recompensed Richard for his share of the inheritance.

The Crusaders wintered in Sicily, which gave plenty of time for them to quarrel over small things and great ones. One of the small things was a row over William de Barre, a French knight who humiliated Richard in an impromptu duel with canes. Richard was so angry at being made to look a fool that he insisted William leave the Crusade; it took the combined diplomacy of the whole leadership, of Church and nobility, to persuade him to relent.

One of the greater things was that Richard was betrothed to Philip's sister Alice, but he and his mother had arranged for him to marry Berengaria, the daughter of the King of Navarre – thereby stabilizing the border between Spain and Aquitaine. Richard tactfully explained to Philip that he could not really be expected to marry Alice, since she had been sent to the English court as a child, where his father Henry had started sleeping with her. Relations between the two kings grew even chillier.

Philip sailed with his army on 30 March 1191, a few hours before Eleanor arrived with Berengaria. He crossed to Tyre and then went on to Acre with Conrad. Philip reorganized the siege and put it in readiness for the final assault. But he had to wait for Richard, who had gone to find his wife and mother. They had been caught in a storm and stranded on the south coast of Cyprus.

Richard's Ideal Honeymoon

Cyprus was in the hands of a bizarre confidence trickster, Isaac Ducas Comnenus. Isaac was a member of the Byzantine imperial family and had been Governor of Cilicia when he staged a revolt against a new emperor in 1182. He had ended up a prisoner of the Turkish ruler of Armenia. Somehow he had persuaded the Templars that if they ransomed him, they would get their money back with substantial interest; all he had to do was go and collect it from his friends in Cyprus. The Templars were not known for their gullibility, but they fell for the deal.

Isaac then turned up in Cyprus with an impressive retinue (courtesy of his brother-in-law, a Sicilian admiral) and forged documents that stated that he was the new Governor sent out from Constantinople. The bemused Governor of Cyprus handed the island over to him and Isaac took control of the fortresses. He then announced that he was going to call himself emperor. He ruled Cyprus as a tyrant and made a treaty with Saladin. The Templars, of course, never saw their money again.

Isaac must have viewed the arrival of Frankish ships off his coast much as a man who has stolen money from the mafia might regard the arrival of a group of cars with darkened windows. Terrified, he arrested those who struggled ashore, refused water to Joan's ship and started strengthening his defences.

Richard arrived seasick, bad-tempered and upset by the way the ladies were being treated. He attacked Limassol. Isaac withdrew and the inhabitants of the town welcomed Richard as their liberator. Isaac then came on a safe-conduct to meet Richard and agreed to release his prisoners, make restitution for goods he had taken from the shipwrecks and generally be helpful. He was, presumably, delighted that no-one mentioned the Knights Templars or the money he owed them.

Isaac then made the mistake of assuming that he was safe after all and, once he had returned to his fastness in the north of the island, he ordered Richard leave. On the very same day, unfortunately, King Guy and his leading supporters at the siege of Acre sailed into Limassol to see what had happened to Richard. With them were, as it happened, many of the leading Templars. Nemesis had come to Isaac. It was not hard to persuade Richard that, before sailing away, he should lead the conquest of Cyprus.

He married Berengaria on 12 May, the day after Guy's arrival. Then he took her on what must have been a medieval prince's idea of the ideal honeymoon – a fortnight's pillage and conquest. At the end of it the whole of Cyprus was his. From now on it would be a tenuous lifeline for the ailing Kingdom of Jerusalem.

12

The Battle of the Heroes: Richard v. Saladin

Richard arrived at Acre on 8 June with twenty-five war galleys, Isaac a prisoner (he had asked not to be put in irons and so Richard had had silver fetters made) and a reputation as an invincible warrior. *'No pen can sufficiently describe the joy of the people on the night of the King's arrival,'* declared the soldier-chronicler Ambroise, who then tried his best to describe the all-night party that followed.

The siege of Acre had lasted for almost two years, and there had been a difficult winter, with acute shortages of food. Now everything was ready to bring it to a conclusion. The siege catapults were completed and had been christened with names like 'Bad Neighbour' and 'God's Own Sling'. There was also a great grappling ladder called 'The Cat'. But two years of doing nothing had sapped the morale of the besiegers and although Philip had done good work, he had not proved an inspirational leader. Besides, he was sick with *arnaldia*, a disease which caused his hair and fingernails to fall out.

When the English King finally arrived, his mere presence seemed to infuse the troops with the energy needed for the final assault. Richard himself, however, fell sick with an attack of *arnaldia* even worse than Philip's. So he simply directed operations from his bed. He stepped up the bombardment and requested a meeting with Saladin; Saladin refused this, but suggested Richard meet his brother, al-Adil.

Saladin's main hope still lay in letting the Europeans quarrel themselves into impotence and he had good reason to think this might happen. Inevitably, Philip supported Conrad against Guy (Conrad was Philip's cousin) and Richard supported Guy against Conrad (Guy's brother was one of Richard's leading vassals).

The siege of Acre from a manuscript written only eighty years later
in 1280. The siege engine is shown as having a counter-balance,
which means that it was capable of hurling heavier and more
damaging ammunition than the human-powered
artillery of the First Crusade.

There was plenty of room for argument because Queen Sibylla and both her daughters had died during the siege. Guy was, of course, King only because of his marriage to Sibylla, so the deaths created a strong argument that Sibylla's half-sister, Isabella, was now the rightful Queen. Conrad thought so much of this argument that he got Isabella's marriage to the effeminate Humphrey of Toron annulled and married her himself. In so doing he certainly didn't make poor Isabella happy (she really seems to have loved Humphrey for all his gentle effeminacy), but it made Conrad a rival for the crown.

And to help matters along, Philip demanded, and was refused, half of Cyprus.

These quarrels bubbled along, but they would not save Acre for Saladin. He could no longer send supplies into the city by sea, because Richard and Philip had enough ships to block the harbour completely. It was now only a matter of time before the Crusaders would take Acre.

Finally, on 11 July, the Turkish garrison capitulated. They not only agreed that they would surrender the entire contents of the city, but that Saladin would release fifteen hundred Frankish prisoners, pay two hundred thousand gold pieces and return the portion of the True Cross which he had captured at Hattin. Saladin only heard of these terms after they had been agreed and understandably he was not happy with them.

The city was occupied by the Crusaders and there was the normal squabbling over who got exactly what and who lived exactly where and exactly who was in charge, Guy or Conrad. Richard and Philip both raised their standards, in recognition of their own agreement that they would share the spoils of the Crusade equally. Leopold of Austria, who commanded the pathetic remnant of Barbarossa's Crusade, also raised his standard. Richard was not going to share any more than he had to. So he acted with his usual flair for diplomacy: he tore down Leopold's standard and threw it in the moat. It was an act that he was bitterly to regret a year later.

But of course the real issue was not which Crusader lord got what buildings, but which Italian city got what trading rights. For Pisa and Genoa, in particular, the struggle for supremacy at Acre was literally a question of life and death — especially now that the Church had outlawed commerce with Egypt. The Pisans were Guy's men and the Genoese were Conrad's.

It was finally agreed that Guy would remain King, which meant that the Pisans were protected in Acre, but Conrad would be Lord of Tyre, which meant that Tyre became a Genoese stronghold. Conrad, however, was also named as heir to the throne. This made the Pisans nervous.

Philip, who was sick, tired and fed up with Richard, packed his bags and went home, after promising not to attack any of Richard's lands in France before Richard got back. Leopold and others who had been cut out of the division of the spoils also left. Those Crusaders who stayed, if they were not Richard's own men (who adored him), were as distrustful of their new commander as was Philip.

Richard Marches on Jerusalem

Richard was anxious to get to Jerusalem and he had no intention of hanging around in Acre for the drawn-out process of ransoming prisoners. He had nearly three thousand captured Moslems on his hands. Saladin, in this situation, would have released the prisoners. In fact Saladin had already been heavily criticized by his own people for releasing so many of the prisoners of Hattin and for allowing Tyre to be reinforced with the men he had freed.

Richard agreed with these critics. He therefore took the first opportunity of a hitch in the ransom arrangements to butcher all his prisoners. Some 2700 survivors of the Moslem garrison, with about three hundred of their wives and children, were taken outside the city walls in chains and slaughtered in cold blood and in the sight of Saladin's army.

Richard then marched his men out of Acre on 22 August, heading south towards Jaffa. They did not want to leave, because Acre had become a very lively, if not decadent, city. Saladin's secretary, for example, described the arrival of a boatload of prostitutes in the finest tradition of tabloid journalism, detailing with relish exactly what he disapproved of:

> Tinted and painted, desirable and appetizing — bold and ardent, with nasal voices and fleshy thighs, they offered their wares for enjoyment, brought their silver anklets up to touch their golden ear-rings, made themselves targets for men's darts, offered themselves to the lance's blows, made javelins rise towards shields. They interwove leg with leg, caught lizard after lizard in their holes, guided pens to inkwells, torrents to the valley bottom, swords to scabbards, firewood to stoves, and they maintained that this was an act of piety without equal, especially to those who were far from home and wives.

Who would trade that for a march through enemy territory, in a region with little food and less water, in the heat of full summer and with no safe haven at the end of the march?

Richard.

It was a demonstration of invincibility.

Richard the Lion-heart ordered the massacre of 2700 survivors of the Moslem garrison at Acre. Here he watches the spectacular show from a grandstand. Interestingly, the Moslems are shown robed as martyrs, while Richard's army is portrayed in black. From *Les Passages faits Outremer . . . , c.* 1490.

The key to the march was strict discipline. Saladin's biographer, Baha' ad-Din, described the column on the move, its flanks *'packed together like a wall'*:

> Every foot-soldier wore armour made of very heavy felt, and so stout a coat of mail that our arrows did no harm ... I saw soldiers with as many as ten arrows in their back, who marched on as usual without breaking rank ... One could not help admiring the patience of these people: they bore the most extreme hardships ... and derived no personal advantage.

In front and behind were the Templars and Hospitallers. Right in the middle was the Royal Standard, a flagpole mounted on a wagon, surrounded by the reserve, a group of noblemen. The fleet, carrying additional food and water, shadowed their movement down the coast.

There was no question of there being camp followers. Richard explicitly forbade women on the march, except for washerwomen, who were there *'to keep the Crusaders' linen clean, to wash their hair and to de-louse them, at which task they were as skilful as monkeys'.* These washerwomen, who were regarded as essential by all Western commanders, created a deep impression on the Moslems. *'Everywhere was full of old women ... They exhorted and incited men to summon their pride, saying that the Cross imposed on them an obligation to resist to the bitter end, and that the combatants would win eternal life only by sacrificing their own lives, and that their God's sepulchre was in enemy hands.'* When they were captured, they were normally sent straight back to the Crusaders.

The Battle of Arsuf

Marching only in the morning, Richard's army covered on average a mere four miles a day. On 7 September, when they reached Arsuf, only about fifteen miles from Jaffa, Saladin launched a full-scale attack. His only hope was to cause so much disruption to the Crusaders that the knights would break out of formation and charge in small groups which could be surrounded and cut down. He threw wave after wave of attackers onto the rearguard, who had to march backwards defending themselves. The Hospitallers were losing horses, which could not be as padded and protected as men. For knights, whose whole ethos was based on valour and whose horses were part of their very identity, the situation was shameful. But the formation held.

Saladin's forces were trained and schooled, and part of their training was devoted to recognizing the complex process by which knights prepared to charge. This was essential, because their response was meant to be to get out of the way – groups scattering to right and left, while a large body would retreat in a straight line, drawing the charging knights as far as possible from the main army so that they could be cut off and destroyed. But when Richard's forces charged on this day, the Moslems were caught completely by surprise. The charge had actually been triggered prematurely, but Richard immediately took control, turned it into an immense charging wall and called a halt before it broke up. The knights returned in order and then made two further disciplined charges.

Saladin's biographer, Baha' ad-Din was in the centre of the Moslem attack which was shattered. He tells how he rode over to the left wing, which he found in full retreat, then rode across several miles to the right wing, where the situation was even worse. He then withdrew to Saladin's formation, *'since this was to be the general rallying point. But I found only seventeen men there, though the banners were flying and the drums were still beating.'*

The Moslems were beaten. Saladin had been brilliantly able to organize *jihad* against a Christian state, but he could not rely on public opinion, popular outrage and religious fervour to destroy a well-commanded military force.

Negotiations

Richard took Jaffa. But to take Jerusalem meant a march inland and his army would be much less effective away from its ships. He therefore opened negotiations with Saladin. Saladin would probably have been happy to negotiate a treaty, but his position was now very weak. He had lost the triumphant aura of his reconquest and he was surrounded by subordinate emirs who were no longer behaving as subordinates. He refused to meet Richard and again sent his brother al-Adil in his place.

Richard enjoyed al-Adil's company and through him he sent a letter to Saladin. *'The Muslims and Franks are bleeding to death, the country is utterly ruined and goods and lives have been sacrificed on both sides. The time has come to stop this. The points at issue are Jerusalem, the Cross and the land.'* Saladin replied that Jerusalem was *'as much ours as yours'*, that the land of the Kingdom of Jerusalem had only fallen to the Franks in recent times and that he would only hand over the Cross if he received something valuable for it. This was not closing the door to an agreement, but it was not taking things forward at all.

Richard knew that Saladin was also quietly negotiating with Conrad, trying to split the Christians (not a hard task), and so he offered al-Adil an extraordinary proposition: that he, Saladin's brother, should marry Richard's sister Joan. They would rule Palestine jointly from Jerusalem, Richard ceding Acre and Jaffa to Joan, and Saladin ceding the rest of Palestine to al-Adil. Conrad and Guy would both be out of it, al-Adil would have a kingdom and Richard could go home.

This was about as far from the ideology of a Crusade as you could get.

Saladin approved the terms, *'knowing quite well that it was a practical joke'*, according to Baha' ad-Din. When Joan got to hear about it, however, she was furious, and swore she would never marry a Moslem thank you very much! So Richard asked al-Adil if he would mind converting to Christianity. Saladin's brother politely declined and the whole affair ended with a lavish banquet and oaths of friendship, but no alliance.

Richard unhorsing Saladin, whose helmet is toppling off to reveal the outlandish features of the Saracen devil-king. The personalization of the conflict into a battle between the two men who never actually met established the legendary status of both of them.

Richard's Dilemma

During the winter, when Saladin had disbanded most of his forces, Richard took the army on an expedition into the hills. They got to within twelve miles of Jerusalem. But it was clear that even if they took the city, there was no way to hold it once Richard and his army had gone. There were not enough Christian knights who wanted to live out their lives in the Holy Land.

Richard withdrew to Ascalon, which Saladin had dismantled, and busied his men with reconstructing it as a mighty fortress. Conrad refused to come and help, and the Duke of Burgundy, whom Philip had left in charge of his troops, took a large French force to Acre. Since the French had always backed Conrad, and Conrad was a tool of the Genoese, the Pisans saw this as a threat. They seized the city just as the French were arriving, drove them off and held it for three days against Genoese galleys, appealing for Richard to come and impose order. Richard went north, patched things up without resolving anything and returned to Ascalon.

←——————————————————————————————→

The French set up a very fashionable camp around Tyre and quite distressed the English soldier/chronicler who saw them there dressed in smooth, tight clothes with gold chains on the sleeves, embroidered belts, jewelled collars and garlands of flowers in their hair. The French were obviously degenerates.

So far as Richard was concerned, there would have to be a treaty with Saladin. Saladin could in theory simply sit and wait for Richard to leave, but in fact he needed a treaty as much as Richard did. Al-Adil was now ambitious and seemed to be negotiating on his own account with Richard and Conrad. If Saladin did not reach an agreement of some sort, al-Adil might – and he might have the support of Saladin's grumbling emirs.

An agreement appeared to have been reached by the end of March. The Christians would keep what they had conquered and have the right of pilgrimage and of maintaining priests at Jerusalem. The Holy Cross would be given back. They could also have Beirut, if its fortifications were dismantled.

Richard announced that he was leaving. His brother John was creating trouble in England and Philip was threatening Normandy. Besides, his success as a diplomat did not cover the fact that he now knew it was entirely pointless to conquer Jerusalem, which had been the whole purpose of coming. It was definitely time to go home. Somehow, though, the Guy-Conrad struggle had to be sorted out. He called a council to ask the knights and barons to choose between Guy and Conrad.

The Murder of Conrad

Conrad had now committed himself completely to the Genoese, and Genoese invest-ment in him was large; this may account for the fact that the Council displayed an extraordinary unanimity in electing him king. Guy had lost and Richard arranged for him to purchase the Kingdom of Cyprus as a consolation prize. More significantly, perhaps, the Pisans had lost. The moment Conrad became king, they could expect the Genoese to be given a monopoly at Acre.

Just as the coronation was being prepared, Conrad was struck down and killed in the street by two Assassins, sent by the Old Man of the Mountains. No-one knew why; many thought it had been arranged by Richard. There were as many theories about this odd murder as there are about the killing of J. F. Kennedy. One oddity was the role of Isabella. Conrad was killed because he had gone out to find someone to dine with, after she had refused to leave her bath to eat with him. The Assassins were waiting for him on the way back; someone had tipped them off.

The most obvious beneficiary was Henry of Champagne and he turned up at Tyre as soon as he heard of the assassination – to be acclaimed immediately by the populace as their new Lord and the man who should marry the newly widowed (and pregnant) Isabella. He was young, popular and the nephew of both Richard and Philip. He and Isabella were married within forty-eight hours of the murder. Richard approved. But although Henry ruled as a king, he was never crowned. No-one knows why.

The chroniclers do not devote many lines to merchants and seamen; they are impressed by knightly valour and religious fervour, not account books and sordid squabbles over money. But it is clear that the other great beneficiaries of Conrad's death were the Pisans. Richard and Henry now confirmed them in privileges which gave them control over the whole of the economically important section of Acre. This was still not enough for them and the following year a Pisan plot was discovered in which Tyre would be seized by force and Guy de Lusignan brought back from Cyprus to rule it. Henry banned all Pisans from the Kingdom.

Two years after the assassination, when the Old Man of the Mountains died, his successor invited Henry of Champagne to pay him a visit at his castle. He apologized for the killing of Conrad and then asked Henry to watch a demonstration. Pairs of men in white robes stood on the ramparts. The Assassin chief explained that these men would obey him more perfectly than any of Henry's soldiers would obey Henry. He shouted, and one pair stepped off the ramparts and plunged to their deaths. Would Henry like the demonstration repeated? Henry declined, badly shaken. He was politely asked if there was anyone the Assassins could kill for him?

Very shortly afterwards, the Pisans were restored to their lands and privileges. There was a tragic coda to this, for not long afterwards Henry himself fell to his death by inadvertently stepping backwards out of a window of his castle.

With Conrad dead, and the faction fighting apparently over, Richard could concentrate on finishing his negotiations with Saladin. He decided to increase the pressure, took Saladin's last fortress on the coast, Daron, and then marched his army once more towards Jerusalem. He waited there for a month, looking threatening but actually impotent.

Richard's Last Great Battle

R ichard had sworn that he would only set eyes on the Holy City as its conqueror, so when he accidentally caught sight of the city walls in the distance, while riding in the hills, he sadly covered his face with his shield. Finally Richard ordered a

←—————————————————————————→

withdrawal to the coast. The French soldiers, who did not understand Richard's reluctance to take the city and did not share his own troops' admiration for him, began singing an obscene song about him. Richard wrote one of his own about them. Unfortunately, neither has survived.

Negotiations seemed to be drawing to a conclusion and Richard moved to Acre, preparing for his departure. Then Saladin's army suddenly appeared at Jaffa and the city surrendered. Saladin's forces, however, had lost enthusiasm for this war; the only thing that was still holding them together was the prospect of plunder. Saladin had agreed that the Christians in Jaffa could leave with their goods, but his troops had very different ideas and began to rampage. Saladin, outraged, put guards at the gates and confiscated the plunder.

Richard, having heard of the attack, immediately sailed to Jaffa with the small force he had to hand. By the time he arrived Saladin's standard was already flying over the town, but a swimmer brought him the news that the garrison had not yet withdrawn. Richard brought his boats close inshore, jumped into the surf with only the top half of his body armoured, and began fighting. His companions followed his example.

Richard was a careful commander but an insanely careless fighter. Three years earlier, fighting against his father, he had pursued a retreating force with such enthusiasm that he had not bothered to put on armour. The warrior who turned to take him on was William Marshal, a celebrated champion, and Richard suddenly realized that he was in mortal danger. *'By the legs of God, Marshal,'* he cried, *'do not kill me! I am not armed!'* Marshal replied that he would not, *'but I hope the Devil may'*, and killed his horse. Now Richard had done it again. To wade ashore fighting with the surf at his back would have been suicidal if the Moslems had made a serious effort to stop him. They did not. They simply ran away.

Jaffa was too badly damaged and the stench of corpses was too great for it to be occupied. Richard and his tiny force (fifty-four knights capable of fighting, with only fifteen horses between them, and some infantrymen) camped outside the walls. A few days later Saladin ordered a full-scale cavalry attack on this little troop.

Richard's chroniclers saw what followed as a heroic battle, a marvellous vision of Richard the perfect warrior in action, triumphant against overwhelming odds.

> *The King was a very giant in the battle and was everywhere in the field — now here, now there, wherever the attacks of the Turks raged the hottest. He slew numbers with his sword which shone like lightning; some of them were cloven in two from their helmets to their teeth, whilst others lost their heads, arms, and other members, which were lopped off at a single blow.*

In fact what happened was not quite like that. Although the Mameluks (slave warriors from Egypt) had charged and been seen off by the crossbowmen, the rest of Saladin's troops had mutinied. Saladin was told that since he had confiscated their booty — presumably for the enrichment of his own family — he should go and fight for himself. They had had enough.

At one point in the battle, al-Adil, seeing that Richard's horse had fallen under him, sent him two replacement horses, requesting that Richard reward him later. One chronicler, staying with his story of a dramatic encounter between two super-heroes, explained that al-Adil was instructed to do this by Saladin and that the horses had been trained to bolt. A likelier explanation is that al-Adil saw more profit in helping Richard than Saladin.

The energy of the *jihad* had evaporated with the conquest of Jerusalem, and Saladin's moment in history was past. Back in 1098 at Antioch, victory against equally impossible odds had been achieved when the Turks similarly refused to fight for their commander. Then, victory had been ascribed to divine intervention; now, almost a hundred years later, it was ascribed to the Hero. God was no longer needed. The energy of the Holy War had evaporated on the Christian side as much as on the Moslem.

Jerusalem would never again be captured by Crusaders. The parts of the Kingdom that would survive were those that mattered to the Italian merchants. There was no port in Jerusalem.

After the battle, Richard and Saladin both fell ill. Both were exhausted and both had failed. Saladin sent fruit and snow to Richard and supplied him with a doctor. On 2 September 1192 they signed a three-year truce. The Christians could keep the coastal strip (but must demolish the fort at Ascalon) and Christian pilgrims would be free to visit Jerusalem. Many knights did so, but not Richard. On 9 October he sailed away.

But that was not the end of his hardships.

Richard was shipwrecked on his way home and forced to travel overland through the territory of Leopold of Austria, whose banner he had cast into the moat at Acre. He disguised himself as a Templar knight, but was recognized while stopping at an inn in Vienna. He was imprisoned by Leopold on the charge of murdering Conrad and then handed over to Emperor Henry VI, who kept him a prisoner for a year. Richard was eventually released only on payment of an enormous ransom.

←───────────────────────────────────→

Saladin – the Model Christian?

Saladin, utterly worn out, died five months after Richard left Acre. To some of his fellow countrymen he remained the 'Upstart', a man more prepared to fight his fellow-Moslems than the Franks and who used the rhetoric of *jihad* simply to fulfil his own ambitions. He brought Nur ed-Din's work to its logical conclusion by recapturing Jerusalem, but was criticized by his contemporaries for not being more ruthless with the Franks and for not driving them out of Palestine altogether. In the West, on the other hand, Saladin became an icon of chivalry. He was celebrated for his sense of honour, his generosity and his distaste for bloodshed.

There is little doubt that he was a man of his word and yet he was also quite capable of hypocrisy. When Amalric died, for example, Saladin wrote to his son, the wretched ten-year-old leper Baldwin: *'The king must know that we have a sincere affection for him, as we had for his father ... let him rely on us.'* But to his own nephew, Saladin punned on the dead king's name, which in Arabic was Maury: *'may God curse him and abandon him and lead him to punishment as bitter* [Murr] *as his name'.*

There is no disputing Saladin's generosity. It was often the despair of his treasurers. *'He was as generous when he was poor as when he was rich,'* recalled one member of his household, *'and his treasurers kept certain reserves concealed from him for fear that some financial emergency might arise.'* When he died, ruler of so many lands, his treasury was virtually empty but for forty-seven drachmas of silver and one piece of gold.

Saladin was generous – to a fault – but his generosity was part of his political method. And while even his enemies found this extremely attractive, the keener-sighted, according to William of Tyre, realized that such generosity was actually one of Saladin's chief weapons: *'He was a man wise in counsel, valiant in war, and generous beyond measure ... for this very reason, he was distrusted by those of our nobles who had keener foresight ... there is no better means by which princes can win the hearts of their subjects ... than by showing lavish bounty towards them.'*

Saladin clearly did not value money for itself, but he needed it, lots of it. His power was based on force – on his army – and without money he could do nothing. He spent five times as much on his military as he did on everything else. This was the whole trouble with being an 'upstart'. He was locked in a cycle of conquest and expansion. He used the wealth of Egypt to conquer Damascus, he used the wealth of Damascus to conquer Aleppo, he used the wealth of Aleppo to conquer the coast, but, as the chronicler al-Fadil remarked, in this sort of system: *'hopes of expansion can never come to an end'.*

Saladin's humanity is perhaps his most attractive feature. His humane treatment of civilians after the conquest of Jerusalem was remarkable and yet it would be a mistake to see him as a humanist in any modern sense. His avoidance of bloodshed at Mosul and Aleppo was a matter of policy: he did not want to alienate the people he was supposed to be rescuing and he also needed the manpower that they represented.

On other occasions, such as the massacre of the Black Regiment in Cairo or when he crucified Fatimid and Shi'ite rebels, he acted with all the brutality that was expected of a ruler of his time. Perhaps most disturbing was his habit of creating an amusing spectacle out of the execution of prisoners. On more than one occasion he ordered a batch of captives to be killed by 'men of piety'. Presumably the terror of those who were about to die matched the terror of the 'men of piety' who were expected to do the killing. This — coupled with the *Sufis'* inexperience in handling the sword and the needless death agonies of the victims as the amateur executioners botched up — must all have made hilarious entertainment for the hard-bitten soldiers watching.

Saladin's biographer, Imad ed-Din, recalled how he himself was once summoned to such an occasion. To his horror, he discovered that the prisoner he was supposed to kill was a boy. This may have been a doubly good joke to Saladin and his 'rough companions', since elsewhere Imad ed-Din is satirized as a homosexual. At all events, Imad ed-Din refused to carry out the deed and instead asked if he could keep the boy as a slave. But he made it clear that he did so not out of compassion but to avoid joining the laughing-stock: *'I turned from that deed, lest the company might laugh at me as they did at the others.'*

Saladin remains a mystery, an attractive and yet ambivalent figure. Even his mausoleum in Damascus contains not one but two tombs — a homely wooden one erected by his fellow countrymen shortly after his death and an elaborate marble one erected by the German Kaiser in the last century to celebrate Saladin as the great romantic hero that the West saw.

In many ways he is the West's hero rather than the East's.

Saladin's death was the death of his empire. It would take ten years for his brother al-Adil to reunite its parts. In the meantime the logic that had persuaded Richard not to attack Jerusalem had lost its force. If he had stayed another six months, with Saladin dead and his coalition army dispersed, Richard could have become the conqueror of the Holy City.

Richard himself died in 1199 from a gangrenous arrow-wound received when he was carelessly inspecting the defences of a tiny castle which he was determined to assault. But there were others who became interested in Jerusalem.

13

The Fourth Crusade

In the long struggle between Pope and Emperor which had been launched by Gregory VII, there were few times when the Papacy found no powerful Emperor. There were even fewer when a Pope in that position had an unequivocal sense of his historic mission to make all secular monarchs the liege-men of the Church.

That day had come.

In 1198 Lothario dei Conti de Segni found himself, aged only thirty-seven, elected Pope in a world where no lay ruler could rival his power. The German Emperor had died leaving a child heir; France and England were locked in debilitating war. The young Lothario took the name of Innocent III and immediately put his own men in key positions in the Church and the administration of Rome. He had come to power from nowhere. He had been a mere deacon and so on his election as Pope he had first to be ordained as a priest.

Like Stalin, he took over power not because he was known for his politics but because he knew how to run the administration and watched all the details. And like Stalin, once he had arrived, he blossomed into a monster seeking unlimited power and ruthlessly destroying anyone who was not completely subservient. Unlike Stalin, the organization which he infused with his personality was already firmly established and would endure for centuries to come.

His ambition was total. He was the heir of the revolution begun by Gregory VII; he was determined that the Pope, representative of the supreme monarch in heaven, must be the supreme monarch on earth. That programme called for the submission of kings, the subjection of the Eastern Church to Rome, the elimination of all but his own interpretation of the Christian message and the reconquest of Jerusalem under his own command.

Pope Innocent III, arguably the most powerful Pope in
the history of the Catholic Church. Fresco in a
monastery at Subiaco in Italy.

In 1199 he wrote to the Patriarch of Jerusalem for information which would help
him direct the Crusade he planned. The Patriarch wrote back to say that no Crusade
was necessary, thank you very much; in his view the Saracens would happily withdraw
from the Holy Land if they could be given guarantees of the security of their other
possessions. The barons wanted to live in peace with al-Adil; the last thing they
wanted was another bunch of knights to come over, make a lot of trouble and then
go away leaving them to live with the results. This was not the information Innocent
wanted to hear. He ignored it.

←————————————————————————————→

The Preaching of the Crusade

A priest by the name of Fulk, from near Paris, had been wandering about France preaching the need for a new Crusade. Fulk was no ragged itinerant like Peter the Hermit. He was respectable, well groomed and with great powers of oratory – a perfectly acceptable representative of papal intentions. Innocent III now gave Fulk's preaching full papal authority. In addition, he sent letters to the clergy and nobility throughout France and northern Italy urging them to take up the Cross. But he sent no letter to any king – not that he would have stopped them going, but why encourage them, since he himself was to be the ultimate commander?

There didn't seem to be quite the same enthusiasm for crusading as there had been in the time of Urban II, so Innocent resorted to unprecedented – even desperate – measures. For the first time ever he announced a tax upon the clergy themselves to pay for the Crusade. There was an outcry, of course. The Cistercians were immediately up in arms and refused to pay. But the fact that the Pope was prepared to put other people's purses where his mouth was changed the whole basis of the Crusade. From now on it was less of a financial burden to go on Crusade; and would-be Crusade leaders who could get the tax assigned to them were even able to show a profit – especially if they did not go after all.

Although a lawyer himself, the Pope also decided to throw Canon Law out of the window by announcing that men no longer needed their wives' consent to go on Crusade to the Holy Land. Innocent believed firmly that the end justified the means. In the name of Divine Law and Christian morality, he would break any law that needed breaking – and any bones.

In November 1199 the first contingent of Crusaders arrived for a grand tournament at the castle of Ércy in Champagne (today it is called Asfeld-la-Ville). Amidst the flying banners, the martial contests and the feasting, the twenty-two-year-old Count Thibald of Champagne and the twenty-seven-year-old Count Louis of Blois took the Cross. They were followed by other lords and vassals, including Count Baldwin of Flanders. These three Counts became the military leaders of the expedition, but they now made diplomatic history by immediately handing over their powers to six envoys, armed with blank charters already sealed and signed by the Counts. This is the first time in history we ever hear of plenipotentiaries given such complete freedom of action.

The Crusaders Proposition Venice

The six envoys (one of whom was the chronicler Geoffrey de Villehardouin) approached the greatest maritime power of the day, Venice, for help in transporting the armies across the sea to the Holy Land. In 1201, in the heart of winter, they arrived at the court of the old, blind Doge, Enrico Dandolo.

Venice was used to huge maritime contracts. In 1187, for example, it had secured the contract to build and man the entire Byzantine navy. But its focus of interest was Constantinople. The specialists in travel to the Holy Land were Genoa and Pisa, but they were now at war with each other and any fleet hired from one stood a good chance of being attacked by the other. The envoys estimated that the total number of Crusaders would be 33 500 men. This was an absurd number, seven times larger than the army King Philip had taken in 1190. It is clear that great lords and chroniclers had only the vaguest idea of the size of armies.

The Grand Council of Venice asked for a week's grace (probably they needed to go somewhere quiet and fall about laughing); once they had composed themselves they offered to build enough ships to carry 4500 knights, each with one horse, 9000 squires and 20 000 foot-soldiers and supply nine months' provisions. The cost would be five marks for each horse and two marks for each man, all of which came to 89 500 marks, but they could offer a five per cent discount for friends, which brought it down to 85 025 – let's call it 85 000 marks.

The army was to be seven times larger than Philip's – and the transport charge fifteen times larger! The Council also expected to receive half of everything captured on land and at sea (the normal deal was a third). Perhaps the Venetians did not want a deal to be struck. Although the leaders of the Crusade said publicly that their destination was Palestine, they had agreed in private that the way to most damage the Moslems in Palestine was to attack Egypt first. Venice had no interest in damaging its large colony of traders in Alexandria.

But the Venetians had another agenda altogether, which led them to offer fifty armed galleys at their own expense. Fifty galleys was a huge addition – as large as the entire Byzantine war fleet – and would have required seven thousand crewmen. But perhaps it *was* the entire Byzantine war fleet! After all, that fleet had been supplied and was still manned by the Venetians, and they were unhappy with the new Emperor. He was offering better deals to the Pisans and Genoese, he was not paying his considerable debts and he was levying tolls on Venetian ships in Constantinople, in breach of treaties.

The envoys accepted the terms. A wonderful pantomime was played out in the Church of San Marco, when they faced the population of the city and Geoffrey de Villehardouin announced that he and the other envoys had been commanded to kneel at the Venetians' feet and not to rise until those noble people agreed *'to take pity on the Holy Land over the sea'.* Whereupon the envoys threw themselves on their knees in tears. The Doge, who was well over eighty, virtually blind but otherwise still in full command of all his faculties, wept. So did all the Venetians gathered there and with one accord they raised their hands to heaven and shouted out: *'We consent! We consent!'* And in the noise and the uproar that then followed you would have thought the whole world was crumbling to pieces, according to Geoffrey.

The envoys borrowed 5000 marks from Venetian bankers so that the shipbuilding could begin, and returned to France with the satisfaction of a job well done.

The Débâcle in Venice

Soon after the envoys arrived back in France, the unofficial leader of the Crusade, the young Count Thibald, died. Without him there was a danger that the whole thing might founder, but it was by no means easy to find a replacement. Eventually Geoffrey de Villehardouin proposed that they offer the command of the army to the Marquis Boniface of Montferrat, the brother of the assassinated Conrad.

From the way Geoffrey puts it, it sounds as if the Marquis had already indicated that he would be prepared to accept. Boniface's main interest, though, was not in Jerusalem but Byzantine Thessalonica. He believed that he had a right to it and a Crusade army might install him there. Since, by coincidence, he had also just been invited to overthrow a usurper in Byzantium, everything seemed to be falling into place for him. He took the job.

From the beginning of June, Crusaders began to arrive in Venice and were given quarters on the island of San Niccolo di Lido. The Venetians set up a market for them with every kind of goods anyone could ever want, and everything seemed to be going according to plan. But as the days passed, the barons began to realize that they had a problem on their hands. The Crusaders were not arriving in anything like the numbers they needed.

In fact the number who did come was enormous – 11 000. But it was a long way short of the anticipated 33 500. And the awful truth began to dawn that to meet the Venetians' bill every man would have to pay three times what he had expected – three kilos of silver per man, seven and a half per horse! Many could not afford it; the barons collected what they could. But even when they added in their table-services of gold and silver plate, and saw them carted off into the Doge's palace, they were still 34 000 marks short.

The Crusaders were stuck. Winter was nearly upon them; there was no way they could keep the army together until the next sailing season and now the Venetians were threatening to cut off their supplies. At this point the blind Doge came up with an offer they could not refuse. This was how he put it to his own people:

> The King of Hungary has taken from us our city of Zara in Slavonia, one of the strongest places in the world; and we shall never recover it, even with all the forces at our disposal, except with the aid of the French. So let us ask them to help us recover it and we will allow them to postpone payment of the 34 000 silver marks they owe us until such time as God shall permit our combined forces to win this money by conquest.

This offer was then put to the barons and a violent debate broke out. Those who objected pointed out that they would be starting their Crusade by attacking a Christian town — not only that, but a town that belonged to one of their fellow Crusaders, for King Emeric of Hungary had recently taken the Cross himself! Faced with this argument, the Doge needed to demonstrate his own commitment to the Crusade. Zara was, after all, very important, since it gave access to the forests of Dalmatia, which supplied the wood for shipbuilding. So one Sunday the blind Doge climbed the steps of the lectern in the Church of San Marco and addressed a huge crowd of Venetians and Crusaders.

'Sirs,' he said, 'I am an old man, weak and in need of rest, and my health is failing. At the same time I realize that no man can control and direct you like myself, your lord. If you will allow it, I will take the Cross so that I can protect and guide you. I shall go to live or die with the pilgrims.' The Venetians cried out: 'We beg you in God's name to take the Cross and go with us!' Then he knelt before the altar and they sewed a cross onto the front of his cotton cap, so that everyone could see it. And suddenly there were lots of Venetian Crusaders. The Crusade was going to Zara.

The Crusade Attacks Zara

The great fleet set out in November 1202. Shields were hung out on the bulwarks and the ships' castles, and banners and pennants were hoisted. Between them, the ships carried more than three hundred siege machines and everything you could need to capture a city.

But as the attack on Zara was about to begin, the Abbot of Vaux stepped forward with a letter from the Pope: *'My lords, in the name of the Pope of Rome I forbid you to attack this city; for the people in it are Christians, and you wear the sign of the Cross.'* The Doge immediately turned to the counts and barons and said: *'You have given me your promise to assist me in conquering this city, and I now summon you to keep your word.'* They did, and the bombardment began. After five days the city capitulated, and was dutifully pillaged. The Doge and the Crusaders took over all the fine houses and divided the city up between them. They decided to winter there, before continuing on their Crusade.

And now we come to the heart of the plot.

In Byzantium, the Emperor, Isaac Angelus, was now the ex-Emperor and was even blinder than the Doge of Venice. When his brother, Alexius, had been captured by the Turks, Isaac had paid off the ransom and brought Alexius back to Constantinople. Alexius then showed his enduring gratitude by turning on his brother and rescuer, tearing out his eyes and having him thrown into prison, along with his son, who was also named Alexius. Alexius the usurper was the man who had so annoyed the Venetians by doing deals with the Pisans and Genoese.

Young Prince Alexius had managed to escape to the west, however, and it was he who had invited Boniface to overthrow the usurper. Boniface, who had thought it prudent to visit Rome rather than participate in the attack on Zara, now rejoined the Crusaders, with envoys of the young Prince Alexius close on his heels. The envoys brought a tempting offer to the Crusaders: restore the Crown Prince to his rightful throne and he would give them . . . the Earth!

> *He will place his whole empire under the authority of Rome, from which it has been long estranged . Secondly, since he is aware you have spent all your money and now have nothing, he will give you 200 000 silver marks and provisions for every man in your army, officers and men alike. Moreover he himself will go in your company to Egypt with 10 000 men, or, if you prefer it, simply send 10 000 men with you; and . . . he will maintain, at his own expense, 500 knights to keep guard in the land oversea.*

The Abbot of Vaux said he would never give his consent, since attacking Constantinople meant attacking their fellow Christians yet again. There were many others who agreed with the Abbot – they wanted to get on to Syria. But the Marquis of Montferrat and the Doge insisted that the only way to recover the Holy Land was to take the offer and then sail against Egypt.

If Venice had one foreign policy objective, it was to have control of the trade concessions in Constantinople. If it had another, it was to have control of Constantinople. And for a third wish . . . .

To Dandolo, it was Constantinople, not Jerusalem, that was the centre of the world. That was the fabled city, that was the fount of wealth and power – that was even where the best holy relics were stored. His own Church of San Marco was a replica of the Church of Haghia Sophia in Constantinople. And Constantinople had placed itself in his power; he had its fighting ships, he had the Crusaders. All he had to do was take it.

The main problem was now holding the army together through the winter in Zara. There were many desertions from both the nobility and the lower ranks. They often escaped aboard merchants ships – in one instance five hundred got away in one ship. Others ran away by land, only to come to a sticky end amongst the Slavs. It is hard to say which of these deserted because they were unhappy with the direction the Crusade was taking, which were impatient to get to Syria and which were simply disillusioned by the whole affair.

Meanwhile the Pope was furious about the capture of Zara. The Crusaders had ignored his specific instructions. He excommunicated the entire expedition – Crusaders and Venetians alike! They were not allowed to attend Mass, or to be confessed; they would die in a state of mortal sin and be dispatched to the fires of everlasting hell.

The bishops in the army hastily granted the Crusaders temporary absolution, while envoys were rushed to the Pope to explain the impossible choice with which the army had been faced: do as the Venetians demand or abandon the whole Crusade. Having brought them to heel, the Pope rescinded the ban of excommunication on the Crusaders. But he did not lift the ban on the Venetians, who were plainly not yet cowed by him; they remained well and truly excommunicated.

Not that that worried the Venetians at all, for the simple reason that the Marquis de Montferrat didn't pass on the news to them that they were still excommunicated! As he later explained to the Pope, there was no use in upsetting them and endangering the whole Crusade yet again.

And so, on Easter Monday, 1203, the Crusaders boarded ship at Zara, while the Venetians razed the city to the ground. On the way they encountered two ships full of knights and pilgrims returning from Syria. When the Marquis sent out a small boat to enquire their business, a sergeant in one of the boats leapt over the side and joined the Crusaders, yelling back to those he had left on deck: *'You can do what you like with anything I've left behind. I'm going with these people, for it certainly seems to me they'll win some land for themselves.'*

←————————————————————→

The Crusade Diverts to Constantinople

The Crusaders were overawed by the sight of *'that city which reigns supreme over all others'*. Geoffrey de Villehardouin reported that those who had never seen it before *'never imagined there could be so fine a place in all the world'*. Alexius III, the usurper, tried to buy them off with provisions and money, but the Crusaders refused to be diverted from their noble mission to restore the imperial throne to its rightful heir. They even sailed up close to the walls of Constantinople, showing off the young Prince on the deck and shouting out to the Greeks: *'Here is your natural lord ... The man you now obey as your lord rules over you without just or fair claim to be your Emperor, in defiance of God and the right.'*

On the appointed day, the Franks and the main army attacked from the land, while the Venetians attacked from the sea. At this point the Doge showed a remarkable degree of courage, according to Geoffrey de Villehardouin. The ancient blind man stood at the prow of his galley with the banner of Saint Mark and demanded that his men put himself and the banner on shore, whereupon his men leapt ashore and the siege began.

That night the usurper Alexius III analysed his position objectively. His people had little love for him. What remained of the imperial army consisted entirely of mercenaries and if things went against them, no soldier could be expected to risk his neck merely for a wage packet. And since the majority of Crusaders were Franks, the Frankish regiments in his pay could not be trusted either. Perhaps he could still count on the Varangian Guard, but even they were mainly Danish and English. The analysis complete, Alexius III took the wisest course of action – he did a bunk.

The Byzantine officials woke up next day to find themselves without an emperor. Their solution, however, was brilliant in its simplicity. They pulled the blinded ex-Emperor Isaac Angelus out of prison, set him back on the throne and announced to the Crusaders that the rightful ruler had been restored, according to their wishes, and there was thus no need for any more of their kind assistance. Would they therefore please stop attacking?

————————————

The Crusader fleet and camp outside Constantinople,
from *Les Passages faits Outremer ...*, c. 1490.

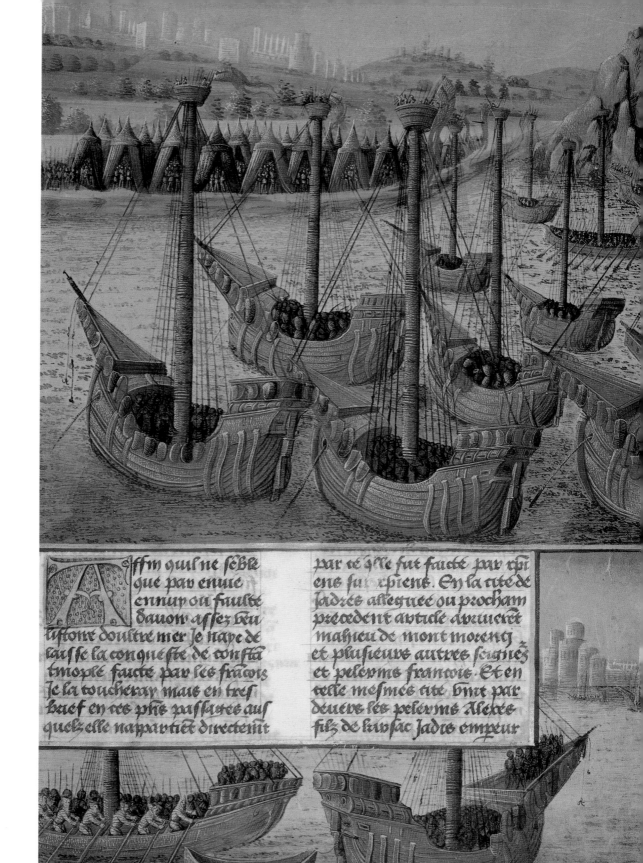

Affin qui ne semble
que par enuie
ennuy ou faulte
dauoir assez veu
listoire doultre mer Je nape de
laisse la conqueste de consta
tinople faicte par les francois
Je la toucheray mais en tres
brief en ces pñs passatres aus
quelz elle napartiet directemt

par ce qlle fut faicte par chi
ens sur chiens. En la cite de
sadres assegnee ou procham
precedent article aruierct
mahieu de mont morenci
et plusieurs autres seigneʒ
et pelerins francois. Et en
celle mesmes cite vint par
deuers les pelerins Alexis
filz de kirsac jadis empeur

But the Crusaders were not to be cheated of their reward. At a private audience Geoffrey de Villehardouin explained to the reinstated Emperor the Crusaders' contract with his son:

> *You know what service we have rendered your son, and you are aware that we have kept the terms of our agreement with him. We cannot, however, allow him to come here until he has given us a guarantee for the covenant he has made with us. He therefore, as your son, asks you to ratify this covenant in the same terms and the same manner as he has done himself.*

Isaac Angelus grumbled that they were indeed hard conditions, but he signed the covenant, and the deal was celebrated with great jubilation and feasting. On 1 August 1203 the Prince was crowned Alexius IV alongside his father in the Church of Haghia Sophia.

The Pay-off that Never Came

The Crusaders now waited for their 200 000 marks and the submission of the Greek Empire to the Pope in Rome. While the blind father shut himself away with his favourite astrologers, the young Alexius IV began to discover that it is one thing to make grand promises as a pretender to the throne, but another to carry them out as emperor. His attempt to enforce submission to Rome naturally roused tremendous resentment amongst both the clergy and the people. As for the money he had promised — it simply did not exist. Byzantium was broke.

Eventually he summoned the Doge and the barons to a meeting. There, in the time-honoured manner of debtors everywhere, he put a counter-proposal to his creditors. *'You are soon to leave,'* he said. *'I cannot hope to carry out all I have promised you in so short a time. The Greeks, I must tell you, hate me because of you. If you leave, I will lose my Empire and they will put me to death.'* He therefore begged them to stay until the following Easter, by which time he should have made his position more secure and, hopefully, raised the promised money.

The suggestion created uproar amongst the Crusaders. The idea of yet another delay seemed insupportable ... and yet what else could they do? They had got themselves into a double-bind. Unable to go forward without more money, unwilling to delay another year .... In the end there was nothing to do but wait.

Alexius toured his Empire exacting submission (and, presumably, cash) from his not altogether willing subjects. In this enterprise he was supported by many of the crusading barons, and this further alienated his people.

Meanwhile the rest of the Crusaders strutted around Constantinople doing nothing to endear themselves to the Greek population. Drunken brawls were frequent, and during one a Frenchman set fire to the city. A terrible fire raged out of control for a week, after which no Latin dared to live in Constantinople. In January anti-Latin sentiment in the city broke out in a riot in which the wonderful statue of Athena, which Phidias the Athenian had made some 1500 years before at the request of Pericles, was utterly destroyed because it seemed to be beckoning to the invaders.

Finally the Doge insisted that matters be brought to a head. A delegation, including Geoffrey de Villehardouin, was given the extremely risky task of delivering an ultimatum to the now increasingly haughty young Emperor at a great assembly. *'The Greeks were much amazed and deeply shocked by this openly defiant message, and declared that no one had ever yet been so bold as to dare issue such a challenge to an Emperor of Constantinople in his own hall'*, Geoffrey reported. Angry voices filled the room. The Emperor scowled and the Franks beat a hasty retreat in fear of being torn limb from limb on the spot.

This was followed by a palace coup. A character by the name of Murzuphlus, who had been one of Alexius' most trusted advisers, now seized the young Emperor as he slept, threw him into prison, and had him strangled. Alexius's father, the blind old Emperor, died a few days later. Murzuphlus then had himself crowned Emperor to the popular acclaim of the Greek population. *'Have you ever heard of any people guilty of such atrocious treachery!'* exclaims Geoffrey de Villehardouin.

The Sack of Constantinople

This turn of events made it easy for the Venetians to persuade the Crusaders that there was now only one course of action open to them: they must put an end to the ancient Roman Empire. Their clergy offered moral justifications – the Greeks had committed a mortal sin in supporting the murder of their Emperor. And besides they were all schismatics who ought to be brought back into the fold of Rome. They even told the soldiers that all those who died in the enterprise would *'benefit from the indulgence granted by the Pope, as though you had completed the Crusade'*. In promising this, of course, the clerics were giving the death knell to the whole Crusade.

The Pope did not forbid the proposed attack; he simply said that Christians were only to be attacked if they were actively hindering the Holy War. Since it was common knowledge throughout the West that Byzantium had never done anything but actively hinder the Holy War, that seemed like a papal blessing.

Venice after the fall of Constantinople. The four bronze horses from the Hippodrome can be seen adorning the façade of St Mark's in the top left of the picture. From a fourteenth-century manuscript.

In March the leaders of the Crusaders and the Venetians met to divide up the spoils to come. A quarter of everything was to go to whoever should be elected Emperor, after the conquest. The rest was to be divided fifty/fifty between the Crusaders and the Venetians.

Crusade to the Holy Land? What Crusade to the Holy Land?

On 6 April 1203 the Crusaders began the attack. On the 12th two of the Venetian ships, the *Pilgrim* and the *Paradise*, were blown by the wind so close to a tower that they were able to get a ladder fixed to it. Then the troops swarmed onto the tower, got ladders against other towers and within a short time had broken into the city. Murzuphlus fled with his wife and family, and by the next morning the Doge and the crusading barons were ensconced in the Great Palace.

The soldiers were then told they had three days to pillage the city. Every house was open to rape and murder. In Haghia Sophia, drunken soldiers tore down the silk hangings. The iconostasis, the screen across the church, was solid silver; they tore it to pieces. A prostitute sat on the Patriarch's throne and sang ribald songs. Nuns were ravished in their convents. Children and women were left to die in the streets. The bloodshed went on and on. Even the Saracens would have been more merciful, cried the historian Nicetas Choniates.

But the booty — ah! the booty! *'Geoffrey de Villehardouin here declares that, to his knowledge, so much booty had never been gained in any city since the creation of the world.'* No one could calculate the treasures that were looted in those three days — gold and silver, table-services and precious stones, satin and silk and the finest furs. Confronted by so much wealth, after all their delays and hardships, the Crusaders went crazy. Nor were those in holy orders exempt from the hysteria.

Abbot Martin from Paris openly threatened to kill one elderly Greek priest from the Church of the Pantocrator unless he immediately revealed the whereabouts of the most precious relics of the saints. The old man opened up an iron chest and Abbot Martin greedily plunged in both his hands. Then he and his chaplain, *'briskly tucking up their skirts, filled the folds with holy sacrilege ... As he hurried to the ships, he was seen by those who knew him. They asked him joyfully whether he had carried anything off. He answered with a smiling face: "We have done well". To which they replied: "Thanks be to God".'* Some of the loot remains on display to this day in Venice, including the most famous piece — the sixth-century Quadriga — the four horses from the Hippodrome, which still adorn the church of San Marco.

The Crusaders celebrated Palm Sunday with hearts full of joy. Nobody mentioned anything more about their pious urge to rescue the Holy Land or about avenging *'the*

←——————————————————————————→

outrage suffered by Our Lord'. Boniface now owned Macedonia. Baldwin, Count of Flanders and Hainault, was elected emperor and the Byzantine Empire was divided up between him, the Marquis and the Doge of Venice.

The Fourth Crusade had done nothing whatever to harm the Moslems. But it had completed another agenda that had been part of the crusading movement from the beginning. Urban had wanted the Eastern Church to be subordinated to the Western; now it was. Bohemond had dreamed of a European conquest of Byzantium; now it was conquered. The pigeons sent out by the Emperor in 1095 had finally come home to roost. The Roman Empire was destroyed.

14

A New Kind of Crusade

Although Pope Innocent was appalled by the slaughter at Constantinople, he had been very pleased indeed by the destruction of the Eastern Church and the imposition of the Latin one. He charged the Crusaders and the clergy *'to defend and hold the Empire of Constantinople'*, through the aid of which the Holy Land could be more easily freed from pagan hands.

Throughout the West there was celebration as the riches of Byzantium began to fill the churches of Europe. Those of tender conscience could always justify the daylight robbery of so many holy relics by the comforting tradition of *furta sacra* or 'sacred thefts'. This doctrine argued that if the theft of a saint's bones were successful, then this very success indicated that the saint in question had sanctioned the theft and clearly wished his bones to be removed and relocated wherever it was the thief wished to relocate them!

But gradually the enormity of what had happened began to sink in. Pope Innocent began to receive more detailed reports and he was horrified by the brutality, barbarism and blasphemy of the sack of Constantinople. His letters to the Crusade leaders now bitterly denounced the bloodthirsty outrage. At the heart of his rage was the realization that the conquerors had divided the spoil and established a new church organization without any reference to him.

The conquest of the Eastern Church should have been part of the process of creating the single, world-wide papal monarchy that was Innocent's goal. Instead, the new Latin Patriarch in Constantinople had been appointed by Venice, not by Rome. The Venetians had taken over the Church of Haghia Sophia and stacked the cathedral staff with their own men (four of whom couldn't even write!).

The Pope's Crusade had been hijacked.

Cathars being ejected from the town of Carcassonne. The artist has portrayed them as
pious in their nakedness, but they are plainly meant to be seen as morally dubious,
while their attackers are shown as non-violent.

The last straw was when Innocent learnt that his legate had absolved the Crusaders from their vow to carry on to the Holy Land. The Crusade was meant to be an instrument of papal supremacy. No one could release them except the Pope.

The Crusade against Christians

A hundred years before, Urban II had told the knights of Europe that it was a crime to kill Christians and it was their purpose to rescue the threatened churches of the East. Innocent III had no compunction about killing Christians who 'actively hindered' his purposes. His Crusade destroyed the churches of the East.

The change became even starker four years after the sack of Constantinople when Innocent launched a Crusade against the Cathars – communities of Christians in southern France who did not accept the authority of the Pope. His language has been echoed by many of Europe's violent demagogues since:

> *The ingrained corruption of abominable heresy grows persistently in areas of Toulouse and does not cease to breed monstrous offspring . . . Let us apply ourselves without cease, and with the help of many, to enforce correction on this vile breed of people . . . ulcers which do not respond to treatment with dressings must be cut out with the knife. Those who hold cheap the correction of the Church must be crushed by the arm of secular power.*

These abominable heretics believed that the material world was sinful and that the ideal life was one of chastity, simplicity and poverty. And they were pacifists. They believed that violence was wicked. No wonder a Christian Pope demanded that they be *'cut out with the knife'*!

Cathari means 'Pure Ones'. The notion that had once been associated with the Tafurs, that the poor and pure were the true followers of Christ, had been linked to the old Christian gnostic idea that the physical world was the realm of Satan. The Cathars developed a local church of their own in which elite believers received a sacrament which cut them off from this evil physical world. They toured the countryside as beggars, living lives of chastity and poverty.

By 1208 Innocent had become so inflamed by the spread of their beliefs that he wrote a public letter explaining that the pacifist heretics *'are not only sharpening their tongues to crush our souls but they are in reality stretching out their hands to kill our bodies'*. He called Christendom to arms against them, assuring all knights that they could seize the heretics' property for themselves. Attacking the Cathars would be an act of piety, guaranteeing release from any sins the killers had committed, just like going on Crusade to the Holy Land; in fact he offered even better indulgences than for

← ———————————————————————————————— →

going on a Crusade against Moslems. Instead of having to complete a pilgrimage to Jerusalem in order to have all his sins annulled, a warrior merely needed to perform forty days' service against the heretics – the normal period of feudal duty!

Papal supremacy had always been at the heart of crusading. The Crusade was a war on behalf of Rome. Its power to move men was intimately linked with the Pope's supposed authority to unlock the gates of heaven. Under Innocent, the Crusade reached its natural flowering. Crusaders were the Pope's Assassins, not individuals but whole armies which could be launched against any enemy he chose, in return not only for earthly rewards, but paradise.

The Popes' concept of the world was genuinely totalitarian; people should have no bonds to each other, only to the Church. Heresy is an expression of shared differentness. In a culture where religion infuses every aspect of life, cultural differences are expressed as religious differences. A war against heresy was a war against differentness.

Provence, Languedoc and Catalonia, where the Cathar belief was widely held and highly respected at every level of society, were the regions of troubadours and sophistication. The southern French resented the economic and political dominance of the northern French, whom they regarded as crude and uncultured. In this region, Catharism spread among noblemen and educated town-dwellers, as well as among the poor. When Innocent instructed the Counts of Toulouse and of Béziers – neither of whom were Cathars themselves – to uproot the 'enemy' in their midst, they flatly refused, and a Papal legate was killed. When the Pope then ordered the faithful to crusade in the land of the heretics, he was in effect ordering the northern French to go to war against southerners and seize their property. They responded with enthusiasm.

The Cathars also challenged the Pope's power. They did not believe that the sacraments were effective; they did not believe that priests or masses had any special powers. What mattered, in their view, was simply how you conducted yourself. Which meant that the Pope was an irrelevance and his claimed powers to unlock the gates of heaven were simply vainglorious boasting.

Rome had sent preachers to convince them of their errors, but the arrogance of these preachers, who displayed the wealth of a very worldly church, was wholly counter-productive. Innocent began to advise preachers to behave like the heretics, dressing in tattered clothes and engaging in itinerant preaching and debates; thus were the Dominican Friars born, in an attempt to 'convert' the Cathars back to Rome. The Cathars did not find it convincing.

That was why the Pope would have to kill them all.

The same machinery was at work as in all Crusades: the demand of the supreme monarch to his liege-men, the guarantee of personal grace through putting the world right in arms and this time not just the chance but the certainty of plunder. In the spring of 1209 the Crusade army, led by the Abbot of Cîteaux, began attacking some of the smaller towns where the pacifist heretics lived. It was easy.

Previous calls from a Pope for a Crusade had always been to take control of the Holy Land. Killing was merely incidental. But this Crusade was not a war for land; those who refused to convert would be liquidated. Mass murder was its only possible goal. Heresy was treason against God, and the Pope was God's stand-in on earth. *'Papa est Deus'*, and the penalty for denying the Pope's power in heaven meant death, dispossession, and the punishment of the heretic's heirs.

On 22 July 1208 Béziers was attacked. *'Our forces spared neither rank nor sex nor age ...'*, rejoiced the Abbot of Cîteaux in a letter to the Pope. *'Thus did divine vengeance vent its wondrous rage.'* An inhabitant of Toulouse, which was besieged by anti-Cathar Crusaders in 1229, saw it rather differently: *'Rome, you do little harm to the Saracens, but you massacre Greeks and Latins. In hell-fire and ruin you have your seat, Rome.'* Every single inhabitant of Béziers was killed. It was said that when soldiers asked the Abbot how they could avoid killing true believers, he replied: *'Kill them all. God will know his own.'*

The penalty was not always death. When the Bishop of Toulouse gave a sermon describing the orthodox as sheep and the heretics as wolves, he was interrupted by an ex-heretic whose nose had been cut off and eyes put out. *'Have you ever seen a wolf so bitten by a sheep?'* he asked.

The south was driven into armed resistance, and the Crusade became a seemingly endless horror that lasted, in fact, for twenty years. *'In what book, Rome, do you find that one should kill Christians?'*

The Children's Crusade

The belief in holy poverty was not limited to the Cathars. As trade increased, especially in northern France and western Germany, a new class of rural poor was created. Overpopulation, the clearance of common woodlands and wasteland for cultivation, the replacement of bonded servitude by wage labour and the growth of taxation on the poor — all these factors helped to produce a dispossessed mass. Increasing numbers of poor families wandered dependent on alms and casual work.

In this situation, resentment at the wealth of the Church, and a belief that poverty and holiness were linked, grew easily. And the old Tafur belief, that it was the poor who would save the Holy Sepulchre, surfaced and resurfaced. There was, however, a great difference between this concept of purity and that of the Tafurs; it included the idea that a true Crusade would be peaceful. The power of God would be their sword, they would need no other. Popular Christianity, as opposed to papal tyranny, looked to the humble and the innocent; that is why the legend of the Children's Crusade grew up in the middle of the thirteenth century.

Slave markets were an important feature of Islamic life, and the Christians of Outremer purchased and sold slaves too (when they were not themselves being bought and sold as prisoners). The final destination of many of the children who went on the Children's Crusade was thought to be Arab slave markets. From an Arab manuscript.

In fact a number of separate accounts of poor people and rural 'street children' processing round Europe like hippy convoys were conflated to produce a heart-wrenching tale of children marching in hope to conquer Jerusalem and dying or being sold into slavery before they arrived. Most of these groups simply dispersed, or became involved in the Crusade against the Cathars; some, dressed as pilgrims, got down to Genoa and plainly hoped to find ships that would give them free passage to the Holy Land. They did not. There is a story that one group did find seven ships at Marseilles, but two of them sank and the other five were sailed to North Africa, where the passengers were sold into slavery. It is told as a story from 'a man who knows a man who says . . . .'

The significance of the story is its immense appeal to the imagination of Europe, then and now. The revolutionary zeal that had launched the Crusades had taught people to see the world in moral terms. It had created a new form of tyrannical authority – the new Papacy – but it had also created the popular critique by which authority would be judged.

The Death of Innocent

Pope Innocent, having been abandoned by the Fourth Crusade, still expected the recovery of the Holy Sepulchre to be the crowning act in his establishment of papal supremacy over all the kings of Christendom. But he needed a new Crusade for another reason, too. So long as people were crusading, they were directly under his control. At the end of 1213 Innocent began to mobilize the entire population of Christendom in the Crusade.

Monthly processions were held throughout Europe, calling on God to help deliver the Holy Land. Preachers distributed the crusading cross not just to men who could fight, but to the old, the blind, to children and to lepers. A kind of Ministry of Information was set up in the papal curia to handle campaigning. Innocent was now using Crusade recruitment as a device to break all the bonds that tied society together and replace them with a tie from each individual to the Pope. He had already decreed, for the Fourth Crusade, that married men no longer needed their wives' consent to go on Crusade. Now he was saying that people should take the Cross without reference to their feudal overlords. At the same time he slammed the gates of heaven in the faces of those who were fighting the Cathars. Their privileges were suspended, so as not to distract from this new effort.

He called a great council at the Lateran in 1215. It was the first universal Council of the Latin Church – the governing body of Christendom, under the Pope, who was now dressed in the scarlet robes of a Byzantine emperor. There were representatives of every part of Christendom, including eight hundred abbots, priors and representatives of monastic institutions, as well as plenipotentiaries of the kings.

Here laws were passed which authenticated the papal dictatorship. Heresy was legally defined and the powers of bishops to enquire into people's beliefs and destroy those who did not conform were redefined. Jews were ordered to wear special clothing. New taxes were ordered. And the rules of the Crusade were laid down. One of the rules confirmed a papal decree made at the start of Innocent's papacy, that any man who equipped a Crusader would receive the same indulgence as if he went on Crusade himself. The Pope saw no particular value in the act of crusading. What mattered was the submission to Crusade ideology. To encourage that, he was prepared to sell the forgiveness of sin.

But Innocent was never to see his last Crusade. He died in 1216. The Crusades he launched had probably killed more people than all earlier Crusades combined. But not a single one of his Crusaders had entered Moslem territory. Their victims had all been Christians.

The Crusade to Damietta

Innocent may have died, but the Crusade he had initiated was all ready to go. The question was: where? Acre, the heart of the remaining Christian enclave called 'the Kingdom of Jerusalem', had now been fully restored as the most successful port in the eastern Mediterranean and enjoyed excellent relations with its Syrian neighbours. In fact the Latins got on far better with the Moslems than with the Syrian Christians, or with each other. It was a city of merchants, traders and opportunists (including many criminals who had been sent to the Holy Land on penitential pilgrimage).

The ruler of Egypt, al-Kamil, also enjoyed good relations with Christians; there were three thousand European merchants in Egypt. But the Italian merchants had decided that the time had come to take control of Alexandria as Venice had taken Constantinople; they would use the Crusaders to do it. In 1216 they pulled out of Alexandria, went to Acre and waited.

Two years later the Crusaders who had responded to Innocent's last call arrived in Acre. They found their services were not really wanted there. But, they were told, if they were to attack Egypt they could break Ayubid power and remove the Egyptian fleet from the sea. Then they could take Jerusalem, couldn't they?

In May the Crusaders obediently sailed for Damietta, on the eastern side of the Nile Delta; in August they succeeded in taking the city's port. Saladin's brother, al-Adil, who had established himself as overlord of all the lands that Saladin had ruled, was so shocked that he died. His son al-Kamil, who was already Lord of Egypt, became overall Sultan and his brother, al-Mu'azzam, became the ruler of Syria. Around this time reinforcements arrived from France, England, Spain and Italy, including the papal legate, a Spanish cardinal called Pelagius. He took command of the siege of Damietta.

The siege was badly organized, badly commanded, and many Crusaders quit. Many more died of disease. Things were no better in the besieged city and the Ayubid brothers decided that this war was not worth the candle. Al-Mu'azzam dismantled the walls of Jerusalem and the major fortresses of Syria, prior to a negotiated settlement. Then al-Kamil offered the Christians the return of the whole former Kingdom of Jerusalem except Transjordan, for which he would pay a tribute of 30 000 bezants. The Crusade had achieved its notional purpose. But Pelagius had come to fight, not to negotiate! The siege went on.

In August al-Kamil won a battle and nearly destroyed the Christian army; he then made an even better offer. He would not only restore the former Kingdom, he would rebuild the walls of Jerusalem and return the True Cross. All he wanted was the right to hold Transjordan, without which he would be cut off from Syria. Again Pelagius said no.

What was he playing at? A great many Crusaders were bewildered. But from a businessman's perspective, Jerusalem was an irrelevance. It was economically useless. The whole point of this war was to take over Egypt and gain control of Alexandria, one of the greatest ports of the Mediterranean.

Pelagius was the merchants' ally in refusing the peace terms, but for very different reasons. For him, for Rome and for many Latins, there could never be peace with the 'infidel'. Jerusalem would always be in danger as long as Egypt was Moslem: in fact any Moslems anywhere were a threat. Crusading had become an institution and an ideology; whether waged against heretics or infidels, it was by its very nature endless.

On everything else, Pelagius and the men of Acre disagreed and he was widely seen as pig-headed and stupid. This view was reinforced when he led his army to complete catastrophe. He marched towards Cairo and made camp in an area subject to the Nile flood. Al-Kamil destroyed the flood barriers. Pelagius found a boat and escaped from the waters that engulfed his army, carrying with him most of their food and medical supplies.

Al-Kamil was generous. He told the wreckage of the Crusade that they could have a five-year truce, the True Cross and their prisoners back. They must simply go away and stay away. But he could not eradicate the deep popular hostility to Christians. And when he sent for the True Cross to give it back, no-one could find it.

Stupor Mundi

Rome had now been humiliated twice in less than twenty years; one Crusade to the Holy Land had gone out of control, the next had been made to look ridiculous. One Frenchman, Guillaume le Clerc, wrote that *'Because of the legate who governed and led the Christians, everyone says in truth, we lost that city through folly and sin ... Greatly should Rome be humiliated for the loss of Damietta'.*

Not everyone shared Rome's enthusiasm for permanent struggle against the infidel and the fact that a Crusade vow had a cash value (enough money to equip a soldier) was deeply resented. People who could never go on Crusade had been induced to take the Cross and then found themselves forced to pay up.

> *By this means secular justice and ecclesiastical censure ruin the old, the weak, and those who took the Cross under prescribed conditions ... This scandal has affected the preaching [of the Crusade] to such an extent that if they [the clergy] again preach the indulgences of the Cross their success is uncertain, although it is certain they shall receive various insults.*

Frederick II, the Holy Roman Emperor and ruler of southern Italy, was, however, enthusiastic to go on Crusade. He had the power and the money to do it, and had taken the Cross at his coronation in 1215, a move which had astonished his own followers. Innocent had ignored him; he did not want kings on his Crusades, they were a challenge to his own authority. Innocent's successor, Honorius III, however, decided that Frederick was just the man for the job. Pope Honorius needed a successful Crusade to wipe out the memory of what had happened at Damietta. Honorius was, with remarkable regularity, expert at misjudging people.

Frederick was, indeed, keen to go on Crusade, but in his own fashion. He certainly did not subscribe to the ideology of the Popes. He did not have any ideas about everlasting war and the destruction of Islam. He wanted to rule in Jerusalem because he was the Emperor, the leader of Christendom, and Jerusalem was the magical heart of his universe. He would never tolerate the idea that the Pope was his sovereign, with rights over himself and his subjects. His appeals for recruits indicated the way he was thinking: *'Remember how the Roman Emperor, in ancient days, with the help of his soldiery, loyal unto death, subdued the whole earth.'*

Frederick was so keen that he successfully urged Pope Honorius to excommunicate anyone who took the vow and had not set out by 24 June 1220. Unfortunately Frederick himself was one of those who had not set out by 1220. He was, in fact, far too busy to go at all. Honorius was able to put increasing pressure on him as the Emperor requested delay after delay. Eventually Frederick agreed that he absolutely, definitely would go to rescue the Holy Land on 15 August 1227, paying for the whole army himself, under absolute pain of excommunication if he did not go. In the meantime he married the Queen of Jerusalem.

Five months before the departure date, Honorius died. His successor, Gregory IX, was a much smarter character who had very serious worries about Frederick. The Emperor got his fleet away in mid-August and set out himself a few days later — very sick. He was forced back to Italy, seriously ill. Gregory promptly excommunicated him and, for good measure, issued a ferocious condemnation of an emperor whom he regarded as extremely dangerous. An excommunicant, of course, could not lead a Crusade.

Frederick recovered by the spring. In the meantime an emissary had come from al-Kamil asking for Frederick's help against his brother al-Mu'azzam, who he believed was trying to seize the Sultanate from him. Al-Kamil offered Frederick the Holy City in exchange for his support. Frederick could see the opportunity for a diplomatic coup and set out for his Kingdom in the East.

For the first time a Crusade was being organized by a secular ruler against the wishes of the Pope. Gregory was enraged and denounced him in ferocious language. Frederick had challenged the very essence of his authority. But then, Frederick was a very odd Christian.

It was odd to find a European ruler who spoke six languages including Arabic, who had read the Koran, who enjoyed philosophy and sciences. It was odd to find any European who put his wife in a harem, who openly enjoyed extravagant eroticism and who had no hesitation in making outrageous comments on morals and religion. He was a true product of Sicily, the cultural mix that had been created by the Norman conquest of the eleventh century.

To Europeans, he was *stupor mundi*, the amazement of the world.

Islamic observers, who heard him comment that while the Caliph was a descendant of the Prophet, the Pope had been found on a dung-heap, decided that he was an atheist. It is true that he was energetic in his persecution of heretics, but he probably did that for the same reason that he banned guilds and associations of townspeople — he did not like the idea of people making their own rules.

Frederick and Jerusalem

When Frederick arrived at Acre he found the situation had changed. Al-Mu'azzam had died, and al-Kamil no longer needed his help. Frederick had to plead with al-Kamil: '*I am your friend. It was you who urged me to make this trip. The Pope and all the kings of the West now know of my mission. If I return empty-handed I will lose much prestige. For pity's sake give me Jerusalem, that I may hold my head high!*'

Al-Kamil had as little interest in the Holy War as Frederick, but he was in an embarrassing position: '*I too must take account of opinion. If I deliver Jerusalem to you it could lead not only to a condemnation of my actions by the Caliph, but also to a religious insurrection that would threaten my throne.*' It was intimated to Frederick that the only way out of the situation was a show of force. If al-Kamil were forced to give up Jerusalem in order to avoid bloodshed, he might save face. And so, in November 1228, Frederick marched at the head of his army of three thousand men and al-Kamil then went through a charade of negotiation.

So, on 18 February 1229, Jerusalem was restored to the Franks, without a drop of blood being spilt. The deal was for ten years and included Bethlehem and some places between the Holy City and the coast. The Dome of the Rock and the al-Aqsa Mosque would remain in Moslem hands. The Holy Sepulchre was in Christian hands once more.

Frederick went to Jerusalem and toured the city. The *qadi* of Nablus was his guide in the Moslem shrines and saw him eject a Christian priest who tried to enter the al-Aqsa Mosque. The next morning the *qadi* went to see the Emperor again.

> He said, 'O qadi, *why did not the muezzins give the call to prayer last night in the usual way?*' '*This humble slave,*' I replied, '*prevented them, out of regard and respect for Your Majesty.*' '*You did wrong to do that,*' he said. '*My chief aim in passing the night in Jerusalem was to hear the call to prayer given by the muezzin.*'

Frederick was determined to be re-crowned in the Holy Sepulchre. He was an excommunicant, but Frederick needed no Pope to justify his actions. He declared '*Behold, now is the day of salvation!*' and issued an address to the world, saying that he stood between God and mankind. He crowned himself in an act of messianic significance. It seemed to connect with mystic prophecies which spoke of the coming of the 'Last Emperor', who would win Jerusalem and unite East and West under his rule.

The following day a message arrived that the Patriarch, in Acre, had laid Jerusalem

Frederick II as depicted in a thirteenth-century manuscript
of his treatise on falconry. Frederick was a man of such energetic
scholarship and encyclopaedic learning that he earned the nickname
Stupor Mundi – the amazement of the world. Of course the name
could equally apply to his behaviour which often shocked and
stunned his contemporaries.

itself under an interdict. All divine services were forbidden in the city. It was suggested that Frederick was not the Last Emperor but Antichrist.

The rage on both sides was incandescent. The Templars and Hospitallers agreed with the Patriarch and the Pope that the purpose of a Crusade was to shed 'infidel' blood, not to do deals with them. Peace was not a price worth paying for the recovery of the Holy Sepulchre. Religious Moslems, for their part, felt utterly betrayed by al-Kamil – and al-Nisir, al-Mu'azzam's successor in Damascus, encouraged them in saying so.

Frederick returned home to find that the Pope had organized an invasion of his realm and he had to drive out the armies drummed up for the purpose. Once he was gone, the merchants and barons of Acre turned the city into a self-governing commune, to protect themselves from his absolutist rule. Frederick had achieved nothing beyond exposing the true nature of the Crusade movement. It was about the shedding of blood and the power of the Pope. Jerusalem was now a side-show.

Ten years later Frederick tried to extend his power over north Italy and Pope Gregory not only excommunicated him once more, but declared a Crusade against him. The same indulgences would be given to warriors against the Emperor as to those who defended the Holy Land. The Holy War was now being preached not against the 'infidel', not even against a heretic – no such charge was made against Frederick – but against a political enemy of the Pope.

The Crusade against Frederick's power-base of Sicily continued long after both he and Gregory were dead. It destroyed the civilization of Sicily and everything it represented. Crusading had become a system for teaching ideological war and intolerance. Its religious significance was hard to grasp – as many Christians bitterly observed. *'Today I see sovereignty held by the clergy by means of robbery, treachery, hypocrisy, violence and preaching . . . They are anxious to make the world theirs.'*

15

Mongols and Mameluks

The weakness of the Ayubids, and their consequent readiness to cede Jerusalem without a fight, was not simply due to the usual fratricidal in-fighting. There were new invaders pressing on the Islamic world from the Asian steppes. The fragmentation of the Seljuk Empire, which opened a door in the West to the First Crusade, opened the Eastern door to the people of the steppes. Unlike the Seljuks, who had accepted Islam when they began moving west, the new peoples on the move were not Moslems. They were pagans and nomadic Buddhists accompanied and supported, strangely enough, by Christians.

Followers of a fifth-century 'heretical' Patriarch of Constantinople, Nestorius, driven out of the Roman Empire, had made their headquarters in Mesopotamia and conducted missionary work in India, Turkestan and China. They believed that Jesus was a divinely inspired teacher, more human than divine. In the 1130s a Mongol people from Manchuria, the Kara Khitai (Black Cathay), with an army that included Nestorian Christians, came westward to the region of Tashkent and Samarkand. Malik Shah's son Sanjar, who was the supreme Seljuk Sultan, tried to stop them, and his army was crushed in 1141.

The story of this invasion enthralled Europe, where it arrived at the same time as news of the fall of Edessa. The chief of the Kara Khitai was called the Gur-Khan which, pronounced Yur-chan, easily became 'Johan' — John. The story grew that an Oriental Christian ruler called Prester John had the power to come to the aid of the Christians in Palestine.

The Gur-Khan did not fulfil their hopes. Instead, Persia was engulfed in a new upheaval. The Khorezm Turks, Moslem farmers in an isolated region south of the Aral Sea, found themselves cut off and surrounded by chaos. Their shahs responded by recruiting a powerful army of pagan Turks from the steppes. Since their only means of subsistence was conquest, these warriors began expanding into central Persia. Sultan Sanjar tried to restrain them too and ended up being taken prisoner in 1153. After Sanjar's imprisonment and death, it was plain that Seljuk power would never recover. It was in this larger framework that Nur ed-Din had created a new Syrian-Egyptian state, and Saladin had established his Kurdish rule over it.

The Khorezm-Shah was now the barrier between the steppes and the Mediterranean — and he was a very flimsy shield. His largely pagan army occupied central Persia, living by a system of robbery aggravated by extreme bodily harm which failed to endear itself to the Persians. Those who lived under Khorezm rule looked for a liberator and found one in the next power coming from the steppes. They welcomed the coming of the hordes of Jenghiz Khan.

The Golden Horde

Unlike any of the previous horde-movements, Jenghiz Khan's Mongols formed a disciplined body under the direction of a single nomad autocrat. He created an army out of the steppe cavalry whose combination of speed, discipline and numbers was previously unknown and apparently irresistible. To those who tried resistance, they showed no mercy whatever. Always on the move, with apparently limitless endurance, they used huge bows with hollow-headed arrows that howled in flight and created terror.

As the Mongol army advanced westward, the Khorezm-Shah's Empire was savagely destroyed. Bokhara was burned; Samarkand was depopulated. Huge cities simply disappeared. Desperate Khorezmian bands, thousands strong, fled into Syria, raiding, pillaging, and selling their services to any emir who could offer them booty.

In 1240 the Egyptian Sultan, needing Christian allies, agreed to return to the Kingdom of Jerusalem all the lands that had been captured by Saladin west of the Jordan, as far south as Gaza, with the exception of Nablus and Transjordan. Moslem power in the Middle East was disintegrating and the Kingdom of Jerusalem suddenly reappeared without a blow being struck! But the Franks were too divided to take advantage of their triumph. The Templars and Hospitallers openly fought each other; Tyre and Acre were in a state of undeclared war. The situation was anarchic.

In 1243 both the ruler of Damascus and the ruler of Cairo offered to withdraw Moslem officials from the Temple area in Jerusalem, in order to win Frankish support. The Franks decided to support Damascus, but did nothing to protect Jerusalem. In

June 1244 ten thousand Khorezmian horsemen swept down on Damascus at the suggestion of the Egyptian Sultan. Since they found they could not capture the city, and so had no booty, they rode on to Jerusalem. It was easy meat. The Christian population was small – only about six thousand. Three hundred Christians reached the coast. The rest were killed. The raiders dug up the bones of the kings, pillaged the houses and burned the churches, including the Church of the Holy Sepulchre.

When everything was gone, and Jerusalem destroyed, the Khorezmians rode on to join the Egyptian army at Gaza. The combined force then took on the armies of Damascus and Acre, and demolished them. The Kingdom of Jerusalem was back where it started when Frederick II had arrived.

That December, the King of France, Louis IX, sick with malaria, vowed that if his life was spared he would set out to rescue the Holy Land. It was. He did. And he failed completely.

So much for suspense.

Saint Louis

The utter destruction of Jerusalem made no significant impression on Europe. There was no great cry of anguish, and the Pope did not even consider having a mild heart tremor. Jerusalem had lost its grip on the European imagination.

Pilgrimages, however, were big business and had become well organized. There were two convoys a year, in spring and autumn, from Marseilles and the Italian cities, and these allowed pilgrims about two weeks to get from Acre to Jerusalem and back. Although knights made the trip as a form of crusading tourism, there was no great feeling that it really mattered whether Moslems or Christians actually controlled Jerusalem. To ordinary pilgrims, the Moslems actually seemed rather better guardians than the scum of Europe who had washed up at Acre: *'They breed sons who imitate the crimes of their fathers, and from bad parents descend worse sons, and from them the worst grandchildren, who tread upon the holy places with polluted feet.'* Even the Patriarch of Jerusalem spoke well of the Saracens, who *'despite frequent occupation of the Christian lands, always maintained the holy places to the best of their ability'*.

Moslems were no longer seen as the dark evil forces they had seemed in 1095; poems had appeared celebrating Saladin as a noble heathen and the conflict between Christian and Saracen seemed to have acquired a sense of tragedy. Crusading had its opponents, too, among them those who argued that if God wanted Christian armies to defeat the Saracens, he would have seen to it by now.

There were, on the other hand, plenty of European Christians who believed that, as a broad general principle, it was their duty to destroy all other religions. King Louis did not take the Cross because the Turks had taken the Holy City. He took it because it was his solemn Christian duty to destroy Islam. He was in his mid-thirties, decisive, just and honest. He was a careful organizer and utterly dedicated. To put it another way, he was a militant religious fanatic, and he had the power to restart the old Pelagian policy of war without end against the infidel.

As usual, this was associated with attacks on Jews – but now these attacks were instigated by the King. He, alone among Christian monarchs, responded with enthusiasm to the Pope's call to destroy Jewish books and had every available copy of the Talmud (the book of rabbinical legal commentaries) burned. The saintly Louis maintained that it was a bad idea to listen to Jews defending their religion; just give them *a good thrust in the belly as far as the sword will go*.

It took four years to prepare his Crusade. It was paid for by the Church and it was entirely an enterprise of his own Kingdom, and under his power. Frederick II advised him not to go and, when Louis insisted, Frederick warned the Egyptian Sultan.

Egypt now controlled Syria, so Louis attacked Egypt. Once more Damietta was

Louis IX attacking Damietta. Here, he is in the forefront
of the assault (but where is everybody else?). From the
fourteenth-century *Chronicle of St Denis*.

assaulted, once more it fell. Once more the Sultan offered to return Jerusalem to the Crusaders, once more the leader of the Crusade rejected the idea of peace. Once more the victorious army pressed its victory too far and was destroyed – this time not by floods, but by the slave-soldiers of the Sultan, the Mameluks, supported by thousands of volunteers. Louis himself was taken prisoner, and had to give back Damietta before he was released. He then tried to continue the Crusade by going on to Acre, but he had no army left.

Never mind. Louis had a plan. To destroy Islam, he would employ the contemporary equivalent of the hydrogen bomb. He would call on the help of the Mongols.

The Wrath of God

Louis knew quite a lot about the Mongols, who had been wreaking havoc in Poland and Hungary. They withdrew from Europe in 1243 to destroy the Seljuk army of Rum, in central Anatolia, and turn the region into a Mongol protectorate. They were annihilation. But that was all right. Some of them were Christians.

Like Gur-Khan ('Prester John') and his Kara Khitai, who had been destroyed by Jenghiz Khan, the new Mongol Empire made use of Nestorian Christians. In 1245, the year after the Khorezmian destruction of Jerusalem, the Pope sent an embassy to Mongolia and in 1247, before its return, he sent another to meet a Mongol general at Tabriz, in north-west Persia.

It was very clear that the Mongol Empire was not Christian, but some Mongols had converted and it was certainly not Moslem. When Jenghiz Khan had taken Bokhara, he had addressed the Moslems in their great mosque: *'I am the Wrath of God. If you had not been so wicked, I would not be here.'* Mongols were clearly murderous savages, who lived on nothing but rancid horse meat and fermented mare's milk, and who were utterly pitiless, but they might still be useful.

The first envoys returned at the end of 1247 with a report that the Mongols were only interested in conquest, not alliances. But the second came back with envoys from the Mongol General, who liked the idea of having the Moslems distracted by a Crusade while he destroyed Baghdad.

In 1248, when Louis was in Cyprus waiting for the right moment to attack Egypt, two Nestorian Christians had visited him with the information that the Great Khan *'was ready to help our King in conquering the Holy Land and delivering Jerusalem from the hands of the Saracens'*. Louis sent two ambassadors of his own, with gifts that included a tent-chapel of rich cloth, full of small statues of Biblical figures which could be used as a teaching aid. Now, in 1251, his ambassadors were back. They had travelled for a year through the Khan's lands to reach Mongolia, past endless vistas of destroyed cities and heaps of bones. When they finally presented their gifts they were told that the great Khan accepted them as tribute and the new vassal, the King of France, should send similar tribute annually.

The Mongol Khans far outdid the Pope or the Emperor in their belief that they were the rulers of the universe. Anyone, they explained, anywhere in the world, who did not submit to their authority would be pursued and slaughtered. They meant it.

Louis can have had no illusions about the nature of the Mongol Empire by now. Anyone concerned with the survival of their own civilization should have considered the Mongols the real threat. But Louis was not concerned with survival; his task was the destruction of Islam. In 1253 he heard a story that Sataq, son of the Khanate's Viceroy of the West, had taken up Christianity. Louis immediately sent ambassadors urging the Mongols to invade Syria. They did. They were coming anyway.

It was a well-prepared campaign. In 1253 an advance army moved into Persia, securing the main towns of the plateau and capturing some Assassin strongholds. The Assassins had killed one of Jenghiz Khan's sons. They would be destroyed. Then the roads through Turkestan and Persia were repaired, bridges were built, carts were found to bring siege-machines and gunpowder from China. Herds were slaughtered to clear pasture for the horses. One thousand Chinese archers, who specialized in fire-arrows, were brought to supplement the great force — one fifth of the entire might of the Mongol confederacy.

In January 1256, when everything was ready, the army came, led by the Great Khan's son, Hulagu. His wife and his leading general were Christians. The army moved slowly and methodically, destroying. The Assassins of Persia were wiped out. Then came Baghdad. In January 1258 the army of Baghdad was annihilated; in February the city fell. The slaughter lasted forty days. Eighty thousand people were butchered. The Caliph was killed by being smothered in a carpet, but the Christians and their churches were left undisturbed. The Nestorian Patriarch was found and was presumably rather surprised to be given a royal palace as his church in the city of corpses.

Louis's dream was realized; the Christians rejoiced. If there had been any serious intention among the Latins to take Jerusalem, this was the moment to act. But the Europeans were embroiled in a civil war between Venetians and Genoese, which dredged up every quarrel in the whole society.

St Louis, shown with a halo, taken
prisoner on his retreat from
Mansurah to Damietta. Damietta
was surrendered to the Mameluks in
return for the King's freedom.
From a fifteenth-century manuscript,
The Life and Miracles of St Louis.

The Mongols moved into Syria. Mosul, Aleppo and Damascus sent messages of submission. That did not protect them. Early in 1260 the Mongol army arrived at Aleppo. Aleppo tried to resist. That was a bigger mistake. The Moslems were killed; the Christians were spared. The army moved on to Antioch.

Antioch was the one Latin state untouched by Saladin. It had never had a large population of European knights and lacked the constant flow of pilgrim-warriors that maintained the Frankish colony in the Holy Land. Inevitably, Antioch had gradually been absorbed into the surrounding landscape, which was dominated by the Armenians. Its prince was the son-in-law of the King of Armenia, a man who had had the insight to understand the true nature of Mongol power and had personally gone to Mongolia to offer himself as a vassal in 1254. This demonstrated unique good sense; he was now in possession of a document from Hulagu's brother saying that his person and kingdom were inviolate, that he was chief Christian adviser on matters concerning western Asia and, what's more, that all Christian churches and monasteries would be exempt from taxes.

Now the Prince of Antioch made humble submission. His name was Bohemond. Hulagu, recognizing that the Greek Orthodox community was the largest in Antioch, insisted that the Latin Patriarch be replaced with a Greek one. Bohemond obeyed. The Franks at Acre, who seemed by now to understand very little, were bewildered and outraged at his subservience. Bohemond was excommunicated. It was gradually dawning on the Franks that the Mongols were not there to help them.

Next came Damascus. The head of the occupying army was General Kitbuqa, who was a Nestorian Christian. With him came the King of Armenia and Bohemond of Antioch. A pagan power, with Christians carrying its banners, was carrying out the Crusade dream of destroying Islam. Moslem Syria no longer existed and the Frankish kingdom was safe – but only so long as it submitted to the Khan. This was not exactly what the barons of the kingdom had in mind.

The Mameluks

The Franks would have inevitably been quickly devoured by the dragon they had been calling to for so long, but for a stroke of luck. The Great Khan died in 1259 and Hulagu felt it prudent to move nearer to Mongolia during the inevitable succession crisis. General Kitbuqa was left to take care of things for a while, with only a fraction of the army. Before leaving, Hulagu sent an embassy to Egypt demanding that the Sultan become his vassal.

Hulagu's ambassador to Cairo walked into a totally unexpected situation. Some-thing new had happened in Egypt. The Mongol ambassador met death at the hands of a new power that was afraid of nothing. The Mameluks had thrown off their masters and created a new kind of country.

The Mameluks had been the military backbone of Egypt, men whose country was the army. They were Turkish slaves, bought as children in the steppes, knowing nothing but the life of a nomad. Once in Egypt they were educated in barracks under a Mameluk sergeant who became, in effect, their father. They were converted to Islam and given a name. Since they no longer had a real father they all bore the same patronym, Ibn Abdullah, 'son of Abdullah' (Mohammed's father). They were freed when they reached arms-bearing age and then they could rise to any position (and expected senior posts). They could often hardly speak Arabic. They could marry, but their children could not be Mameluks. Their children were Moslems, and therefore not enslavable, but more importantly, they were unsuitable because they had not been weaned in the wild steppes and then removed from everything they knew. The Mameluk system needed a constant supply of freshly bought children.

In the 1240s, when the Khorezmians were rampaging, the Egyptian Sultan had refined and developed the system; fearful of his relatives, he completely sur-rounded himself with Mameluk guards. In the world of Moslem politics, the Mameluks' personal loyalty to their commander was a precious treasure. But it was such a very personal loyalty that when the Sultan died his Mameluks had to be replaced.

The Sultan had died during the campaign against Louis. But before his successor could do the traditional thing and replace them, the Mameluks had realized that they were now numerous and powerful enough not to be replaced. They killed the new Sultan and took over.

The Mameluks were a war machine running a kingdom. And now they had someone to fight. The Mongol ambassador was killed and the Mameluk army moved north. It was directed by the Mameluk Sultan, Kutuz ibn Abdullah, and in the van marched the man who had struck the first blow at the Ayubid Sultan, Baibars ibn Abdullah. In between there were thousands of them – all called Ibn Abdullah.

The Franks decided to let the Mameluk army pass unmolested through their territory. They were going to enjoy being spectators in a struggle between Titans. The Mameluks went to Acre and when they heard that the Mongols had crossed the Jordan, they set out to meet them. The Mameluks had the greater numbers and most of them remained out of sight while Baibars attacked. When he retreated again, the Mongol army pursued him and ran straight into the trap. The Mongols were obliterated.

This battle, which took place at Ain Jalut, the Pools of Goliath, ended the Mongol threat to Islam. The Mongols had never before been defeated in a significant battle and as the Mameluks went on to take Damascus and Aleppo, they became a power that the Mongols would never be able to challenge successfully. And they were soon to be led by a leader every bit as ruthless as Jenghiz Khan.

Opposite Jenghiz Khan's army, shown here storming through the mountains into China, before turning its attentions westward.

Below Even the Mongols were no match for the Mameluks — the slave-warriors of Egypt. This fourteenth-century Mameluk manual on horsemanship belongs to an extensive Islamic literature on the science of warfare. European cavalry fought quite differently, with saddles that gripped the rider to sustain the shock of direct impact.

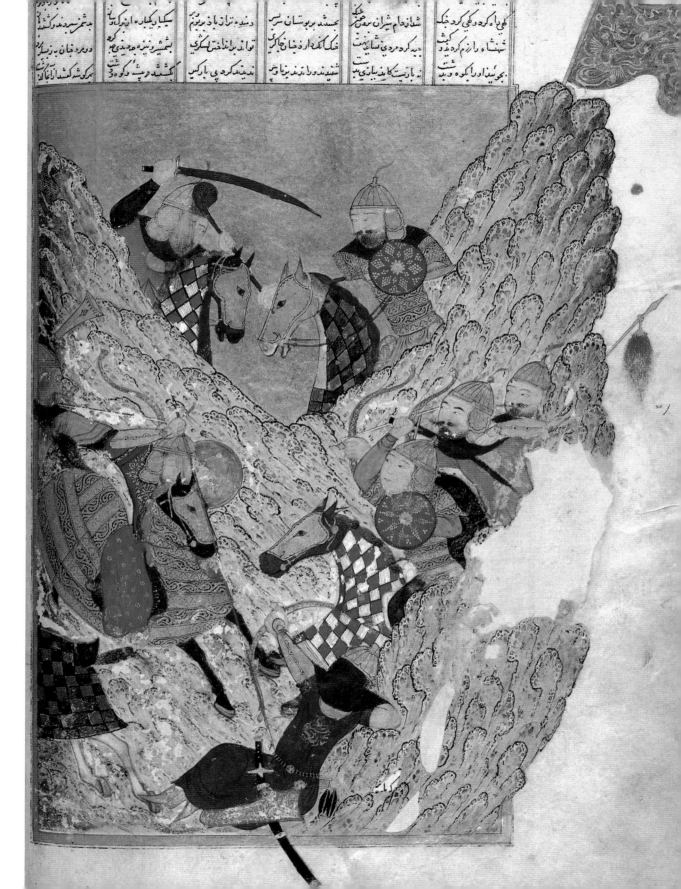

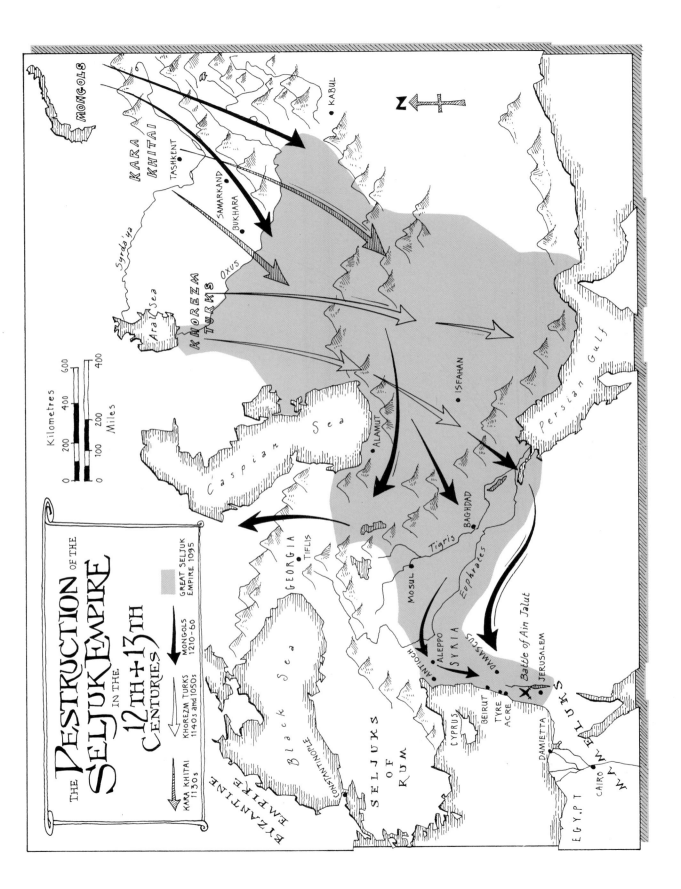

THE DESTRUCTION OF THE SELJUK EMPIRE IN THE 12TH + 13TH CENTURIES

GREAT SELJUK EMPIRE 1095

MONGOLS 1210-60

KHOREZM TURKS 1140s and 1050s

KARA KHITAI 1130s

Kilometres
0   200   400   600

Miles
0   100   200   400

MONGOLS

KARA KHITAI

KABUL

TASHKENT

SAMARKAND

BUKHARA

Syr da'ya

Aral Sea

Oxus

KHOREZM TURKS

Caspian Sea

ALAMUT

ISFAHAN

Persian Gulf

GEORGIA

TIFLIS

Mosul

Tigris

BAGHDAD

Euphrates

Black Sea

CONSTANTINOPLE

BYZANTINE EMPIRE

SELJUKS OF RUM

ANTIOCH

ALEPPO

SYRIA

DAMASCUS

Battle of Ain Jalut

JERUSALEM

CYPRUS

BEIRUT

TYRE

ACRE

DAMIETTA

CAIRO

EGYPT

FATIMIDS

Sultan Baibars

Baibars asked if he could be Governor of Aleppo and Sultan Kutuz said no. Baibars then killed him. When the Mameluk army returned to Cairo, it marched back under the command of Sultan Rukn ad-Din Baibars Bundukdari ibn Abdullah. The Mameluk state was a kind of military occupation. Only Mameluks could be Men of the Sword. Men of the Pen (the civil administration) and Men of the Turban (the religious and legal establishment) were non-Mameluks and were subject to regular inspection.

The Frankish kingdom was doomed. Lacking numbers, it had put its faith in thick walls. But the siege engines of the thirteenth century were not the puny objects of the First Crusade. They were now heavy artillery, hurling quarter-ton missiles, and they were available in numbers.

In 1265 it began. First was Caesarea. Baibars took it and dismantled it completely. Then Haifa. Those who did not escape were massacred and once more the town and citadel were taken apart. Arsuf was smashed; the commander surrendered on a promise that the survivors would go free. The promise was a lie. The Franks now held nothing south of Acre except for Jaffa (held by John of Ibelin, who had excellent relations with the Moslems) and an immensely strong fort on the shore at Atlit. Baibars returned to Egypt.

The next year it was the turn of Safed, the huge Templar castle that dominated upper Galilee. The Templars surrendered when they were told they could return safely to Acre. They were beheaded. Toron, on the coast, fell without resistance. Then Baibars marched south, killing every Christian he encountered. A second Mameluk army meanwhile moved into Cilicia. They returned to Aleppo with forty thousand prisoners, having removed Cilicia from the political map.

In 1267 Baibars moved to Acre, but he had not brought enough siege equipment to break through the walls. When the Franks asked for a truce they arrived at the castle of Safed to find it completely encircled with the skulls of Christian prisoners. Baibars had a nasty sense of humour.

In Europe, Louis IX tried to set up a rescue Crusade, while the good people of Acre returned to trying to kill each other in the hope of controlling the trade of the port. Much of that trade was, as you might guess, with Baibars. The Venetians were selling him military supplies (importing timber and iron from northern Europe for his siege machines), while the Genoese handled the slave trade. They were doing all this under licence from the High Court at Acre!

The End of the Kingdom

In 1268 Baibars struck again. John of Ibelin had died and the Mameluks took Jaffa to pieces. The better bits of the castle became part of a new mosque in Cairo. Next was the castle of Beaufort, where the Templars were enslaved, but women and children were allowed to retreat to Tyre. Was Baibars going soft? No.

It was time to deal with Antioch. He split his army into three, one part taking the port of St Symeon, one covering the mountain pass to Cilicia and the third knocking down the wall and walking in. The gates of the city were then locked and everyone in it either killed or made prisoner and taken away. Antioch has never recovered. Bohemond was at Tripoli, so Baibars ordered his biographer, Ibn Abdazzahir, to drop him a note:

> Our purpose here is to give you news of what we have just done, to inform you of the utter catastrophe that has befallen you ... You would have seen your knights prostrate beneath the horses' hooves, your houses stormed by pillagers and ransacked by looters ... You would have seen the crosses in your churches smashed, the pages of the false Testaments scattered, the Patriarch's tombs overturned. You would have seen your Moslem enemy trampling on the place where you celebrate the mass, cutting the throats of monks, priests and deacons upon the altars ... Since no survivor has come forward to tell you what happened, we have informed you of it, and since no one is in a position to give you the good news that you have saved your life at the loss of everything else, we bring you the tidings in a personal letter.

Years of Christian crusading had finally produced this monstrosity: a Moslem state run by ex-slaves who had learnt to be the mirror-image of the enemy they fought and whose pleasure in destruction and slaughter was the exact image of the delight the Crusaders themselves had once taken in butchering Moslems.

Saladin may have been a model of Islamic moderation, and may have taught the West the meaning of chivalry. Baibars was a model of religious fanaticism and the Franks had been his teacher. He continued with his programme of demolition, now taking on the formidable fortifications of the Krak des Chevaliers. Modern siege-engines made short work of it.

Acre would survive until the Mameluk Sultan decided to destroy it. Baibars died in 1277 and the final attack did not come for fourteen years. When it did, the Sultan brought more siege-engines than had ever been gathered before at one place. The walls of Acre had been rebuilt. Women, children and old men were shipped off to Cyprus if they could afford the fare. Some thousand mounted men, fourteen thousand foot-soldiers and thirty thousand non-combatants prepared to meet their fate.

There were said to be one thousand Moslem engineers allocated to the destruction of each of the city's towers. The final assault came six weeks after the siege began. Acre was smashed to pieces, so that it could never again be used as a Frankish base. Babies were killed; women who had surrendered were massacred; prisoners were beheaded. No one knows how many died or were enslaved.

By the middle of August 1291 there was not a single building in Palestine held by the Franks. Then the whole coast was completely stripped of buildings and vegetation. The Franks disappeared. And the native Christians, whose cause had been so trumpeted by Pope Urban in 1095 and whose tragedy had moved his hearers to go on Crusade, were now the victims of a Moslem religious zealotry that had not existed before.

Six years after the fall of Acre the Pope declared that King Louis IX, who had died crusading to wipe Islam from the face of the earth, was a saint. Ten years later Dante Alighieri began writing the *Divine Comedy*; he placed Frederick II, whose Crusade had won Jerusalem without a war, in Hell.

In Mongolia, the terrible monsters who had spawned Jenghiz Khan, the self-styled Wrath of God, turned their backs on the West and became Buddhist pacifists. They still are.

Crusaders, their crosses stripped from them and trampled
underfoot, are led away into captivity.

Notes on Sources

Most references are given here in a shortened form. Full details can be found in the bibliography.

Introduction

P. 9   'The world is divided' Abu 'l-'Ala al-Maarri, quoted in Nicholson, p.167

1   The World of a Crusader

P. 11   'more than forty' Ibn al-Athir in Gabrieli, p.11

P. 14   'with an impiety' Migne, quoted in Norwich, p.83

P. 18   'Frequently he burned' Radulph of Caen quoted in Riley-Smith, *The First Crusade*, p.36

P. 21   'They have circumcised' Robert the Monk, RHC Occ. III, pp.727–30

P. 21   'Whoever for devotion' R. Somerville, quoted in Ibid.

P. 24   'Until now' Guibert of Nogent, RHC Occ. IV pp.137–10

P. 25   'At last' Radulph of Caen quoted in Riley-Smith, *The First Crusade*, p.36

P. 25   'This land' Robert the Monk, RHC Occ. III pp.727–30

2   The Great Adventure

P. 28   'Full of enthusiasm' Anna Comnena, p.309

P. 29   'All the Saracens' Fulcher of Chartres, p.118

P. 38   'When they gathered' Ibid., p.312

P. 38   'Know, Emperor' Ibid., p.313

P. 40   'soft, effeminate' Southern, p.34

P. 41   'lifted his foot' Norwich, p.277

P. 43   'Bohemond's appearance' Anna Comnena, p.422

P. 43   'I come of' Ibid., p.327

P. 43   'If I had' Ibid., p.328

P. 44   'Your father,' Stephen of Blois, quoted in Hallam, pp.72–4

3   War in Anatolia

P. 46   'a Frank on horseback' Anna Comnena, p.416

P. 48   'In five weeks' Stephen of Blois, quoted in Hallam, pp.72–74

P. 49   'These Turks began' Guibert of Nogent, in *Gesta Francorum*, p.19

P. 52   'many who had' Albert of Aachen III, 2

P. 57   'You may be very' Stephen of Blois, quoted in Hallam, pp.78–81

P. 57   'We have endured' Ibid.
P. 59   'We shall restore' Albert of Aachen III, 59
P. 61   'there appeared' *Gesta Francorum* X, 29
P. 62   'Then we called' Ibid.
P. 62   'Let the cupidinous' Bohemond, quoted in Hallam, p.84

4   *The March to Jerusalem*

P. 64   'a sign to show' Cohn, p.66
P. 64   'Some of the poorest' Guibert of Nogent, quoted in Hallam, p.85
P. 64   'our troops' Radulph of Caen, quoted in Hallam, p.89
P. 66   'All of us' Cohn, p.67
P. 71   'He had almost' Radulph of Caen, quoted in Hallam, p.89
P. 74   'This peace' Payne, p.98
P. 74   'Our squires' Fulcher of Chartres, p.122
P. 74   'among them a large' Gabrieli, p.11
P. 74–5 'Oh day so ardently' Fulcher of Chartres, p.123
P. 75   'They also ordered' *Gesta Francorum*, p.92

5   *The Arab Response*

P. 81   'This is war' Abu al-Muzaffar al-Abiwardi, trans. A. Ereira
P. 83   'In former times' William of Tyre II, p.407
P. 88   'I do not know' Imad ed-Din, trans. A. Ereira
P. 90   'I come from' Imad ed-Din, trans. A. Ereira
P. 91   'They wept' Ibn al-Qalanisi, quoted in Gabrieli, p.29
P. 91   'on the Caliph's' Ibid., p.29
P. 91   'At that time' Fulcher of Chartres, p.208
P. 92   'Mawdud never' Ibn al-Qalanisi, quoted in Maalouf, p.87

P. 92   'The Lord permitted' Fulcher of Chartres, p.209
P. 94   'to see what' Ibid., p.215
P. 94   'When they told' Ibid., p.216
P. 94   'We who were' Fulcher of Chartres, p.271
P. 97   'in less than' Ibn al-Qalanisi, quoted in Galonelli, p.39
P. 98   'After God' Maalouf, p.94
P. 99   'That blow' Kemal ad-Din, quoted in Maalouf, p.97
P. 99   'And we all' Fulcher of Chartres
P. 99   'Syria would have' Ibn al-Athir, quoted in Gabrieli, p.41

6   *The Fight Back Begins*

P. 100   'Before he came' Kemal ad-Din, quoted in Gabrieli, p.54
P. 100   'they seemed' Kemal ad-Din, quoted in Ibid., p.54 n. 2
P. 100   'He had only' Ibn al-Athir, quoted in Ibid., p.54
P. 101   'Zengi, mightily' William of Tyre II, p.105
P. 101   'this cruel enemy' Ibid., p.105
P. 101   'Then might have' Ibid.
P. 102   'each rejoiced' Ibid., p.141
P. 102   'far from the' William of Tyre II, p.140
P. 102   'were utterly' Ibid., p.141
P. 102   'Although he was' Ibid., p.143
P. 102   'walls, towers' Ibid., p.142
P. 103   'an unsavoury' Ibid., p.143
P. 103   'The Emir' Ibn al-Qalanisi, quoted in Maalouf, p.137
P. 103   'gorged with wine' William of Tyre II, p.146
P. 104   'And yet he' Ibn al-Qalanisi, quoted in Maalouf, p.138
P. 104   'His treasures' Ibid., p.139
P. 104   'Nur ed-Din' Ibn al-Athir, quoted in Gabrieli, p.70
P. 104   'rise to his' Ibn al-Athir, quoted in Gabrieli, p.72

P. 104 'the tambourine' Ibn al-Athir, quoted in Maalouf, p.145

P. 104 'I have read' Ibn al-Athir, quoted in Gabrieli, p.70

P. 106 'and so he' Ibid., pp.71–2

P. 106 'Nur ed-Din' Kemal al-Din, quoted in Maalouf, p.145

P. 106 'O God, grant' Ibid., p.145

P. 106 'Nureddin . . . was' William of Tyre, II, p.146

P. 107 'a lazy, idle' Ibid. II, p.201

P. 110 'a great multitude' Ibid. II, p.160

P. 110 'There might have' Ibid. II, p.160

P. 110 'and our people' Ibid. II, p.160

7 St Bernard's Dogs

P. 111 'mothers hid' St Bernard of Clairvaux, quoted in the *Encyclopedia Britannica*, vol. 3, 1969, p.523

P. 114 'award to those' St Bernard of Clairvaux, *Opera*, ed. J. Leclerq and H. Rochais, quoted in J. Riley-Smith, *Crusades*, pp.97–8

P. 114 'If you are' J. Riley-Smith, *Crusades*, p.97

P. 114 'This is a plan' Ibid., p.95

P. 114 'It would be' St Bernard of Clairvaux, quoted in the *Encyclopedia Britannica*, vol. 3, 1969, p.524

P. 114 'I opened my mouth' St Bernard of Clairvaux, *Epistolae*, MPL vol. CLXXXII quoted in Runciman vol. II, p.254

P. 114 'Man, what ought' St Bernard of Clairvaux in Otto of Freising, *Gesta Friderici*, quoted in Runciman, vol. II, p.256

P. 115 'Reports kept coming' Ibn al-Qalanisi, quoted in Maalouf, p.146

P. 115 'It was common' William of Tyre II, p.170

P. 115 'these great' Ibid. II, p.171

P. 116 'perchance he' Ibid. II, p.174

P. 117 'in fact the survivors' Ibid. II, p.179

P. 118 'felt a lively' Ibid. II, p.180

P. 119 'they might endeavour' Ibid. II, p.186

P. 121 'the orchards stretched' Ibid. II, p.187

P. 122 'I have offered' Ibn al-Athir, quoted in Gabrieli, p.60

P. 122 'With one blow' William of Tyre II, p.190

P. 122 'in miserable confusion' Ibn al-Qalanisi, quoted in Gabrieli, p.59

P. 122 'the bodies stinking' Ibid., p.59

P. 122 'often interviewed' William of Tyre II, p.193

P. 123 'They preferred' Ibid. II, p.194

P. 123 'pseudo-prophets' *Monumenta Germaniae Historica Scriptores in Folio et Quarto*, ed. G. H. Pertz et al., 1826, quoted in J. Riley-Smith, *Crusades*, p.103

P. 123 'looked askance' William of Tyre II, pp.192–3

8 Arab Unity

P. 124 'I have no intention' Abu Shama, quoted in Sivan, *L'Islam et La Croisade*, p.77

P. 126 'Between you and us' Ibn al-Qalanisi, quoted in Sivan, p.78

P. 126 'the goodness' Quoted in Maalouf, p.171, also al-Qalanisi, quoted in Sivan *op. cit.*, p.79

P. 126 'plunged upright' Ibn al-Qalanisi, quoted in Sivan, p.78

P. 127 'For it is' William of Tyre II, p.305

P. 127 'was excessively' Ibid., p.300

P. 129 'What a marvel' al-Qadi al-Fadil, quoted in Sivan *op. cit.*, p.81

P. 129 'like the lowest' William of Tyre II, p.308

P. 129   'They were cast' Ibid. II, p.308

P. 129   'My uncle Shirkuh' Maalouf, p.159

P. 129   'In the end' Ibid.

P. 130   'The men dared' William of Tyre II, p.317

P. 130   'The Frankish enemy' Maalouf, p.165

P. 130   'guarantee with his' William of Tyre II, p.318

P. 130   'We are wasting' Ibid., p.340

P. 131   'You have exerted' Imad ed-Din, quoted in Lyons & Jackson, p.20

P. 131   'I suffered' Abu Shama, quoted in Lyons & Jackson, p.20

P. 131   'claim that all' William of Tyre II, p.350

P. 134   'Thus strong' Ibid. II, p.357

9   *Saladin the Upstart*

P. 135   'Upon the death' Ibn al-Athir, quoted in Maalouf, p.170

P. 136   'They thought' Imad ed-Din, quoted in Lyons & Jackson, p.34

P. 136   'to suspect' Ibn Abi Tayy, quoted in Lyons & Jackson, p.44

P. 138   'convinced that' William of Tyre II, p.389

P. 138   'Nur ed-Din' Ibn al-Athir, quoted in Lyons & Jackson, p.48

P. 138   'I am your father' Ibn al-Athir, quoted in Maalouf, pp.173-4

P. 139   'since the time' Imad ed-Din, quoted in Lyons & Jackson, p.62

P. 139   'We did not' Ibid., p.62

P. 139   'God knows' Ibn al-Athir, quoted in Gabrieli, p.69

P. 139   'there came a' Ibid., p.69

P. 141   'was secretly' William of Tyre II, p.404

P. 141   'We dawned on' Saladin's correspondence, quoted in Lyons & Jackson, p.83

P. 141   'They knew that' Lyons & Jackson, pp.82-3

P. 141   'This Saladin' William of Tyre II, p.408

P. 141   'Saladin in defiance' Ibid. II, p.408

P. 141   'Saladin was' Boccaccio, quoted in *Dictionary of Proper Names & etc. in the Works of Dante*, Paget Toynbee (Oxford 1968), p.556

P. 142   'You go too far' Maalouf, p.176

P. 143   'We have only' al-Fadil, quoted in Lyons & Jackson, p.86.

P. 143   'Behold this unjust' Maalouf, p.181

P. 146   'Tell him to' Imad ed-Din, quoted in Lyons & Jackson, p.105

P. 147   'one of the' Ibn Abi Tayy, quoted in Lyons & Jackson, pp.159-60

P. 147   'the eye of' Saladin's correspondence, quoted in Lyons & Jackson, p.199

P. 147   'Redoubled fear' William of Tyre II, p.490

10   *The Fall of Jerusalem*

P. 148   'in a perpetual' Ibid. II, p.491

P. 148   'unequal to the' Ibid. II, p.493

P. 149   'Plain people' Ibid. II, p.497

P. 150   'Lady Constance' Ibid. II, p.224

P. 151   'He then completely' Ibid. II, p.254

P. 154   'he threw himself' Ibid. II, p.277

P. 155   'the enemy would' Lyons & Jackson, p.187

P. 155   'Great crowds' William of Tyre II, pp.500-1

P. 158   'even those' Ibid. II, pp.503-4

P. 158   'I, Sibylla' Roger of Hoveden, *Gesta*, quoted in Kedar, et. al., pp.195-8

P. 159   'He broke the' Baha' ad-Din, quoted in Gabrieli, p.112

P. 159   'he would kill' Ibid., p.112

P. 160   'We have routed' Ibn al-Athir,
          quoted in Gabrieli, p.123

11   *To the Rescue*

P. 169   'We and our' Benedict of
          Peterborough, quoted in Hallam,
          p.163

P. 169   'A Frankish' Ibn al-Athir, quoted
          in Gabrieli, p.183

P. 169   'except perhaps' *Recueil des Actes
          de Philip Augustus*
          ed. A. F. Delaborde, quoted in
          Hallam, p.167

P. 169   'No-one in all' Ansbert, quoted in
          Setton 11, p.90

P. 171   'Thus did God' Ibn al-Athir,
          quoted in Maalouf, p.207

P. 172   'I would sell' Gillingham, p.56

P. 174   'For townsfolk' Ambroise,
          Crusade of Richard Lion-Heart

12   *The Battle of Heroes:
     Richard v. Saladin*

P. 180   'No pen can' Ambroise, *Third
          Crusade*, p.59

P. 183   'Tinted and' Baha' ad-Din,
          quoted in Gabrieli, p.204

P. 186   'Every foot-soldier' Baha' ad-Din,
          quoted in Verbruggen, p.215

P. 186   'to keep the' Verbruggen,
          pp.212–3

P. 186   'Everywhere was' Imad ad-Din,
          quoted in Gabrieli, p.207

P. 187   'since this was' Imad ed-Din,
          quoted in Verbruggen, p.219

P. 187   'The Muslims and' Baha' ad-Din,
          quoted in Gabrieli, p.226

P. 188   'knowing quite well' Baha' ad-
          Din, quoted in Gabrieli, p.227

P. 192   'By the legs' Gillingham, p.48

P. 192   'The King was' Ambroise, *Third
          Crusade*, p.153

P. 194   'The king must' Saladin, quoted
          in Lyons & Jackson, p.75

P. 194   'may God curse' Ibid., p.75

P. 194   'He was as' Baha' ad-Din, quoted
          in Gabrieli, p.96

P. 194   'He was a' William of Tyre 11,
          p.405

P. 195   'hopes of' al-Qadi al-Fadil, quoted
          in Lyons & Jackson, p.369

P. 195   'I turned' Imad ed-Din, quoted in
          Lyons & Jackson, p.132

13   *The Fourth Crusade*

P. 200   'to take pity' Villehardouin,
          p.32

P. 200   'We consent' Ibid., p.34

P. 201   'The King of' Ibid., p.43

P. 201   'Sirs, I am' Ibid., p.44

P. 201   'We beg you' Ibid., p.44

P. 202   'My lords' Ibid., p.48

P. 202   'You have given' Ibid., p.48

P. 202   'He will place' Ibid., p.50

P. 203   'You can do,' Ibid., p.57

P. 204   'that city' Ibid., p.59

P. 204   'never imagined' Ibid., p.59

P. 204   'Here is your' Ibid., p.64

P. 206   'You know what' Ibid., p.75

P. 206   'You are soon' Ibid., p.77

P. 207   'The Greeks' Ibid., p.82

P. 207   'Have you' Ibid., p.84

P. 207   'benefit from' Ibid., p.85

P. 210   'Geoffrey de' Ibid., p.92

P. 210   'briskly tucking' Ibid., Gunther of
          Paris, quoted in Hallam

14   *A New Kind of Crusade*

P. 212   'to defend and' Anon., *The Deeds
          of Innocent III*, quoted in Hallam,
          pp.228–9

P. 214   'The ingrained' J. & L. Riley-
          Smith, pp.78–80

P. 214   'are not only' Innocent III, quoted
          in Throop, p.46

P. 216 'Our forces' Letter from Abbot of Cîteaux to Innocent III in M P L vol. C C V X, quoted in Hallam, p.232

P. 216 'Rome, you do' Guillem Figueira, *D'um sirventes far*, written in Toulouse in 1229 when the town was besieged by Crusaders, quoted in Throop, p.38

P. 216 'Have you ever' Ibid., p.38

P. 216 'In what book,' Ibid., p.50

P. 221 'Because of the' Guillaume le Clerc, quoted in Throop, p.32

P. 221 'By this means' Throop, p.82

P. 221 'Remember how' Setton, p.698

P. 223 'I am your friend' Maalouf, p.228

P. 223 'I too must' Ibid., p.228

P. 223 'he said "O qadi"' Ibn Wasil, quoted in Gabrieli, p.272

P. 225 'Today I see' J. Riley-Smith, *The Atlas of the Crusades*, p.81

15 Mongols and Mameluks

P. 228 'They breed sons' *Peregrinationes medii aevi quatuor*, quoted in Kedar et al., p.293

P. 228 'despite frequent' Matthew Paris, quoted in Hallam, p.265

P. 229 'a good thrust' Armstrong

P. 230 'I am the' Marshall, pp.53–4

P. 230 'was ready to' Joinville, p.197

P. 240 'Our purpose here' Ibn Abdazzahir, quoted in Gabrieli, p.310

Bibliography

Primary Sources

MGH   *Monumenta Germaniae historica*, Hanover, 1826–

MPL   Migne, J. P., *Patrologia Latina*, Paris, 1844–55

RHC Occ.   *RHC Historiens Occidentaux*, 1844–95

COLLECTIONS

Bédier J. and Aubry P. (ed.), *Chansons de Croisade* (Paris 1909)

Gabrieli, Francesco, *Arab Historians of the Crusades*, tr. E. J. Costello (Routledge & Kegan Paul 1984)

Hagenmeyer, H., *Die Kretzzugsbriefe aus den Jahren 1081–1100* (Innsbruck 1901)

Migne, J. P., *Patrologia Latina*, 221 vols, Paris 1844–55 (MPL)

Monumenta Germaniae historica, eds. G. H. Pertz, T. Mommsen and others, Reichsinstitute tür ältere deutsche Geschichtskunde, Hanover, 1826 and ff. (MGH: SS = *scriptores*, etc)

Monumenta Germaniae historica. Scriptores errum germanicarum, new series, 10 vols, 1922 and ff.

Muratori, L. A., *Rerum Italicarum Scriptores*, 25 vols., Milan 1723–51 (RIS)

Re. G. Del. *Recueil des Historiens des Croisades*, Publ. Académie des Inscriptions et Belles Lettres, Paris, 1841–1906. *Historiens Occidenteaux*, 5 vols. (RHC Occ.)

SINGLE SOURCES

Albert of Aachen, *Historia Hierosolymitana*, in RHC Occ. I

Ambroise, *The Crusade of Richard Lion-Heart*, tr. & ed. M. J. Hubert and J. L. LaMonte, Records of Civilization, XXXIV (Columbia University Press 1941)

Ambroise, *The Third Crusade*, ed. Kenneth Fenwick (Folio Society 1958)

Anna Comnena, *The Alexiad*, tr. E. R. A. Sewter (Penguin 1969)

Ansbert, *Historia de expeditione Frederici imperatoris*, ed. Anton Chroust, MGH, SS, n.s. (1827, 1928)

Benedict of Peterborough, *Gesta Regis Henrici II*, ed. W. Stubbs, Rolls Series (Longman 1867)

Estoire d'Eracles, RHC Occ., vols. I & II

Eusebius of Caesarea, *The Life of the Blessed Emperor Constantine* (S. Bagster & Sons 1845)

Fulcher of Chartres, *A History of the Expedition to Jerusalem 1095–1127*, tr. Frances Rita Ryan (University of Tennessee Press 1969)

Gesta Francorum et aliorum Hierosolimitanorum, ed. R. Hill (Oxford University Press 1962)

Guibert of Nogent, *Historia quae dicitur Gesta Dei per Francos*, in RHC Occ. IV

Ibn al-Qalanisi, *The Damascus Chronicle of the Crusades*, selected and tr. H. A. R. Gibb (Lusack & Co. 1932)

Ibn al-Athir, *The Perfect History*, 1231,
ed. Tornberg (Leiden 1853–64)
Ibn Munqidh, Usamah, *Autobiography, 'An
Arab-Syrian Gentleman and Warrior in the
Period of the Crusades'* (ed. Hitti) (New York
1929)
Innocent III 'Epistilae', in MPL, vol. CCXV
Malaterra, Geoffrey, 'Historia Sicula', in
MPL, vol 149 and RIS., vol. V
Radulph of Cadomensis, *Gesta Tancredi Siciliae
Regis in Expeditione Hierosolymitana*
Raymond of Aguilers, *Historia Francorum qui
ceperunt Jerusalem*, XX, 300, in RHC Occ.
vol. III
Recueil des actes de Philippe Auguste,
ed. H. F. Delaborde (Paris 1916–43)
Robert of Rheims, *Historia Iherosolimitana*, in
RHC Occ. III
Roger of Hovedon, *Chronica*, ed. W. Stubbs,
Rolls Series (London 1868–71)
Somerville, R., *The Councils of Urban II*, I.
Decreta Claromontensia (Annuarium
Historiae Conciliorum. Supplementum I.
Amsterdam)
Thomas Aquinas, *Summa Theologica*
(Methuen 1989)
Vegetius, *De Re Militari*, abridged *c.* AD 856
by Rabanus Maurus as *Epitome of Military
Science* (Liverpool University Press 1993)
Villehardouin, 'The Conquest of
Constantinople', in Joinville &
Villehardouin, *Chronicles of the Crusades*,
tr. M. R. B. Shaw (Penguin 1963)
Wiederhold, W., 'Papsturkunden in Florenz',
*Nachrichten von der Gesellschaft der
Wissenschaften zu Gottingen*, Phil.-hist.
Kl. (Gottingen 1901)
William, Archbishop of Tyre, *A History of
Deeds Done Beyond the Sea*, tr. Emily
Atwater Babcock and A. C. Krey
(© Columbia University Press 1943)
Extracts in *Crusades* are reprinted with
permission of the publisher.

Secondary Sources

Armstrong, Karen, *Holy War: the Crusades and
their Impact on Today's World* (Macmillan
1992)
Bachrach, Bernard S., 'Animals and Warfare
in Early Medieval Europe', *Settimane*,
XXXI (1983)
Bahat, Dan, *The Illustrated Atlas of Jerusalem*
(Macmillan Academic and Professional
1990)
Billings, Michael, *The Cross and the Crescent:
History of the Crusades* (BBC Books 1987)
Bull, Marcus, *Knightly Piety and the Lay Response
to the First Crusade: the Limousin and Gascony
c. 970–1130* (Clarendon Press 1993)
Cohn, Norman, *The Pursuit of the Millennium:
Revolutionary Millenarians and Mystical
Anarchists of the Middle Ages* (rev. ed. Pimlico
1993)
Davis, R. H. C., *The Medieval Warhorse:
Origin, Development and Redevelopment*,
(Thames & Hudson 1989)
Ebersolt, J., *Les Sanctuaires de Byzance* (Paris
1921)
Gillingham, John, *The Life and Times of
Richard I* (Weidenfeld & Nicolson 1973)
Hallam, Elizabeth (ed.), *Chronicles of the
Crusades* (Weidenfeld & Nicolson 1989)
Kedar, B. Z., Mayer, H. E., Smail, R. C.
(eds.), *Outremer: Studies in the History of the
Crusading Kingdom of Jerusalem* (Yad Izhak
Ben-Zvi Institute, Jerusalem 1982)
Loomis, R. S. (ed.), *Arthurian Literature in the
Middle Ages* (Clarendon Press 1959)
Lyons, M. C. and Jackson, D. E. P., *Saladin:
The Politics of the Holy War* (Cambridge
University Press 1982)
Maalouf, Amin, *The Crusades Through Arab
Eyes* (Al Saqi Books 1984)
Mayer, H. E., *The Crusades*, tr. John
Gillingham (Oxford University Press
1988)
Nicholson, Reynold A., *Studies in Islamic
Poetry* (Cambridge University Press 1921)

←——————————————————→

Norwich, John Julius, *The Normans in Sicily* (Penguin 1992)

Payne, Robert, *The History of Islam* (Dorset Press 1987)

Riley-Smith, J. (ed.), *The Atlas of the Crusades* (Times Books 1991)

Riley-Smith, J. and L., *The Crusades: Idea and Reality 1095–1274* (Edward Arnold 1981)

Riley-Smith, J., *The First Crusade and the Idea of Crusading* (Athlone Press 1986)

Riley-Smith, J., *The Crusades: A Short History* (Athlone Press 1987)

Rouche, M., 'Cannibalisme sacré chez les croisés populaires', *La religion populaire*, ed. Y. M. Hilaire (1981)

Runciman, Sir Stephen, *A History of the Crusades*, 3 vols. (Penguin, rev. eds. 1990 and 1991)

Setton, Kenneth M., *The Papacy and The Levant (1204–1571)*, 4 vols. (American Philosophical Society 1976–84)

Setton, Kenneth M. (ed.), *A History of the Crusades*, 6 vols. (University of Wisconsin Press 1955–86)

Sivan, Emmanuel, *Modern Arab Historiography of the Crusades* (Tel Aviv University Occasional Papers August 1973)

Sivan, Emmanuel, *L'Islam et la Croisade: Idéologie et Propagande dans les Réactions Musulmanes aux Croisades* (Librarie d'Amérique et d'Orient 1968)

Sivan, Emmanuel, 'Réfugiés Syro-Palestiniens au Temps des Croisades', *Revue des Études Islamiques* 35 (1967)

Southern, R. W., *The Making of the Middle Ages* (Pimlico 1993)

Sumbereg, L. A. M., 'The "Tafurs" and the First Crusade', *Medieval Studies*, 21 (1959)

Throop, Palmer A., *Criticism of the Crusade: a Study of Public Opinion and Crusade Propaganda* (Amsterdam, 1940; Porcupine Press 1977)

Ullmann, Walter, *Principles of Government and Politics in the Middle Ages* (Methuen 1961 & 1974)

Verbruggen, J. F., *The Art of Warfare in Western Europe during the Middle Ages, from the Eight Century to 1340*, tr. Sumner Willard and S. C. M. Southern (Oxford: North Holland Publishing Co. 1977)

Picture Credits

BBC Books would like to thank the following for providing photographs and for permission to reproduce copyright material. While every effort has been made to trace and acknowledge all copyright holders, we would like to apologize should there have been any errors or omissions.

Abbreviation: BNP = © Bibliothèque Nationale, Paris

PP. 2–3 BNP Ms Fr. 5594, f.19.
P. 7 BNP Ms Fr. 5594, f.241.
P. 10 © 1994 Comstock, Inc.
P. 15 The Master and Fellows of Corpus Christi, Cambridge. CCCC Ms. 26, f.i R;
P. 19 BNP/Bridgeman Art Library. Ms Fr. 22495, f.9.
P. 23 The British Library. Ms Add. 28681, f.9.
P. 26 British Library/Bridgeman Art Library. Ms Egerton 1500, f.45v.
P. 30 BNP Ms Fr. 5594, f.19.
PP. 34–5 © David South.
P. 39 BNP Ms Fr. 5594, f.34v.
P. 42 Biblioteca Apostolica Vaticana. Ms Vat. gr.666, f.12v.
P. 47 BNP/Bridgeman Art Library. Ms Fr. 2630, f.22v.
PP. 50–1 BNP/Bridgeman Art Library. Ms Fr. 22495, f.235v.
PP. 54–5 BNP Ms. Fr. 5594, f.59v.
P. 55 BNP Ms Fr. 5594 f.50v.
P. 58 BNP Ms Fr. 5594, f.67v.
P 65 British Library/Bridgeman Art Library. Ms. Egerton 1070, f.5.
P. 69 BNP. Ms Fr. 352, f.62.
PP. 72–3 © David South.
PP. 76–7 BNP/Bridgeman Art Library. Ms Fr. 20124, f.331.
P. 80 Telegraph Colour Library.
P. 84 BNP Ms Arabe 5847, f.5v.

P. 85 BNP Ms Arabe 5847, f.138.
P. 89 © David South.
P. 96 El Escorial, Monasterio Biblioteca, Madrid/Arxiu Mas. Libro de los Juegos de Ajedrez.
P. 105 British Library. Ms Roy 16 G VI, f.74.
PP. 108–9 © David South.
PP. 112–13 BNP Ms Fr. 5594, f.138.
PP. 116–17 Giraudon/ Bridgeman Art Library.
P. 120 Bibliothèque Municipale de Lyon/Bridgeman Art Library. Ms 828, f.189r.
P. 125 Frank Spooner Pictures.
P. 128 BNP Ms Fr. 5594, f.153v.
PP. 132–3 BNP Ms Fr. 22495, f.229v.
P. 137 British Library/ Bridgeman Art Library. Add. 30359, fig.86.
P. 140 BNP Ms Arabe 5847, f.79.
PP. 144–5 & 152–3 © David South.
PP. 156–7 BNP Ms Fr. 5594, f.197.
PP. 157 BNP Ms. Res M Y 2395.
P. 161 BNP Ms Fr. 5594, f.202v.
PP. 164–5 BNP/Bridgeman Art Library. Ms Fr. 4274, f.6.
P. 168 Biblioteca Apostolica Vaticana. Ms Vat. Lat. 2001, f.1r.

P. 173 British Library/ Bridgeman Art Library. Ms Cotton Claud D VI, f.9v.
PP. 176–7 © David South.
PP. 180–1 Bibliothèque Municipale de Lyon/Bridgeman Art Library. Ms 828, f.33r.
PP. 184–5 BNP Ms Fr. 5594, f.213.
PP. 188–9 British Library/ Bridgeman Art Library. Ms Add. 42130, f.82.
P. 197 Sacro Speco, Subiaco/ SCALA.
P. 205 BNP Ms Fr. 5594, f.217.
PP. 208–9 © Bodleian Library, Oxford. Ms Bodley 264, f.218r (top).
P. 213 British Library/ Bridgeman Art Library. Ms Cotton Nero E 11 pt.2, f.20v.
P. 217 BNP Ms Arabe 5847, f.105.
P. 224 Biblioteca Apostolica Vaticana. Ms Pal. Lat.1071, f.1v.
P. 229 British Library/ Bridgeman Art Library. Ms Roy 16. G. VI, f.409v.
P. 232 British Library. Ms Add. 18866, f.135.
P. 233 British Library. Ms Or 2780, f.49r.
PP. 236–7 & 241 BNP/Sonia Halliday Photographs. Ms Fr. 2829, f.41v (xxxix).

Index

Figures in *italic* refer to pages with illustrations.

←——————————————→